Exploring macOS

A Journey Through the Mac Ecosystem

Sagar Rastogi
Jasdeep Singh

Apress®

Exploring macOS: A Journey Through the Mac Ecosystem

Sagar Rastogi
Meerut, Uttar Pradesh, India

Jasdeep Singh
Delhi, India

ISBN-13 (pbk): 978-1-4842-9881-7
https://doi.org/10.1007/978-1-4842-9882-4

ISBN-13 (electronic): 978-1-4842-9882-4

Managing Director, Apress Media LLC: Welmoed Spahr
Acquisitions Editor: Divya Modi
Development Editor: James Markham
Editorial Assistant: Divya Modi
Copy Editor: Mary Behr
Technical Reviewer: Utkarsh Handa

Cover designed by eStudioCalamar

Cover image designed by Freepik (www.freepik.com)

Distributed to the book trade worldwide by Springer Science+Business Media New York, 1 New York Plaza, Suite 4600, New York, NY 10004-1562, USA. Phone 1-800-SPRINGER, fax (201) 348-4505, e-mail orders-ny@springer-sbm.com, or visit www.springeronline.com. Apress Media, LLC is a California LLC and the sole member (owner) is Springer Science + Business Media Finance Inc (SSBM Finance Inc). SSBM Finance Inc is a **Delaware** corporation.

For information on translations, please e-mail booktranslations@springernature.com; for reprint, paperback, or audio rights, please e-mail bookpermissions@springernature.com.

Apress titles may be purchased in bulk for academic, corporate, or promotional use. eBook versions and licenses are also available for most titles. For more information, reference our Print and eBook Bulk Sales web page at www.apress.com/bulk-sales.

Any source code or other supplementary material referenced by the author in this book is available to readers on GitHub (github.com/apress). For more detailed information, please visit https://www.apress.com/gp/services/source-code.

Paper in this product is recyclable

Table of Contents

About the Authors

Sagar Rastogi has been a technology evangelist with strong skills centered around Apple macOS, iOS, and Microsoft products since 2012. He is a passionate geek with big ideas to sell. Sagar is an Enterprise Apple Desktop Architect, Jamf Mobile Device Management Subject Matter Expert, and Office 365 Mobility Architect. He is a Jamf Certified Expert, Jamf Certified Admin, and Jamf Certified Endpoint Security Admin. He is certified in Cybersecurity (ISC2) and has also earned certifications in AWS Cloud, Office 365, and ITIL Service Transition. He's also an Android Enterprise Certified Associate.

He has a history of sharing his expertise via white papers and blogs, some of which have been published by Jamf. His easy-going personality and ability to control a room make him an excellent presenter and teacher. He enjoys helping others and sharing his knowledge with them.

He has created unique workflows using Apple devices, specifically macOS, in a variety of industries from manufacturing to retail and healthcare. He builds solutions that emphasize the end user's experience. In addition, he provides in-person and remote device and application support for Windows and mobile end points within his organization.

Jasdeep Singh has been working on and providing training for the Apple ecosystem since 2007. He's a Principal Architect, senior consultant, course developer, trainer, and Apple Enterprise Management Architect in the Digital Workplace Services domain. Jasdeep provides coaching and mentoring for people who use Apple devices (macOS/iOS/iPadOS/tvOS) in complicated environments. He has provided architectural support to multiple organizations across the globe in Enterprise Mobility Management in complex environments, inclusive of Apple devices management via leading Enterprise Mobility suites like Jamf, Microsoft Intune (MEM), Kandji, and Addigy, while acting as a quality transformations, migration, and modernization consultant for Apple devices. He has extensive experience in enterprise architectural activities, digital workplace services, transition and transformation frameworks, and more. He possesses knowledge around solution designing, scripting, security hardening on Apple devices, and automation. He has written handful of technical blogs, architectural documents, and technical SOPs, and he has provided technical expertise in various type of businesses including fintech, healthcare, and commercial.

Introduction

Welcome to *Exploring macOS*. We will take you through the Mac ecosystem. We'll start with macOS fundamentals and, as we progress through subsequent chapters, we'll demonstrate advanced techniques, including how to use scripts to automate tasks. Further, we will cover essential applications and utilities for common goals and guide you through transitioning from Windows to macOS. We will highlight ground-breaking information about Apple hardware architecture with Apple Silicon Chip's impact. Additionally, we will cover the significance of Apple ID and iCloud in the Apple ecosystem. You will learn how to maximize your Mac experience. This book sets the stage for an enriching exploration of Mac devices and their profound impact on organizational workflows. Automation plays a vital role in enterprises, so you will also learn about scripting and its significance to make use of Macs to the best of their capability. Join us on this exciting journey as we unlock the mysteries of Mac devices and uncover the potential of the Mac ecosystem. Let's embark on this adventure together!

CHAPTER 1

macOS Management Settings and Reinstallation Process

In this chapter, we delve into the various aspects of macOS functionality, with a special focus on customizing the operating system to suit individual user preferences. We begin by exploring how users can tailor macOS settings at the operating system level to optimize their overall experience.

Furthermore, we shed light on the essential process of updating Mac devices with the latest security patches and combo updates. By understanding the significance of these updates, users can ensure their systems remain secure and up to date.

Another crucial topic we address is the major operating system upgrades. We guide users through the seamless transition from one macOS version to another, such as upgrading from the familiar macOS Big Sur to the newer and exciting macOS Monterey.

Moreover, we discuss how the Mac recovery system can prove invaluable for troubleshooting purposes. Understanding how to use this system efficiently empowers users to resolve various issues that may arise during their macOS journey.

Finally, we conclude the chapter by focusing on the post reinstallation setup of a Mac. With a fresh operating system in place, we explain the essential steps users must take to configure their systems to their liking, ensuring a personalized and efficient workspace.

Join us on this comprehensive exploration of macOS, where we uncover the inner workings of the operating system and empower users to optimize their Mac experience to the fullest.

© Sagar Rastogi and Jasdeep Singh 2023
S. Rastogi and J. Singh, *Exploring macOS*, https://doi.org/10.1007/978-1-4842-9882-4_1

> **Note**   A significant portion of the information below is quite basic and might already be familiar to many users, even those who have never used a Mac. This is because iOS/iPadOS and macOS now share quite a similar look, feel, and functionality, and since iPhones/iPads are widespread, users may already be acquainted with these similarities. Further, Apple is aligning its product line and OS.

Mac Architecture Transitions

Apple had three principal hardware architecture transitions for Macs. Apple's first computer systems ran on Motorola processors. However, in 1994, Apple transitioned to the latest architecture named PowerPC. While the transition delivered advantages, later the PowerPC processors did not deliver as per the expectations of Apple.

In 2005, Apple decided to transition from PowerPC to Intel. Intel processors were more efficient and quicker compared to PowerPC ones, which empowered the expansion of Mac devices. Apple announced that this transition would start in June of 2006 and be completed in the last quarter of 2007. However, the process went ahead rapidly and as a result it was completed in August of 2006. The transition to the Intel architecture happened when the PowerMac platform was substituted with Mac Pro consisting of the Intel platform.

After successful years with Intel, Apple again decided to add influential and proficient processors to Macs as Apple's iPhones and iPads were already functioning on self-developed chipsets. In June of 2020, Apple announced that the hardware architecture of the Macs would be transitioned to their proprietary ARM-based chipsets from Intel, which would be known as Apple Silicon.

In November of 2020, the first set of Apple Silicon-based Macs inclusive of the first M1 chipset were announced. Apple said this transition was to be completed by the end of 2022.

In October of 2021, Apple presented two new chipsets named M1 Pro and M1 Max as successors of M1, with the capacity to deliver more robust performance. The M1 Pro chip comes with an impressive hardware (10 core CPUs, 16 core GPUs, with an option to be customized with up to 32 GB of RAM). The M1 Max chip consists of 32 core GPUs, with an option to be customized with up to 64 GB of RAM.

In March 2022, Apple unveiled the M1 Ultra as a successor to previous M1 chips, which is more powerful with 48- or 64-core GPU with an option to be customized with 64GB or 128GB of RAM. See Figure 1-1.

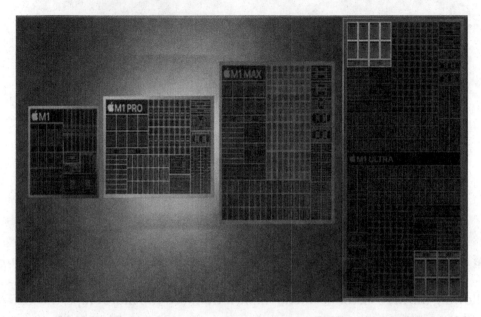

Figure 1-1. *First set of Apple Silicon chipsets architectures designed by Apple, the M1 lineup*

During the Worldwide Developers Conference (WWDC) on June 6, 2022, Apple unveiled its highly anticipated M2 chip, which powers the latest models of the MacBook Air and the 13-inch MacBook Pro. The M2 chip is manufactured using TSMC's Enhanced 5-nanometer technology N5P process and incorporates an impressive 20 billion transistors, representing a 25% increase from its predecessor, the M1 chip. Apple claims that the M2 offers substantial CPU improvements of up to 18% and GPU improvements of up to 35% compared to the M1. See Figure 1-2.

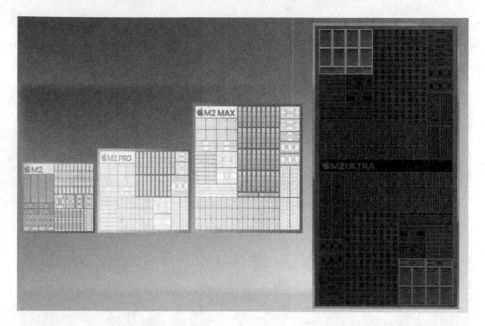

Figure 1-2. *Successor of M1 Apple Silicon chipsets architectures, the M2 lineup*

Following the M2's announcement, Apple introduced two more chips, the M2 Pro and M2 Max, in January 2023, targeted at professional users. The M2 Max boasts additional GPU cores and memory bandwidth, along with a larger die size, making it a more powerful version of the M2 Pro. In June 2023, Apple launched the M2 Ultra, which combines two M2 Max chips within a single package, delivering unparalleled performance for advanced computing needs.

Apple Silicon and Intel Processor Lineup

Table 1-1 shows the entire lineup of processors designed by Apple and Intel, along with the year in which the respective processor was released. Each year Apple announces the successor of previous products, followed by its release. Likewise, Intel keeps working on its product lineup and launches them once they are ready for public release.

Table 1-1. *Apple Silicon and Intel Processors Lineup*

Apple	Year	Intel	Year
M2 Ultra	2023	11th Generation - Tiger Lake	2020
M2 Max	2023	10th Generation - Ice Lake	2019
M2 Pro	2023	9th Generation – Coffee Lake Refresh	2018
M2	2022	8th Generation – Coffee Lake	2018
M1 Ultra	2022	7th Generation – Kaby Lake	2017
M1 Max	2021	6th Generation – Skylake	2015
M1 Pro	2021	5th Generation – Broadwell	2015
M1	2020	4th Generation – Haswell	2013
		3rd Generation – Ivy Bridge	2012
		2nd Generation – Sandy Bridge	2011
		1st Generation – Nehalem	2011

Apple Silicon vs. Intel Processors

The Intel processors that Apple embedded in Mac devices are x86 chips. Apple's proprietary processors are based on ARM (Advanced RISC Machine), inclusive of various technologies designed by Apple.

Apple silicon chipsets are SoC (system-on-a-chip) and self-designed by Apple for Mac devices. Apple is transitioning from Intel to its own chipset on Macs like iPhones and iPads.

Apple claims that the ARM-based M1 chip provides superior performance in comparison to Intel. Further, Apple considers the M1 chip as the fastest in the industry. The M1 chip is an octa-core processor with 4 performance and 4 efficiency cores. In addition, it comes with 8-core graphics and 16-core Neutral Engine, which is designed to deliver up to 15 times quicker performance.

Because of the 8-core GPU, M1-based Macs excel in graphics performance, beating the onboard quad-core Intel chips that were available on older Mac devices.

Distinctions Between the Windows and macOS Operating Systems

As someone who has explored both Windows and Mac machines, you're undoubtedly familiar with the similarities and noteworthy disparities between these operating systems. Let's delve into the primary divergences that set apart the Windows operating system from macOS.

Windows

Microsoft Inc. designed, developed, and created Windows. The preliminary version of Windows was released on November 20, 1985. At present, Windows 11 is the newest version. Windows 365, which supports cloud PC, was released on July 16, 2021 and Windows 11 was released on October 5, 2021.

macOS

Mac is designed, developed, and created by Apple Inc. It's an operating system based on Unix called Macintosh. The Mac operating system is written in C, C++, C-objective, and Swift assembly. It's presently offered in 39 different languages. Formerly, macOS was named Mac OSX.

The preliminary version of macOS was released on March 24, 2001, and the latest release of macOS was on October 25, 2022 (which is macOS 13, known as Ventura).

Quick Differentiation

Windows OS is offered in more languages as compared to macOS.

As compared to Windows OS, the scope of troubleshooting on macOS is easier.

Windows is more widely used globally, with macOS being the second most-used operating system.

For software updates consisting of critical operating system updates, macOS uses Software Update and Windows uses Windows Update.

Supported File Systems

Macs: APFS, HFS, HFS+, UFS, AFP, UDF, NFS, FAT, SMBFS, NTFS, FTP, WebDAV, and ZFS

Windows: NTFS, APFS, UDF, HFS+, FATX, and HFS

Supported Architectures

Macs: Intel-based processors and Apple Silicon chipsets

Windows: Intel- and AMD-based processors

Performance

Macs: Apple has complete control of the hardware and software because both are developed by Apple. As a result, Mac devices provide superior functioning as compared to expensive Windows-based computers.

Windows: It's easier to customize a Windows-based computer as per the different hardware requirements for extreme performance. However, if multiple OEM hardware is embedded in one PC, issues may result related to compatibility and availability of drivers required for each module to function appropriately. This can unfavorably affect functionality and performance of the device.

Applications/Utilities of Windows and Mac with Common Goals

In the ever-evolving landscape of computing, the Windows and Mac operating systems have become integral to our digital lives. Despite their unique features, they share common goals when it comes to providing essential applications and utilities. From enhancing productivity to ensuring system security, these common objectives unite the two platforms in their pursuit of delivering a seamless user experience.

In this exploration, we will delve into the applications and utilities of Windows and Mac that have common goals, revealing how they align in their commitment to meeting the needs of modern users.

Command-Line Application

In the realm of computer programming and system administration, the command-line application stands as a venerable and indispensable tool. Providing users with direct access to a computer's operating system, this powerful interface allows for precise control and execution of various tasks through text-based commands. Command-line applications have a rich history and continue to play a crucial role in modern computing, catering to developers, power users, and administrators alike.

Both applications end up with the common functionality of executing the commands to achieve the certain results.

In Windows, it's called the *CMD (Command Prompt)*.

In Macs, it's known as *Terminal.*

For instance, consider following commands to continuously ping any website via the command line:

Windows: `ping google.com -t`

macOS: `ping google.com`

File Manager/Explorer

The File Manager/Explorer emerges as a fundamental tool. It provides users with an intuitive and efficient way to navigate, organize, and interact with their computer's files and directories. As a cornerstone of modern operating systems, this essential application offers a graphical interface that simplifies file manipulation, enabling users to effortlessly create, move, copy, and delete files and folders. It can be used to quickly find and access files and folders.

The Windows-based application is called File *Explorer.*

The application in a Mac is called *Finder.*

Encryption

Encryption in Mac and Windows systems serves as a crucial line of defense, safeguarding sensitive data from unauthorized access and potential security breaches. Both platforms offer robust built-in encryption features that allow users to protect their files, folders, and communications. Each have a technology to encrypt the hard drive for data security and to prevent any unauthorized access into the device.

8

In Windows, the encryption technology is known as *BitLocker*.

In macOS, the equivalent is called *FileVault*.

System Settings

System settings in both the Mac and Windows operating systems serves as a vital control center, enabling users to personalize and configure their devices according to their preferences and requirements. These settings provide an intuitive interface to manage various aspects, including display settings, sound preferences, network configurations, user accounts, security options, and more. Whether it's adjusting screen resolution, customizing notifications, or managing power-saving modes, system settings empower users to fine-tune their devices to optimize performance, enhance usability, and ensure a seamless computing experience. It can be used to view and change entire system settings, such as network, printer, mouse, and keyboard.

To change system settings in Windows OS, you need to access the *Control Panel*.

In Macs, system settings can be modified or managed via *System Preferences*.

Note   In the new version of macOS 13 (Ventura), System Preferences is rebranded as System Settings by Apple.

Media Player

In the Mac and Windows operating systems, media players play a central role in providing users with a seamless multimedia experience. These versatile applications allow users to enjoy various types of media content, including music, videos, and images, all within a user-friendly interface. Whether it's organizing music libraries, creating playlists, or streaming videos, media players offer a range of features to enhance the entertainment experience.

In Windows, the media player application is called *Windows Media Player*.

In Macs, the media player application is known as *QuickTime Player*.

Web Browser

Browsers play a crucial role in both the Mac and Windows operating systems, serving as gateways to the vast world of the Internet. These powerful applications enable users to access websites, search for information, stream videos, and interact with online content seamlessly. With user-friendly interfaces and a multitude of features, browsers offer a personalized and immersive web browsing experience.

Whether it is *Safari* on Macs or *Microsoft Edge* on Windows, these browsers cater to user's needs, providing fast, secure, and efficient access to the Internet.

Deleting Files

An ability to delete files is a fundamental feature in the Mac and Windows operating systems, allowing users to manage their digital data efficiently. Whether it's removing unnecessary files to free up storage space or eliminating sensitive information securely, the process of deleting files is simple and intuitive. Any deleted files get stored in specific applications as per their respective operating systems. Later you can restore the files or permanently delete them.

When you delete any file or folder in Windows, they get stored within the *Recycle Bin*.

Executing a similar action within macOS moves this data to an application called *Bin*.

System Logs Viewer

The System Logs Viewer is a powerful utility available in both Mac and Windows operating systems, providing users with a comprehensive view of critical system events and activities. By accessing detailed log files, users can monitor system performance, troubleshoot issues, and track important system events. Whether it's reviewing error messages, diagnosing software conflicts, or identifying security breaches, the System Logs Viewer serves as a valuable tool for system administrators and advanced users. There's a dedicated utility or application available in both operating systems that is used to view system wide logs for troubleshooting or detailed information.

In the Windows operating system, you can use an application named *Event Viewer*. In a Mac, it's known as *Console*.

Checking the Use of Resources

Checking the use of resources is an essential task in both Mac and Windows operating systems, empowering users to monitor their device's performance and optimize efficiency. Resource monitoring tools provide real-time insights into CPU, memory, disk, and network usage, enabling users to identify resource-intensive processes and potential bottlenecks. By understanding how system resources are used, users can make informed decisions to improve overall system performance and ensure a smooth computing experience. There's a dedicated utility or application available in both operating systems, which is used to get information about the services or applications utilizing maximum resources of a machine, like CPU or RAM usage.

The application with this dedicated task in Windows is called *Task Manager*.

In macOS it is called *Activity Monitor*.

Switching from Windows to macOS

Switching from a Windows OS to a macOS can be an exciting transition, offering a new and user-friendly computing experience. Here are a few tips Windows users can follow while switching to Mac.

Right-Click

Right-click on Apple's (magic) mouse and two-finger click on Apple's trackpad. These settings can be changed in System Preferences > Mouse preferences and Trackpad preferences.

Swipe, Scroll, and Click

Preferences for scroll directions, swipe gestures, or button assignments are available in Mouse and Trackpad preferences.

Close, Minimize, and Resize Window

Options (like radio buttons) to close, minimize, or maximize any window are available on the top left corner.

Change Volume

Volume controls on the Menu bar or the Volume keys on Apple's keyboard can be used to change volume.

Change Mac Settings

You use the Control Panel in Windows to change any settings; System Preferences can be used in Macs.

Open Apps

Launchpad and Dock can be used to open apps (programs).

Find files

Spotlight is used to swiftly search and open applications, docs, and more.

Browse for Files

As with Windows File Explorer in Windows devices, Finder can be used in Macs.

Delete Files

As with the Recycle Bin in Windows, Trash/Bin can be used in Macs.

Rename Files

Click any file/folder to highlight and press the Return key to rename a file. After entering the name, press the Return key again.

Preview Files

The Quick Look feature is used to preview files swiftly. To use this feature, highlight the file and press the Space key on the keyboard.

Back Up Files

Time Machine is used to back up the files present in Mac. It creates a snapshot of the entire Mac operating system including customized settings and files.

Apple ID

Apple ID is an essential part of the Apple ecosystem. It helps keep the device secure and it manages the data effectively within Apple devices connected to the same Apple ID.

An Apple ID allows access to the iTunes (Music) Store, App Store, Apple Books, iCloud, FaceTime, and other Apple services.

An Apple ID can be created using an email account like Gmail or Yahoo or iCloud (for instance, abc@icloud.com). It is recommended to use one Apple ID in all of your Apple devices and Apple services for seamless user experience.

To create an Apple ID, you can use devices like Macs, iPhones, or iPads, or you can create one at `https://appleid.apple.com/`.

Note   In a few countries and regions, a phone number is allowed for creating an Apple ID instead of an email address.

Create an Apple ID on a Mac Device

On a Mac device, click the Apple menu at the top left corner, open System Preferences, and then click Sign In at the top right corner. See Figure 1-3.

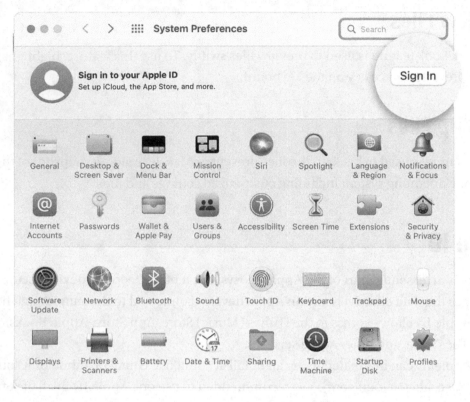

Figure 1-3. *Apple ID Sign In*

Click the Create Apple ID option and follow the on-screen directions to complete the process. See Figure 1-4.

Figure 1-4. *Create an Apple ID*

Once successfully signed in with an Apple ID, you can set up your preferences. Apple ID allows access to all of the Apple services, inclusive of iTunes (Music) Store, Books, App Store for applications or games, your iCloud account, and other essential Apple Services. After a successful sign in, Apple ID preferences are used to edit the account name, photo, contact details, password and security preferences, payment, shipping details, and more. See Figure 1-5.

Figure 1-5. *Successful sign in with Apple ID*

Sidebar Options for Setting Up Apple ID Preferences on a Mac

Overview: These options can be used for reviewing an Apple ID, privacy policies, and to log out from an Apple ID.

Name, Phone, Email: These options allow you to set up a name, phone number, email info, and other contact details linked with the user's Apple ID.

Password & Security: These options allow you to change password and security information linked with the user's Apple ID.

Payment & Shipping: These options allow you to set up payment and shipping details linked with the user's Apple ID.

iCloud: These options allow you to choose the iCloud features and to manage iCloud storage.

Media & Purchases: These options allow you to edit or set up media and purchase preferences linked with the user's Apple ID.

Trusted devices: This section displays the list of trusted devices linked with the same Apple ID and to change these trusted devices' options.

iCloud

iCloud is the service provided by Apple for saving a user's data on cloud storage, such as pictures, videos, documents, music, and apps. Further, it allows sharing the same updated data on Apple devices to be linked with the user's same Apple ID. By using an iCloud account, users can easily share data like pictures and calendars with others (family members or friends).

As a security feature, iCloud also helps in finding a lost Apple device. By default, Apple provides 5GB of free iCloud storage, and users can buy more storage as per the requirements and plans available.

iCloud Preferences on a Mac

After a successful sign in using an Apple ID, System Preferences enables the option for managing iCloud preferences. On a Mac device, click the Apple logo at the top left side corner and then open System Preferences. Click the Apple ID followed by the iCloud option. See Figure 1-6.

Figure 1-6. *iCloud preferences access*

Further, check or uncheck the options to use in iCloud. See Figure 1-7.

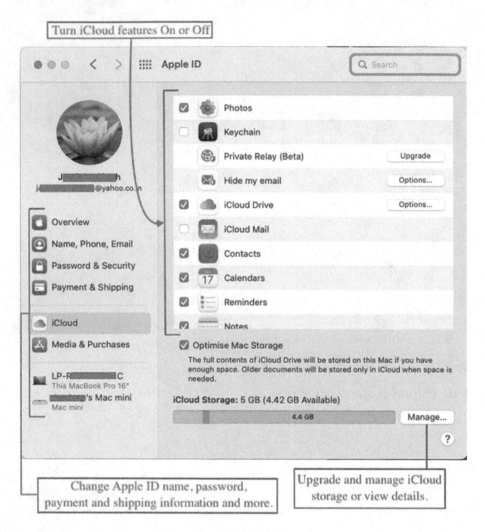

Figure 1-7. *iCloud preferences management*

Information About Important iCloud Icons and Usability

Usability is a crucial aspect of iCloud, as it simplifies data management and ensures seamless access to your information across devices. Through the use of these icons and intuitive interfaces, iCloud offers a user-friendly experience, empowering you to effortlessly sync, access, and share your data, photos, notes, and more across your entire Apple ecosystem. Table 1-2 provides information about available iCloud options with icons and usability.

Table 1-2. *iCloud Icons and Usability*

iCloud options	Details
Photos	Pictures and videos are always available.
iCloud Drive	Share your desktop and documents on all Apple devices linked with the same account.
Family Sharing	Share music, books, apps, and subscriptions with family members.
Find My Mac	Find My Mac is used to trace an active Mac device on the map. Further, remote commands can be pushed on the lost Mac device, like playing a sound, screen locking, or erasing entire data.
Calendars, Contacts, Reminders and more	Keep mail, calendars, notes, contacts, reminders, messages, news, and stocks updated, including HomeKit accessories preferences, by using applications on Macs, iPhones or iPads, and iCloud.
Safari	iCloud Tabs, bookmarks, and reading details in Safari
iCloud Keychain	It helps keep passwords, payment information, and more securely saved, and allows for the automatic filling of these fields on Apple devices linked with the same iCloud account.
iCloud Storage	Apple provides 5GB of free iCloud storage, and users can buy more storage any time as per requirements and plans available.

Mac Desktop

When you log into your Mac, you will find yourself on the Mac Desktop—a familiar and essential starting point for all your computing endeavors. In this chapter, we delve into the various components that make up the Mac Desktop, each serving a unique purpose to enhance your overall user experience.

The Mac Desktop is an organized space that encompasses several key elements designed to provide quick access and easy navigation. Among these elements, the Menu bar takes a prominent position, offering an array of options and features that cater to your computing needs.

Beyond the Menu bar, we will explore Spotlight, a powerful tool that allows you to swiftly search and find applications, documents, and more with just a few keystrokes. As you progress, you will encounter the Control Center, where you can access essential system settings and preferences effortlessly.

Siri, Apple's intelligent virtual assistant, is also present on the Mac Desktop, ready to lend a hand with tasks, answer questions, and facilitate smooth interactions between you and your device. Furthermore, the Notification Center ensures you stay informed about essential updates, messages, and notifications, all neatly organized for your convenience.

Of course, the heart of the Mac Desktop lies in the Desktop itself—a customizable canvas where you can organize files, folders, and shortcuts to frequently used applications. And, not to be overlooked, the Dock remains a steadfast companion at the bottom of your screen, providing quick access to your most frequently used apps and documents.

Last but not least, we acquaint you with the Finder—an essential file management tool that empowers you to navigate your Mac, access files, and effortlessly manage your digital world. See Figure 1-8.

Join us on this journey of discovery as we unravel the intricacies of the Mac Desktop. By understanding each element and its functionality, you'll be equipped to make the most of your Mac experience, creating an efficient and personalized workspace tailored to your needs.

Figure 1-8. *Default screen of a Mac's Desktop*

Menu Bar

The Menu Bar is placed at the top of the desktop window. You can use the menu along with the icons in the Menu Bar to select certain commands, execute the jobs, get required information, and check the status of mentioned features. See Figure 1-9.

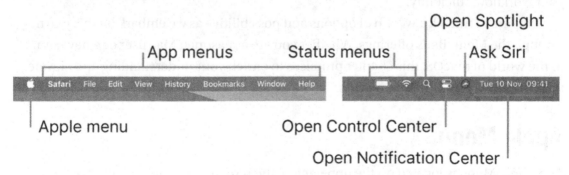

Figure 1-9. *The menu bar segregated into different menus and items*

The Menu Bar is an integral part of your Mac's graphical user interface, offering a range of essential options and controls accessible from the top of your screen. Within this chapter, you will embark on a detailed exploration of the various items that compose the Menu Bar, each serving a unique purpose to enhance your overall Mac experience.

First and foremost is the Apple menu, a symbol of the iconic Apple brand, which provides a gateway to essential system-wide functions and preferences. This menu allows you to access critical actions such as system updates, software installations, and more.

Next, you will delve into the App menu, which dynamically changes to reflect the currently active application. You will uncover the wealth of options it provides, specific to each app, enabling you to manipulate files, adjust settings, and make the most of your software.

Additionally, you will encounter status menus, which are small icons situated on the right side of the Menu Bar, each representing various system status indicators. You will learn how these unobtrusive icons convey crucial information about your Mac's network connectivity, battery life, and other important metrics at a glance.

Intriguingly, you will encounter shortcut icons for Siri, Spotlight, Control Center, and other noteworthy items nestled within the Menu Bar. You will unravel the potential of these quick-access icons, empowering you to harness the full capabilities of your Mac with a single click.

Further, you will examine each Menu Bar item in great detail, exploring their functionalities along with tips and tricks to optimize your Mac navigation and productivity. By the end of this exploration, you will possess a comprehensive understanding of the Menu Bar's significance and how to make it work in tandem with your workflow efficiently.

Prepare to unlock a wealth of options and possibilities as we embark on this journey through the Menu Bar's offerings. Whether you are a seasoned Mac user or a newcomer to the world of macOS, this chapter promises to enrich your understanding and elevate your Mac proficiency to new heights.

Apple Menu

The Apple Menu is located on the upper left of the screen's edge and it includes commands for various tasks to perform in regular intervals, such as updating applications, opening System Preferences, and performing shutdown, restarting, or locking a Mac.

Table 1-3 offers details about each item available within the Apple menu. Every Apple menu item has its own significance for usability. It provides an overview about macOS.

Table 1-3. *Details About Apple Menu Items*

Apple Menu Items	Description
About This Mac	To see details of the Mac, including macOS info with version number, processor, memory (RAM), and optimization of storage Also, access to the manual of the Mac and to obtain service or repair details
System Preferences	System Preferences is used to customize settings on the Mac and to update/upgrade the macOS.
App Store	App Store is used to update and install applications.
Recent Items	When you use apps, files, and network computers, their names are automatically included in a list for easy access in the future. To control the number of items displayed in the list, you can adjust the settings in the General preferences. To access these settings, select the Apple menu, click System Preferences, and navigate to General.
Force Quit	It is used when any application is frozen and not responding. **Important:** *If you force quit any application, there could be a loss of any unsaved data.*
Sleep	To decrease power consumption and lower the screen's brightness without completely powering off the Mac
Restart	Reboot the device.
Shut Down	Completely turn off the Mac.
Lock Screen	Lock the machine and reach the user log-in window.
Log Out	Log out from the current logged in user without turning off the Mac. This is useful if multiple users are provisioned in a single machine.

App Menus

App menus are a fundamental aspect of macOS. They are adjacent to the iconic Apple menu/logo. App menus play a vital role in every application you use, providing a rich set of options and commands to streamline your tasks and workflows. As you explore your Mac's interface, you'll notice that the active application's name is displayed in bold, followed by a series of other menus, commonly bearing typical labels such as File, Edit, Format, Window, and Help.

Within each application, you'll find the indispensable Help menu, a valuable resource for obtaining detailed information about the application's functionalities and other useful insights. Whether you are a newcomer to an application or a seasoned user looking to delve deeper into its capabilities, the Help menu is an invaluable companion.

Each of these menus boasts a collection of commands tailored to the specific application's functionality, offering you a consistent experience across various apps. While certain commands may vary depending on the application's purpose, many commands are available in most apps, facilitating seamless navigation and enhancing your overall efficiency.

Throughout this chapter, we unravel the intricacies of app menus, providing you with comprehensive insights into their organization, options, and usage. By understanding how to leverage these menus effectively, you'll gain mastery over your favorite applications and discover new ways to maximize productivity.

Join us as we unlock the potential of App-menus and dive into the world of commands and possibilities they present. From discovering hidden shortcuts to uncovering advanced features, this chapter promises to empower you with the knowledge to navigate macOS with finesse and confidence. Whether you're a creative professional, a business user, or an enthusiast, the principles explored here will prove indispensable on your journey to becoming a Mac power user.

Status Menu

At the right end of the Menu Bar lies a cluster of icons representing a diverse collection of status menu items. These unobtrusive yet powerful icons let you monitor various aspects of your Mac's status and swiftly adjust essential features to suit your preferences. In this chapter, you embark on a journey to understand the significance of these status menus and how they empower you to stay in control of your Mac experience.

Each status menu icon provides valuable information at a glance. From monitoring battery charge levels to adjusting keyboard brightness, these icons offer quick insights into your Mac's vital statistics. However, their true potential lies in the wealth of options and functionality they provide when clicked upon.

Clicking a status menu icon opens up a world of possibilities. For instance, a simple click of the Wi-Fi icon grants you access to a list of available networks, allowing you to seamlessly connect to the Internet. Similarly, clicking the Display icon unveils options to enable or disable Dark Mode or Night Shift, catering to your visual preferences.

The versatility of status menus extends beyond mere monitoring, as you can customize their arrangement to suit your needs. By holding down the Command key and dragging an icon to a new location, you can rearrange these status menus to optimize your Mac's status monitoring and control.

For those moments when you no longer require a particular status menu, removing it from the Menu Bar is just as straightforward. By pressing and holding the Command key and simultaneously dragging the icon away from the Menu Bar, you can promptly bid farewell to the status menu, decluttering your workspace.

You will explore the hidden potential of status menus and learn to harness their power for a more seamless and personalized Mac experience. Whether you seek to streamline your system monitoring or fine-tune your device's settings, this chapter equips you with the knowledge to navigate the world of status menus with ease and efficiency. Embrace the possibilities as you take charge of your Mac, making it truly your own.

Spotlight

The Spotlight icon, $\mathcal{Q}$, is generally visible in the menu bar. Click this icon to access Spotlight and search various objects/items/directories on Mac and on the Internet.

Nestled within the Menu Bar, the Spotlight icon stands ready to serve as your portal to a world of seamless searching and discovery on your Mac and the vast expanse of the Internet. In this chapter, you embark on a journey to unravel the capabilities of Spotlight, empowering you with the tools to swiftly find files, applications, directories, and much more with ease.

With a simple click on the Spotlight icon, you open the door to a versatile search interface where you can input your queries and uncover a wealth of relevant results. Whether you're seeking a specific document buried in the depths of your Mac's storage or exploring new information online, Spotlight is your trusted companion.

The power of Spotlight extends beyond its presence in the Menu Bar. By utilizing a keyboard shortcut, you can summon Spotlight instantly with the press of Command–Space bar. This effortless combination opens or closes the Spotlight search, offering a seamless and quick way to access the search functionality whenever you need it. See Figure 1-10.

Figure 1-10. Spotlight search

Throughout this section, you will delve into the nuances of Spotlight, providing practical tips to refine your searches and make the most of this remarkable tool. From mastering search operators to customizing Spotlight preferences, you'll discover how to tailor Spotlight to suit your unique needs and streamline your productivity.

As shown in Figure 1-11, you can search for anything within the Spotlight and you will get the search results on different places, such as search result of your macOS or the Internet.

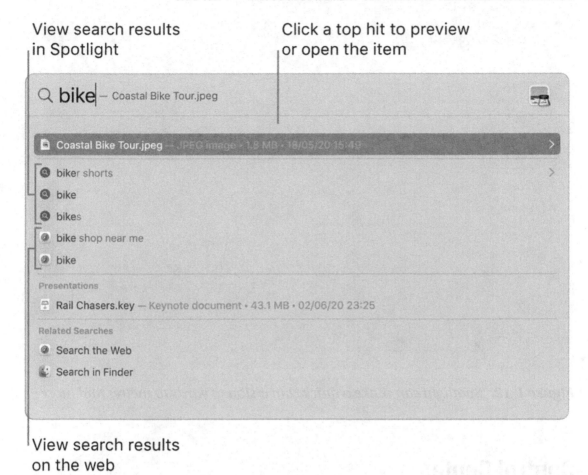

Figure 1-11. *Spotlight search details with an example*

Further, Spotlight can perform quick tasks, as shown in Figure 1-12, such as a quick calculation or converting different types of measurements.

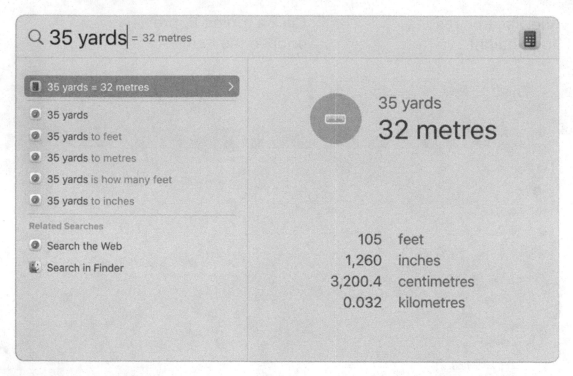

Figure 1-12. *Spotlight can make a quick conversion of yards to metres and more*

Control Center

The Control Center icon, ![toggle icon], is available in the menu bar. To open Control Center, click the icon. With Control Center you can access the features that are frequently in use, such as AirDrop, Wi-Fi, Do Not Disturb, Bluetooth, display brightness, sound, and more.

Control Center is a very helpful feature for accessing required information. It can also help the HelpDesk team to get information quickly from the Mac with the help of the end user. Further, it's very easy for end users to provide the relevant information quickly to the HelpDesk team.

Figure 1-13 shows Control Center.

Figure 1-13. *Default Control Center in Mac with multiple options*

Siri

Siri is virtual voice assistant software that is included in every Mac's operating system. It is designed to respond to voice commands and perform various tasks on the user's behalf, such as launching applications, setting reminders, sending messages, searching the web, providing information, and more.

The Siri icon, ⬤, is usually available in the menu bar. To open Siri, click the icon. To use Siri for tasks such as opening files or apps or for searching for things on the Mac or the Internet, simply click the Siri icon in the menu bar if it is displayed.

Siri can assist you with various day-to-day tasks such as providing prompt answers to inquiries, playing music, and more. Siri can accomplish almost anything you request, whether it be setting up a meeting at a particular date and time or providing answers to your questions.

In certain applications, Siri is capable of presenting suggestions even before you ask for them. For instance, if you receive an invitation in Mail or book a flight in Safari, Siri may recommend adding the event to your calendar. Similarly, while you are browsing web pages, Siri can suggest relevant web pages to explore.

As shown in Figure 1-14, you can ask Siri how many centimeters are in an inch by accessing it via the menu bar and then it will provide the results.

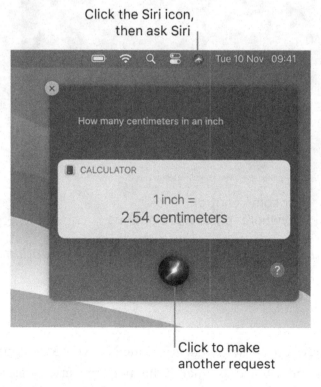

Figure 1-14. *Asking Siri a question*

Notification Center

The Notification Center is a place where you can view pending notifications, appointments, birthdays, and more.

To access the Notification Center, click the Date and Time at the top, extreme right-hand side on the menu bar. Once clicked, all the pending notifications will be visible to access quickly. You can clear all the notifications from the same place.

Figure 1-15 shows the way to access the Notification Center and further interaction with the available notifications. You view and clear the notification with ease.

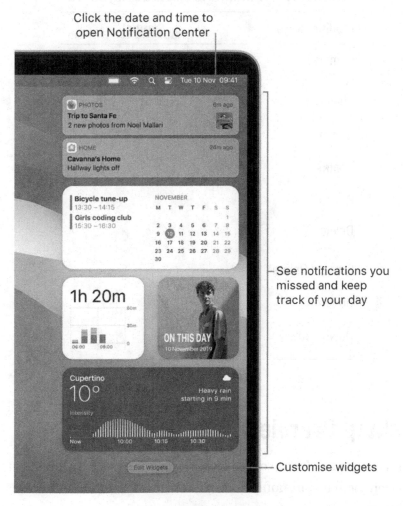

Figure 1-15. Notification Center in a Mac with multiple notifications

Details About the Symbols/Icons in the Menu

Many application menus displays certain symbols, icons, and key combinations, such as ⌘N. These key combinations represents distinct keyboard keys, which are known as *modifier keys*. You can use the key combinations in different menus to execute certain actions, instead of initiating a specific menu. These key combinations save time when opening specific applications, menus, or windows. Table 1-4 shows certain keys that can be used for any specific key combinations.

Table 1-4. *Symbol Keys of a Mac Keyboard*

Modifier keys	Symbol
Command	⌘
Shift	⇧
Option	⌥
Control	⌃
Return	↵
Delete	⌫
Forward Delete	⌦
Up Arrow	↑
Down Arrow	↓

Mac Desktop Overview

The menu bar is located at the top of the screen, while the Dock is situated at the bottom. The area between them is commonly referred to as the desktop, which serves as your primary workspace.

Figure 1-16 shows the default view of the Mac Desktop screen along with the Preview application in the open state and other desktop items, like the Menu Bar and Dock.

Figure 1-16. *Default Mac Desktop overview with an example of an open application and stacks*

Desktop Image

Your macOS desktop is more than just a workspace; it's a reflection of your personality and taste. We will now delve into the realm of desktop customization, exploring the options available to make your Mac experience uniquely yours.

One of the simplest yet most impactful ways to personalize your desktop is by selecting an alternative macOS desktop image. Apple offers an impressive array of stunning wallpapers, including dynamic ones that change automatically as the day progresses. Whether it's the serene beauty of nature or a mesmerizing cityscape, these dynamic images breathe life into your desktop, providing a refreshing visual treat with each passing moment.

However, personalization extends beyond the preloaded collection. If you seek to infuse your desktop with a touch of nostalgia or fond memories, you can opt to use one of your personal photos as the backdrop.

You will delve into the step-by-step process of customizing your desktop image, ensuring that your Mac reflects your style and aspirations. From selecting the perfect dynamic wallpaper to setting up a slideshow of your most treasured photos, we guide you through the vast array of customization options available.

Let's unlock the power of desktop personalization, giving you the tools to create a Mac experience that resonates with your individuality. Whether you seek tranquility, inspiration, or a constant reminder of what truly matters, this chapter empowers you to curate your desktop to perfection, fostering an environment that brings joy and motivation to every interaction with your beloved Mac.

Desktop Appearance

On a Mac, you have the ability to select either a light or dark appearance for the Menu Bar, Dock, windows, and built-in apps. As shown in Figure 1-17, alternatively, you may opt for an automatic adjustment that switches from light to dark mode depending on the time of day.

Figure 1-17. *Options available for your desktop appearance in System Preferences – General*

Organizing Files and Folders

To maintain a tidy workspace, you can use stacks on the desktop to neatly organize files into groups. As soon as a file is saved on the desktop, it will automatically be sorted in the organized stack. Additionally, the Dock features a Downloads stack for grouping files that you download from the Internet.

Turning on Stacks

Click in the desktop space to get the Finder menu, select the View menu, and click Use Stacks or press the Control+Command+0 keys on the keyboard.

You can also Control-click on the desktop space and then select the Use Stacks option. Once done, as displayed in Figure 1-18, the relevant files get organized automagically.

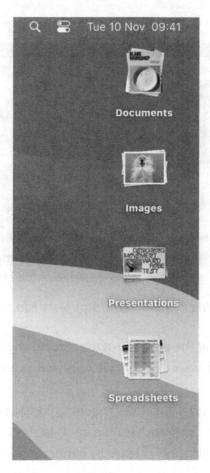

Figure 1-18. *Stacks overview*

Finding an Active Window

If you have numerous open windows cluttering your desktop, you can employ Mission Control to swiftly access the desktop or to view a simplified display of all open windows on the desktop. This makes it easy to locate the window you require. Mission Control presents a comprehensive view of all open windows on your Mac's desktop, arranged in a singular layer to simplify the process of locating the desired window. See Figure 1-19.

Figure 1-19.   *The way to check active windows on a Mac via Mission Control*

The Spaces bar, situated at the top edge of the screen, showcases thumbnails of any apps that are currently in full screen or split view, as well as any desktop spaces that you have created.

From a trackpad: Swipe up using three fingers to enter and swipe down to leave. To modify or disable the trackpad gesture, you can do so in the Trackpad preferences.

From a keyboard: You can enter or leave by either pressing the Mission Control key ⊞ or using the shortcut Control-Up Arrow.

Using Several Desktop Spaces

Creating additional desktop spaces on your computer allows you to better organize your tasks. By assigning specific tasks to each desktop, you can focus on one thing at a time and easily switch between them. For instance, you can have one desktop dedicated to managing your emails while using another desktop for working on a project. Each desktop can be customized to suit the task you're working on, providing a more personalized and efficient work experience. This feature can significantly increase your productivity and help you stay organized while multitasking.

When you have multiple app windows open on your Mac's desktop, it can become cluttered and difficult to manage. To solve this problem, you can use the Mission Control feature to create new desktops, which are known as spaces; they help in organizing several windows.

With this feature, each space contains only the windows that are relevant to the current task, helping you focus and work more efficiently. By separating your workspaces, you can prevent distractions and maintain a clearer overview of your tasks.

Mission Control is a useful tool for keeping your work organized and optimizing your productivity.

Steps for Creating Desktop Spaces

Desktop Spaces is a powerful tool that enables you to organize your workspace efficiently, fostering a seamless and focused computing experience.

To access the world of Desktop Spaces, venture into Mission Control, where a visual representation of your various app windows and full-screen or split view mode thumbnails awaits you in the Spaces bar. Each thumbnail represents a distinct space where you can group related apps and tasks, minimizing distractions and maximizing productivity.

As shown in Figure 1-20, creating a new space is very seamless; you just click the Add button located in the Spaces bar. With this feature, you can tailor up to 16 spaces to your unique requirements, ensuring each space serves a specific purpose, be it work-related tasks, creative endeavors, or personal projects.

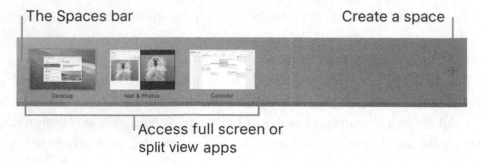

Figure 1-20. *The way to create additional desktop work spaces in a Mac*

Once you have meticulously set up your spaces, navigating between them is a breeze. A simple click on the respective thumbnails in the Spaces bar allows you to seamlessly transition from one virtual space to another, facilitating smooth multitasking and effortless focus.

Furthermore, the flexibility of Desktop Spaces allows you to optimize your workflow and create a personalized environment tailored to your specific needs. By dedicating spaces for specific tasks or projects, you can eliminate clutter and immerse yourself fully in each undertaking.

Using Dock

The Dock is a helpful feature on the Mac desktop that allows easy access to applications, frequently used applications, and features like Launchpad and Bin/Trash. As shown in Figure 1-21, by default Dock consists of applications, downloads, and the Bin.

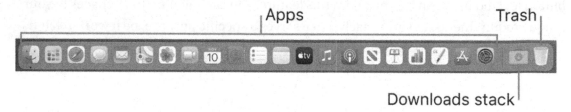

Figure 1-21. *Default view of the Dock in a Mac*

The Dock is a customizable feature on the Mac desktop that can display up to three recently used apps, as well as a folder for downloaded items from the Internet.

By default, the Dock is located at the bottom of the screen; however, it can be adjusted to appear along the left or right edge as well. This makes it easier for users to access their favorite apps and files quickly and efficiently.

With the ability to customize the Dock, users can tailor their Mac desktop to suit their individual preferences and optimize their workflow.

Figure 1-22 shows that you can add more applications in Dock within Apps section. If you have been using any application frequently, it gets added to the Recent section for swift use.

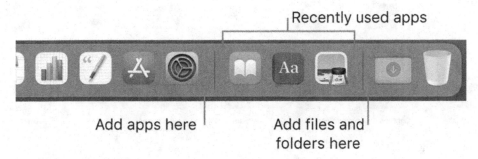

Figure 1-22. *Different sections of the Dock in Mac*

Organizing Files and Folders in Finder

The Finder is a central feature of the Mac operating system, accessible through the blue "smiling face" icon, , in the Dock. It is placed as the first icon on the Dock. As displayed in Figure 1-23, clicking this icon opens a Finder window, which serves as the hub for managing files and folders on Mac.

Figure 1-23. *Finder on a Mac*

Finder windows are the primary means of managing and retrieving nearly all content on your Mac. Figure 1-24 shows the different sections of Finder windows.

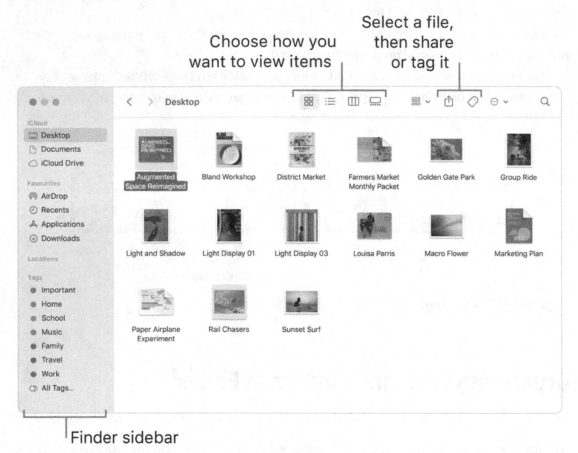

Figure 1-24. Finder view on a Mac with multiple items

System Preferences

Note   In the new macOS version 13 (Ventura), Apple renamed System Preferences to System Settings.

Accessing System Preferences/Settings on Mac

The System Preferences application, which provides access to the settings on Macs and is shown in Figure 1-25, can be accessed in a number of ways.

Figure 1-25. *System Preferences icon*

It can be found in the Applications folder and in the Apple menu located at the top-left of the screen or in the Dock at the bottom of the screen.

Additionally, you can quickly search for it using Spotlight by pressing CMD+Space and typing in System Preferences.

With multiple options for accessing the System Preferences app, adjusting Mac settings has never been easier. It makes it convenient for you to access and customize you Mac as per your liking.

Customizing a Mac via System Preferences

Customizing a Mac is easy with the ability to change system settings. You can personalize features such as the Dock's size and location, appearance with light or dark mode themes, desktop wallpaper, screensaver, security settings, and much more.

Exploring System Preferences/Settings

Multiple features or functions on a Mac are organized into preferences. For instance, settings for Spotlight/Language and Region can be accessed through the Spotlight/Language and Region preferences panel.

As Figure 1-26 shows, preferences are presented in a grid of icons on your Mac. The specific icons vary depending on your Mac and installed apps. Selecting an icon opens the corresponding preference pane, allowing you to view and modify its associated options.

Figure 1-26. *Default view of System Preferences with multiple options*

Options in System Preferences/Settings

When searching for options in System Preferences, use the search field situated at the top of the window. After typing in search text, the options that match will be displayed and their location within preference panes will be highlighted. This is especially useful when navigating through a large number of options or when you are unsure which preference pane the option is located in.

As shown in Figure 1-27, by using the search field, you can quickly and efficiently locate the option needed without having to manually search through each preference pane.

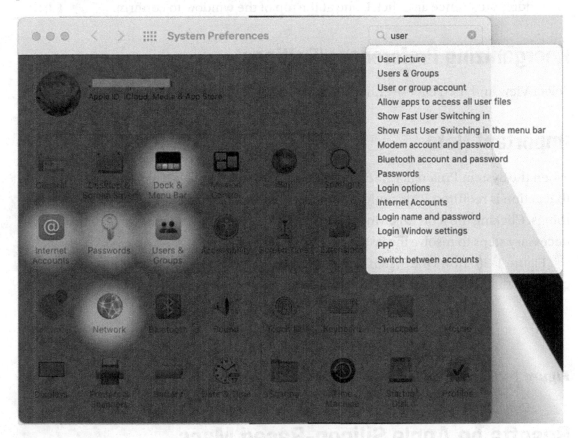

Figure 1-27. *Search field use in System Preferences*

Customizing System Preferences/Settings

Hiding a Particular Preference/Setting

To hide a preference, go to View and select Customize. Deselect the preference's tick box and click Done at the window's top to apply changes.

Showing a Hidden Preference/Setting

To show a hidden preference, select View and then Customize. Check the checkbox for the hidden preference and click Done at the top of the window to confirm.

Reorganizing Preferences/Settings

Select View and then choose either Organize by Categories or Organize Alphabetically.

Important Note

When the System Preferences/Settings icon in the Dock displays a red badge, it indicates that action is required. This could mean installing software updates, among other things. Clicking the icon will bring up the preferences/settings so that you can take the necessary steps to resolve the issue.

Figure 1-28 shows the System Preferences icon. The notification badge in red circle confirms that there is a pending item that requires action.

Figure 1-28. *Notification badge on System Preferences*

Rosetta on Apple Silicon-Based Macs

Rosetta is a translation process that enables users to run apps containing x86_64 instructions on Apple silicon. This means that a Mac with an Apple processor can use apps designed for Intel-based Macs.

Rosetta 2 is the improved version of this technology, which allows for even smoother and faster app translation on Apple Silicon.

Installing Rosetta/Rosetta2

Upon opening an app that is designed for Intel-based Macs on a Mac with Apple Silicon, you will be prompted to install Rosetta. To proceed, simply click the Install button and enter your username and password. This installation process allows for the seamless use of Intel-based apps on Apple Silicon-based Macs.

Once Rosetta is installed, it becomes available for any other apps that require it, eliminating the need for another installation. However, if you choose not to install Rosetta upon the prompt, the system will ask again the next time you try to open an app that requires it. This ensures that you can seamlessly use any app designed for Intel-based Macs on your Apple Silicon-based Mac without any compatibility issues. See Figure 1-29.

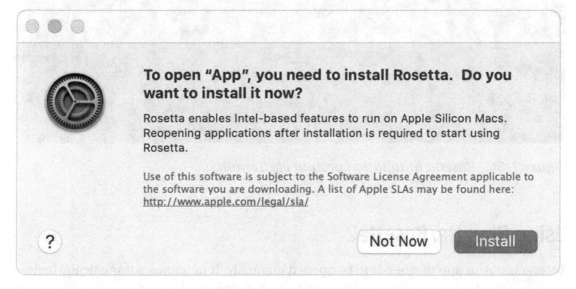

Figure 1-29. *Rosetta installation via the GUI*

Rosetta/Rosetta 2 can also be installed via commands, which can be executed in Terminal with Admin rights. Use this command and see Figure 1-30:

`softwareupdate --install-rosetta`

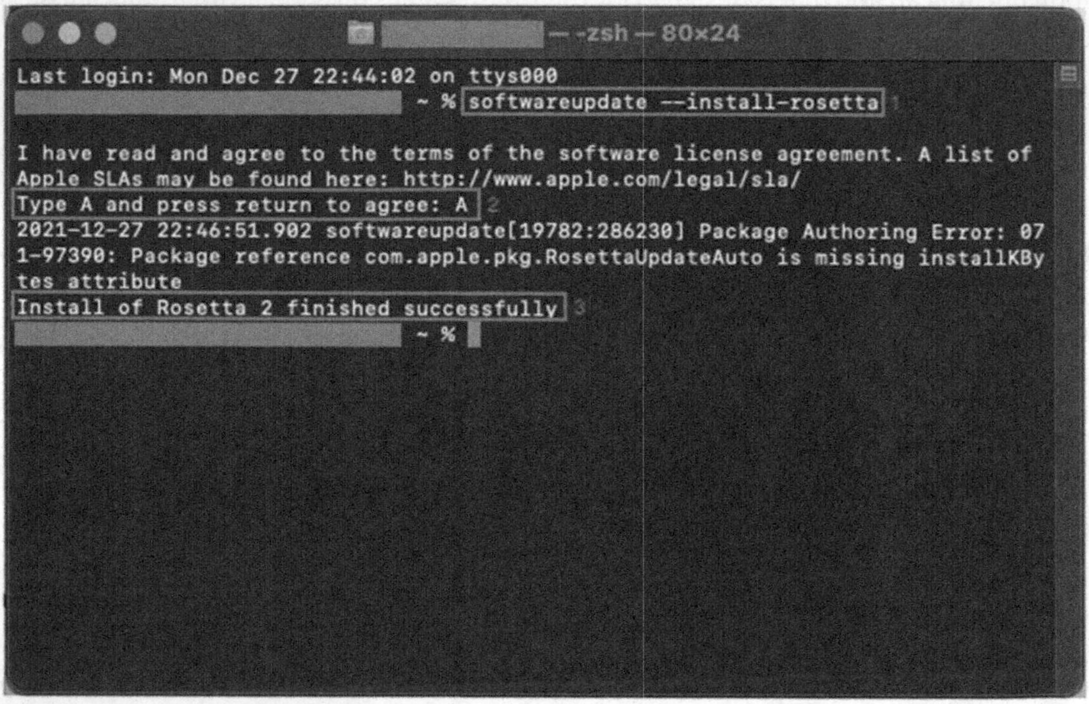

Figure 1-30. *Rosetta installation prompt via Terminal*

Using Rosetta/Rosetta2

Rosetta is not an app that needs to be opened manually. It functions automatically in the background whenever an app designed exclusively for Macs with an Intel processor is launched onto a Mac device that has an Apple Silicon chipset.

Rosetta's purpose is to translate the app for use with Apple Silicon, allowing for a seamless experience for the user. Therefore, you don't need to worry about manually enabling Rosetta each time you use an Intel-based app, as it will function automatically in the background to ensure compatibility.

Which Applications Need Rosetta/Rosetta2?

To determine whether an app requires Rosetta/Rosetta2 or is compatible with it, you can use the Get Info function as follows:

- First, select the app in the Finder.

- From the File menu on the menu bar, select Get Info.

- Look for the information labeled Kind.

  - Application (Intel) indicates that the app is designed only for Intel processors and needs Rosetta to function on a Mac with Apple Silicon.

  - Application (Universal) indicates that the app is compatible with both Apple Silicon and Intel processors, and it will use Apple Silicon by default. See Figure 1-31.

Universal apps include an option in the Info window called Open using Rosetta that enables compatibility with plug-ins, extensions, and other add-ons that have not yet been updated to support Apple Silicon. This setting is particularly useful for apps like web browsers or email clients that rely on add-ons.

If a universal app fails to recognize an add-on that has been installed, users can quit the app, select the Open using Rosetta option, and try again.

This feature allows users to continue using their favorite add-ons on universal apps until the add-ons are updated to support Apple Silicon.

Figure 1-31. Checking the application file type and other details

Minor Updates of macOS

Apple periodically releases updates for macOS that can include important security updates, vulnerability updates, and updates to the preinstalled apps that come with a Mac. These are the updates available for the existing macOS version that is installed, which may or may not include point release updates such as for version 12.5 to 12.5.1.

When a notification appears on a Mac stating that software updates are available, you have the option to select when the installation of the updates happens or be reminded at a later time. Additionally, you can manually check macOS updates by accessing the Software Update section in System Preferences.

If you want to check the updates of applications that were installed via the App Store, simply open App Store and it should show the available updates of the installed applications.

Checking macOS Updates Manually

To download macOS software updates, go to System Preferences by clicking the Apple menu and selecting the Software Update option. The count of available updates, if any, will be displayed besides the System Preferences option.

If you want to update the software that has been downloaded via the App Store, simply go to the Apple menu, and the count of available updates will be visible beside the App Store option. Click the App Store option to continue updating the software within the App Store app.

Checking for Software Updates Automatically

To access the Software Update options on a Mac, go to the Apple menu, choose System Preferences, and then click Software Update.

To enable automatic installation of macOS updates, check the Automatically keep my Mac up to date option.

For advance update options, click the Advanced button and select one of the options mentioned below.

To check the updates automatically, click Check for updates.

To download the updates without any prompt, click Download new updates when available.

To install the updates automatically, choose Install macOS updates.

To install app updates from the App Store automatically, select Install app updates from the App Store.

To install system files along with security updates automatically, select Install system data files and security updates.

After selecting any of the options above, click OK, as displayed in Figure 1-32.

Figure 1-32. *Advanced options in Software Update via System Preferences*

Recommendations

It is advisable to choose the Check for updates, Download new updates when available, and Install system data files and security updates options so that your Mac can get the newest updates automatically.

For automatic downloads of updates, MacBooks, MacBook Pros, and MacBook Airs should be connected to the power adapter.

Table 1-5 provides detailed information about Software Update preferences and the use of each option.

Table 1-5. *Details About Software Update Options*

Option	Description
Update Now	For installation of the entire system software and updates shown in the Software Update pane, click the Update Now button located at the top-right corner. If the Update Now button is not visible, your Mac is already up to date.
More info	If updates are available, click More info to access information about them. • To view information about a particular update, click it. • If you wish to install updates, mark the checkboxes beside the updates you require and click Install Now.
Automatically keep my Mac up to date	To enable automatic installation of updates, select the mentioned checkbox.
Advanced	To access more settings for automatic installation of system software and updates, click the Advanced button.

Note   Rosetta is built-in software in macOS that allows Macs with Apple Silicon to run applications designed for Intel-based Macs.

Major Upgrade of a macOS

Sometimes an upgrade on a Mac involves installing a more recent version of macOS, such as upgrading from Big Sur to Monterey.

Here's a checklist to follow before starting the upgrade:

- Verify compatibility.

- Back up data.

- Clear up storage space.

- Ensure application compatibility.

Check and upgrade your macOS and built-in apps like Safari by using Software Update. To access Software Update, select it within the System Preferences. Then, choose either Update Now or Upgrade Now.

As shown in Figure 1-33, the Update Now option will install the newest available updates of the macOS version installed on the machine, such as going from macOS Monterey 12.6.4 to 12.6.5.

Figure 1-33. *Availability of macOS updates via Software Update*

As displayed in Figure 1-34, by selecting Upgrade Now, you initiate the installation of a significant new version that bears a new name, such as macOS Monterey.

Figure 1-34. *Availability of macOS upgrade via Software Update*

Recovery of a macOS

macOS Recovery is an essential built-in recovery system available on every Mac. It offers a range of utilities that can help you with various tasks, like restoring your data via Time Machine, reinstalling the macOS, accessing online support, repairing or erasing your hard disk, and more. It's an efficient tool for troubleshooting and fixing any issues you may face with your Mac's operating system.

The process of accessing recovery mode varies between Intel-based Macs and Apple Silicon so we cover the process of accessing recovery in both hardware architectures. You will often find a mix of both hardware architectures in enterprises.

Apple Silicon

Many of the recovery options in Apple Silicon-based Macs can be accessed via use of the power button. Firstly, shut down the Mac device. Then, turn on the Mac and keep holding power button until it shows the startup options screen. See Figure 1-35.

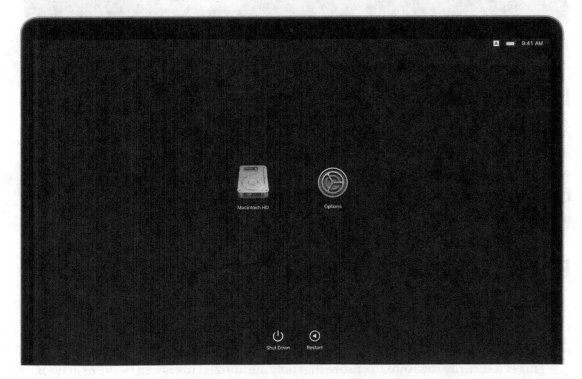

Figure 1-35. *Accessing the recovery system in an Apple Silicon Mac*

As displayed in Figure 1-36, click the Options gear icon and select Continue to proceed.

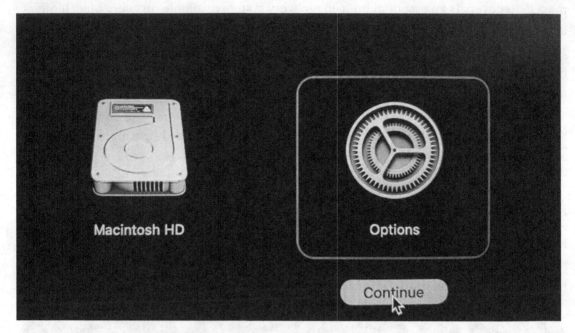

Figure 1-36. Recovery options in an Apple Silicon Mac

Intel Processor

Accessing recovery options in Intel-based Macs is completely different compared to Apple Silicon-based Macs. It requires the use of several keyboard key combinations.

Firstly, shut down your Mac. As soon as you power on your Mac, hold down Command (⌘)-R without delay. Keep holding the keys until you see an Apple logo or any other image.

Recovery Mode

When accessing certain features or making system changes, your Mac may require the password of an administrator user. If prompted, simply enter the requested password to continue.

This is a security measure to ensure that only authorized users can perform actions that could potentially impact the system or compromise its data. Figure 1-37 shows the pop-up to provide admin credentials to access the recovery system options.

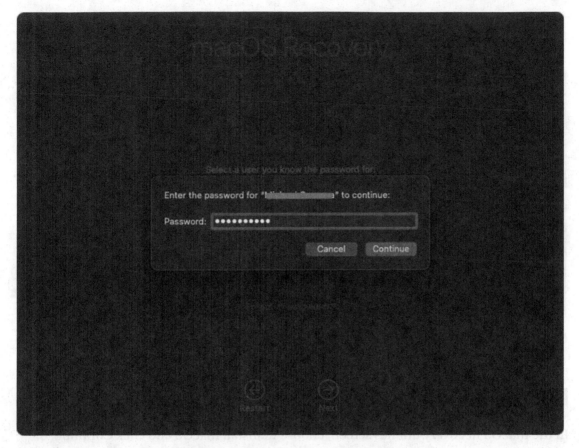

Figure 1-37. *Further prompt to access the recovery system*

The utilities window indicates that the start-up process has finished.

Restore from Time Machine: Retrieve your data from a backup made by Time Machine.

Reinstall macOS: Obtain and reinstall the macOS operating system.

Safari (or Get Help Online): Access Safari to surf the Internet and find assistance for your Mac. The links to Apple's support webpage are provided. Browser extensions and add-ons are turned off.

Disk Utility: Use Disk Utility to mend or wipe your hard drive or other storage devices. See Figure 1-38.

Figure 1-38. *Utilities in the recovery system of a Mac*

Reinstallation of macOS

In the macOS Recovery utilities screen, choose Reinstall macOS and click Continue. Then, follow the instructions provided on your screen to complete the reinstallation process.

Importance of Key Combinations

By pressing Command (⌘)+R, you can start your Mac from the built-in macOS Recovery system.

Alternatively, you can use Option+Command+R or Shift+Option+Command+R to start up the machine from macOS Recovery over the Internet.

Depending on key combinations, macOS Recovery can install a different versions of the macOS.

Installing a macOS from Recovery usually provides the current version of macOS, with a few exceptions. If the start-up disk is wiped using Disk Utility, then probably the previous compatible version of macOS will be offered for installation.

On Intel-based Macs, pressing Option+Command+R at the time of startup may provide the newest compatible macOS version.

Pressing Shift+Option+Command-R may offer the original macOS version or the nearest version available.

If the logic board was recently changed, then probably the newest compatible version of macOS will be offered for installation.

During the Installation Process, Please Adhere to the Following Guidelines

If prompted, enter your Mac login password to unlock the disk during installation.

If installation fails due to an issue recognizing your disk or computer, use Disk Utility to erase the disk before proceeding with the installation.

If given the option to choose between Macintosh HD or Macintosh HD – Data during installation, choose Macintosh HD.

Ensure that the Mac is not put to sleep and its lid is not closed during the installation process. If either happens, this may require multiple restarts with a progress bar and intermittent empty screens.

Erasing and Reinstalling a macOS

To reset your Mac to its original factory settings, you can erase your device and then use the macOS Recovery system that is preinstalled on your Mac to reinstall macOS.

Note   To reinstall macOS on a Mac notebook, make sure the device is connected to the Internet and the power adapter is plugged in.

To access Disk Utility, boot your computer into macOS Recovery mode. You may be prompted to select a user and enter the administrator password.

Once you are in the utilities window, choose Disk Utility and click the Continue button. See Figure 1-39.

Figure 1-39. *Disk utility access via Utilities in the Recovery System of a Mac*

To erase your startup disk and reinstall macOS, follow these steps:

- Open Disk Utility from the utilities window in macOS Recovery. In the sidebar, select Macintosh HD or the name of your start-up disk. Click the Erase button, available in the toolbar. In the Name field, type Macintosh HD or choose a name you prefer. Select the recommended format type, which is APFS.

- If you come across the option called Erase Volume Group, click it instead of Erase.

- After the erase process finishes, select Done and click the Quit Disk Utility under the Disk Utility menu. In the Recovery app window, choose Reinstall macOS and press the Continue button. Afterwards, just follow the instructions displayed on the screen. See Figure 1-40.

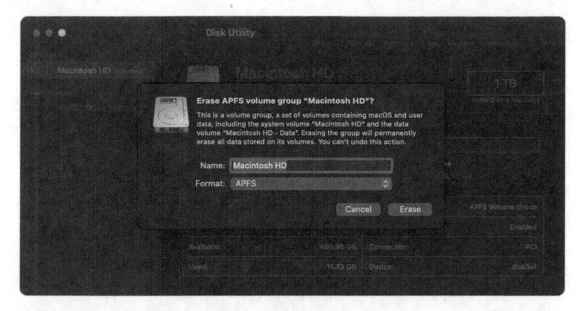

Figure 1-40. *Disk utility to erase a Macintosh HD*

Mac Setup

Post reinstallation of the macOS, complete the setup of your Mac. The macOS Setup Assistant is a tool that guides users through the process of setting up their Mac for the first time or after erasing and reinstalling the operating system.

It includes various steps such as choosing the language and region, setting up a Wi-Fi network, signing in with an Apple ID, setting up iCloud, enabling Siri and Hey Siri, setting up Touch ID, and more.

During setup, users can also choose their preferred desktop appearance with options for Light, Dark, or Auto. Additionally, users are eligible to set up Apple Pay for individual user accounts on their Macs, monitor their computer's use with Screen Time, and set up accessibility options for vision, motor, hearing, and cognitive abilities.

The macOS Setup Assistant ensures that users have a smooth and easy experience setting up their Mac, making it ready to use in no time.

Here are the macOS Setup Assistant steps:

- Choose your country or region and click Continue.

- Select your language and continue.

- Accessibility options encourage users to customize their computer according to their cognitive, hearing, motor, and vision needs. Select whether you want to transfer information from a different Mac device, Time Machine backup, or a Windows PC, or if you want to start fresh, and then click on Continue. Sign in with an Apple ID or skip this step if you don't have one. Agree to the terms and conditions.

- Create a user account and password and set up iCloud Keychain, which allows you to store your passwords and credit card information securely in iCloud.

- Choose whether to enable Siri and Hey Siri. Choose whether to use Screen Time, which allows you to monitor and control the use of your computer. Choose whether to share analytics data with Apple. Choose your preferred appearance for the desktop: Light, Dark, or Auto. Click Continue and then wait for the setup process to be completed.

- Once the setup is completed, you will reach the Mac desktop. See Figure 1-41.

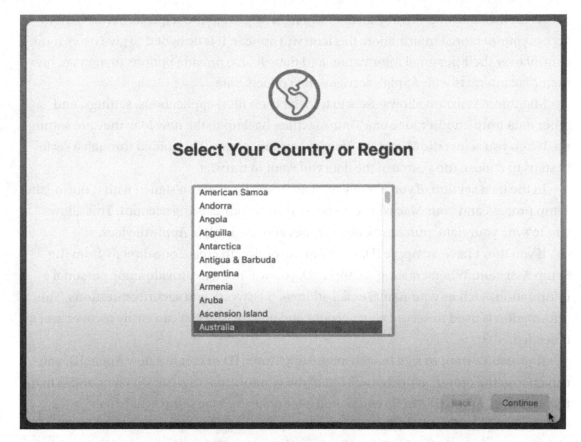

Figure 1-41. *The beginning of Setup Assistant with selection of country or region*

The Setup Assistant window of a Mac typically presents users with a prompt to select their country or region during the initial setup process. This step allows you to specify your geographical location, which can be essential for configuring various settings, such as language, time zone, and regional formats. The chosen country or region will influence the default language, keyboard layout, date and time format, and other regional preferences.

In the next prompt, you will typically see a list of languages supported by macOS. This step allows you to choose the language you want to use for the macOS interface and system settings. The chosen language is used as the default display language for menus, dialog boxes, notifications, and other system-related text.

Moving further, the Accessibility section allows you to configure accessibility settings, making it easier for individuals with disabilities to use and interact with Macs. The Accessibility settings provide a range of features and options to enhance the user experience for people with various needs.

As for the Data and Privacy section, when an Apple feature requests permission to access your personal information, this icon will appear. It is designed to give users more control over their personal information and data. It also provide options to manage how their Mac interacts with Apple's services and collects data.

Migration Assistant allows users to transfer their files, applications, settings, and other data from another Mac or a Time Machine backup to the new Mac they are setting up. When you select the Migration Assistant option, you will be guided through a series of steps to choose the source of the data you want to transfer.

In the next section, if you already have an Apple ID, you can sign in with it during the setup process and your Mac will be associated with your existing account. This allows you to sync your data, purchases, and settings across multiple Apple devices.

If you don't have an Apple ID, you have the option to create one directly from the Setup Assistant. When creating an Apple ID, you will need to provide some personal information, such as your name, email address, password, and security questions. This information is used to secure your account and ensure that you can easily recover access if needed.

If you don't want to sign in with an existing Apple ID or create a new Apple ID, you can choose the option at the bottom left of the window that says Set Up Later and skip to the next step. Apple ID can be configured later once the Mac setup is finished.

The Setup Assistant window includes a step where you are presented with the Terms and Conditions for using Apple's software and services. This step is crucial because it outlines the legal agreement between the user and Apple regarding the usage of their products and services. Agree to the Terms and Conditions because it is a mandatory step to complete the setup of your Mac.

You will be presented with a screen to create an account on your Mac. This will help to configure your Mac as per your choices and to create more user accounts. The account that is created during the Mac setup has administrator privileges by default. In the next screen, an Express Setup is a streamlined and simplified way to configure your Mac quickly, making it ready for use with just a few essential choices.

The Screen Time section allows you to review and configure preferences regarding the collection and sharing of diagnostic and usage data by Apple.

Screen Time is a feature that allows you to monitor and manage your use of your Mac, helping you better understand your digital habits and set healthier screen time limits. It provides insights into your app and website usage, allowing you to track how you spend your time on your Mac. It also offers monitoring capabilities, giving you the ability to supervise and manage your kids' activities on their Apple devices.

Moving ahead, Siri can be activated by your voice, enabling you to accomplish various tasks. For instance, you can schedule meetings, modify preferences, seek answers, send messages, make calls, and add calendar events. Its capabilities extend to a wide range of functions, enhancing your productivity and convenience.

You can also choose whether you want to help Apple improve Siri and Dictation features by providing voice recordings and usage data. When you select the Improve Siri & Dictation option, you allow Apple to collect and store voice recordings and transcripts of your interactions with Siri and Dictation. These recordings are used by Apple to enhance the accuracy and performance of these features. The data is anonymized and dissociated from your Apple ID, ensuring privacy and confidentiality.

During the initial setup process of a Mac you also get an option to choose between three appearance options: Light, Dark, and Auto mode. These choices affect the overall look and feel of the macOS interface.

Figure 1-42 shows the final screen of the Mac Setup Assistant, and it confirms that you have successfully followed all the required steps and your Mac is ready to set up as per the selections made. It may take 2-3 minutes on this screen and then you will reach the Mac desktop.

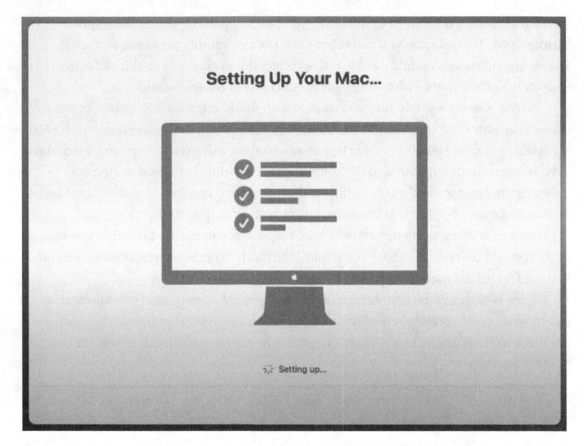

Figure 1-42. Setup Assistant window: the final screen to complete the setup of the Mac

Summary

In this chapter, we explored various aspects of macOS functionality, focusing on customization to cater to individual preferences. We discussed how users can optimize their experience by tailoring macOS settings. Additionally, we emphasized the significance of security updates and major operating system upgrades to keep systems secure and up to date. The Mac recovery system's troubleshooting capabilities were highlighted as invaluable, helping users resolve issues effectively. Lastly, we covered post reinstallation setup, empowering users to personalize their workspace efficiently. As Apple aligns its product line and operating systems, staying informed is essential.

Our comprehensive exploration aimed to empower users in maximizing their Mac experience and adapting to evolving features. In the next chapter, we will focus around the types of user accounts and file systems, along with built-in applications and utilities of macOS and the usability of these tools to troubleshoot the issues.

Glossary

Abbreviation	Description
ADE	Automatic Device Enrollment
ABM	Apple Business Manager
VPP	Volume Purchase Program
APNs	Apple Push Notification Service
FV	File Vault
ACE	Apple Care for Enterprise
ASP	Apple Seed Program

CHAPTER 2

Applications and Utilities Introduction

In this chapter, we will delve into the usability of applications and utilities within macOS so that you can have a comprehensive understanding of their functions and features. We will begin with an exploration of the various types of user accounts and file systems (application and formatting) that are supported on Mac devices, which are essential for effectively managing macOS.

Then we will guide you through the process of installing applications and becoming acquainted with the built-in macOS applications and utilities. This knowledge will prove valuable in navigating the macOS environment efficiently.

Additionally, we will focus on the significance of important preinstalled utilities in macOS, highlighting how these tools can aid in troubleshooting and gathering essential information when needed. By gaining insights into these utilities, you will enhance your ability to handle various technical challenges that may arise.

Throughout this chapter, we will cover a range of topics, including an overview of user accounts, supported file systems on the application level, installation procedures for applications, and an in-depth exploration of the built-in macOS applications and utilities. Furthermore, we will shed light on the supported macOS file format systems as well as techniques to view/hide hidden files and folders using keyboard shortcuts.

By the end of this chapter, you will have a comprehensive grasp of the applications and utilities ecosystem within macOS, equipping you with the knowledge and skills to navigate and troubleshoot effectively within the operating system. Let's begin your journey into the world of macOS usability and functionality.

S. Rastogi and J. Singh, *Exploring macOS*, https://doi.org/10.1007/978-1-4842-9882-4_2

User Accounts Overview

A user account in Mac refers to a personalized and secure profile created for an individual user on a macOS-based computer. It provides a set of settings, preferences, and permissions that are unique as per the logged in user. Each user account on a Mac device is separate from others, allowing different users to have their own customized desktop environment, applications, and files.

A user account on a Mac device includes the following components:

- **Username**: It is the name assigned to the user and is used to log into the Mac.

- **Password**: A password is set by the user during the account creation process. It serves as a security measure to protect the user's account and data from unauthorized access.

- **Home directory**: Each user account has its own home directory, which acts as a personal folder for storing documents, preferences, and settings specific to that user.

- **Access privileges**: User accounts can have different access privileges, determining the level of control and permissions a user has on the system. Accounts can be set as administrators, allowing full control over the Mac, or as standard users with limited privileges.

- **Preferences**: User accounts allow customization of various settings, such as desktop wallpaper, screensaver, language, time zone, and more. These preferences can be adjusted individually for each user account.

- **Applications and files**: Each user account has its own set of applications and files. This means that users can install and use applications specific to their needs, and their personal files are stored separately from other users.

User accounts on a Mac serve as a fundamental mechanism for facilitating a highly personalized computing experience while upholding stringent privacy standards. This is accomplished by guaranteeing that every user is allocated a dedicated environment tailored to their specific requirements and ensuring exclusive access to their individual data.

Consequently, user accounts assume a paramount role in accommodating multi-user environments and scenarios where multiple individuals partake in the shared use of a computer system.

Types of User Accounts

The types of user accounts you can create are shown in Figure 2-1.

Figure 2-1. *Types of user accounts*

Administrator Account

By default, an administrator account on a macOS device possesses unrestricted access to the entirety of its functionalities. This encompasses the ability to oversee and administer user accounts, facilitate the addition or removal of applications, manipulate system files, and regulate security settings.

Essentially, any administrative task can be seamlessly executed by an account endowed with administrative privileges. It is feasible to establish multiple administrator accounts according to your requirements. However, it is imperative to maintain at least one administrator account on a macOS device because it serves as an indispensable element of system operation and management.

The administrator account stands as the utmost authority in terms of privileges and control within the Mac system. It has the ability to generate and oversee additional user accounts, carry out software installations and removals, make alterations to system settings, and undertake administrative duties such as updating the operating system and managing security configurations.

The administrator account plays a vital role in the management and upkeep of the Mac system, ensuring its smooth operation and overall maintenance. See Figure 2-2.

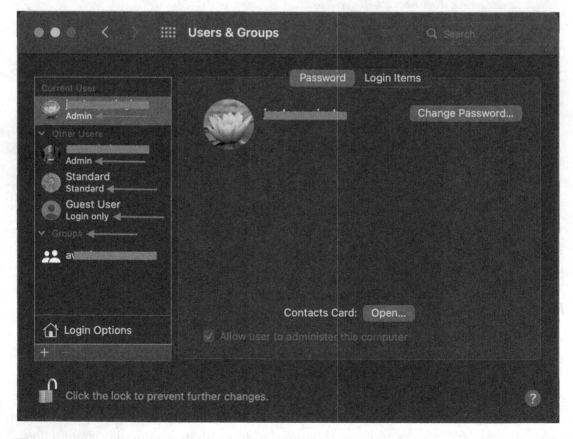

Figure 2-2. *List of user accounts in the Users & Groups preferences*

Standard Account

Standard accounts are entry-level user accounts that grant end users the ability to personalize settings exclusive to their own account. These accounts come with certain limitations in terms of modifying system settings, accessing files belonging to other users, and altering macOS security settings.

It is worth noting that standard accounts retain the capability to execute administrator-level modifications to the system by inputting the username and password of an administrator account. However, they lack the authority to modify settings of other users, create new user accounts, or delete any existing user accounts on the Mac.

A standard user account is specifically tailored for routine use and caters to regular users who do not need administrative privileges. Individuals with a standard account possess the ability to access and employ most applications and files on the Mac; however, they are unable to enact system-wide alterations or execute administrative duties.

This type of account is suited for individuals whose computer activities predominantly revolve around personal tasks like web browsing, word processing, or multimedia consumption. See Figure 2-3.

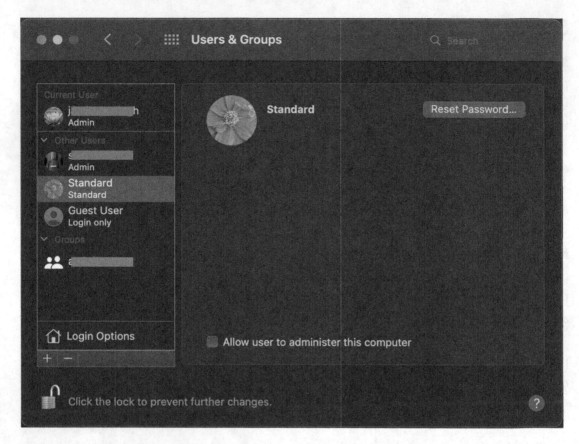

Figure 2-3. *Standard user account*

Sharing Only Account

A sharing only account enables a user to access particular shared folders on your Mac. If you engage in file sharing activities at home or in a work environment, you may find it useful to create user accounts that solely grant access to files on the computer without allowing any other actions.

You can grant access to specific folders by utilizing the Sharing preference pane in the System Preferences. See Figure 2-4.

It's important to note that a sharing-only user cannot log in or make any changes on the Mac. This type of account is primarily intended for remote access to shared files.

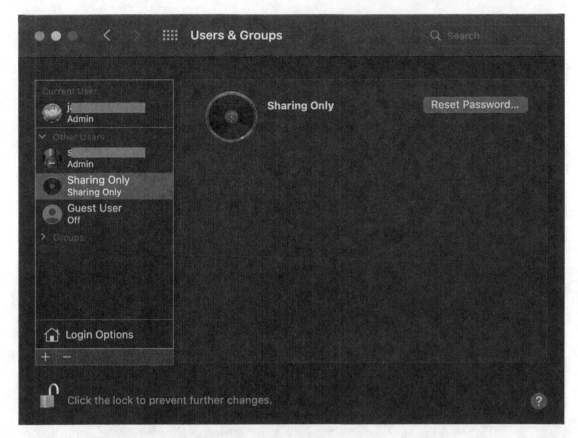

Figure 2-4. Sharing only user account

Guest Account

The guest user account is inherently present on your Mac, requiring only activation to make it accessible. This account permits guests to log in effortlessly without the need for a password.

However, it is important to note that guests using the guest user account are unable to modify settings or make any changes to the system configuration. Additionally, any files saved by the guest user during their session are automatically erased once they log out.

The guest user account provides a temporary and restricted user experience, ensuring that guests can utilize the Mac while maintaining the system's integrity and safeguarding user privacy.

The guest account serves as a transitory and constrained account, affording users the ability to access the Mac system without the need for a dedicated user account. Its primary purpose lies in providing temporary access to individuals who lack their own user account, such as visiting friends, family, or colleagues with a short-term presence. The guest account generally offers limited access to applications and files, ensuring a controlled user experience. Importantly, any modifications made during the guest session are automatically discarded and erased once the user logs out, ensuring the privacy and integrity of the Mac system. See Figure 2-5.

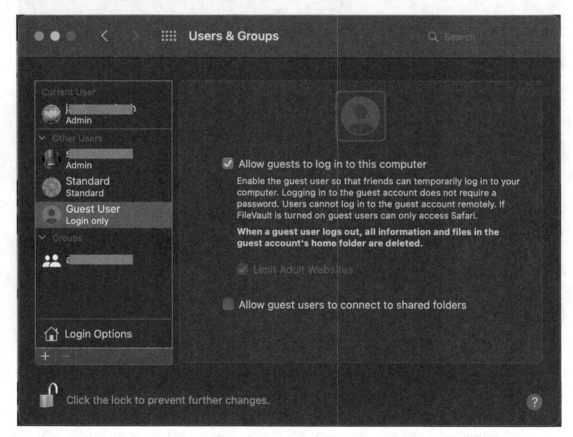

Figure 2-5. *Guest user account*

Important note   The sharing only and guest users do not possess a home folder associated with their accounts.

Groups

On Mac, groups within user accounts serve as a feature that enables the collective organization and management of users based on shared access privileges, permissions, and roles. By assigning users to specific groups, administrators can streamline the process of administering and allocating permissions within the macOS ecosystem.

Groups can be established for various purposes, such as granting access to particular files, folders, or applications, or for defining specific roles and responsibilities within a shared computing environment. Users have the capability to be members of multiple groups, allowing them to inherit the combined privileges and permissions associated with each group they are part of.

The group management functionality in macOS empowers administrators to set access controls, define permissions for files and folders, and determine the extent of system-level privileges for groups of users. This simplifies the task of granting or revoking permissions, as any changes made at the group level automatically propagate to all members of the respective group.

In essence, groups in user accounts on a Mac offer a convenient and efficient means of managing user access, permissions, and privileges within the macOS environment. This ensures the appropriate allocation of resources while upholding security measures and maintaining control over shared computing resources. See Figure 2-6.

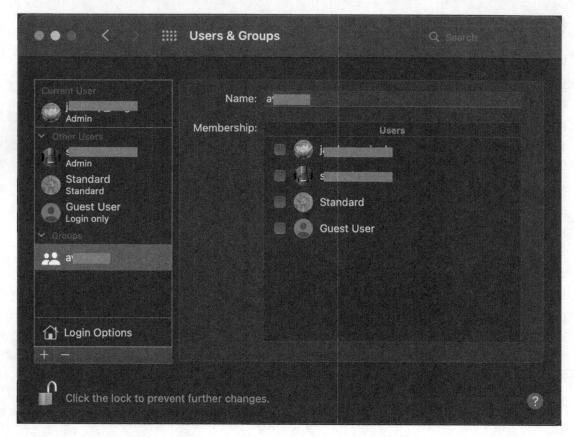

Figure 2-6. *Users group*

Let's talk about other type of accounts that can be used for specific and enterprise-level requirements within an organization.

Sudo User Account

A sudo user account refers to a user account that has been granted elevated administrative privileges through the utilization of the sudo (superuser do) command. This command, derived from Unix, permits a user to temporarily assume the authority and privileges of the system's superuser or administrator.

When setting up a Mac, the first user account created is automatically endowed with administrative privileges, thus enabling the execution of administrative tasks without the need for a separate administrator username and password. This initial user account is commonly known as the primary sudo user.

Additional user accounts can also be assigned sudo privileges by the primary sudo user or an existing administrator account. This allocation enables these users to perform administrative tasks utilizing the sudo command, which requires entering their own account password for verification.

By employing the sudo command, a non-administrative user can temporarily elevate their privileges, enabling the execution of tasks that typically require administrative access. These tasks may include software installation, system file modifications, or the execution of commands at the system level.

The capability to assign sudo privileges to specific user accounts offers a refined level of control over administrative access on a Mac. This feature allows multiple users to engage in administrative tasks while upholding the security and integrity of the system.

Active Directory Mobile Account

An Active Directory mobile account allows for remote access to an Active Directory user account that is housed on the AD server, even in the absence of network connectivity. By using the Active Directory connector in Directory Utility, your mobile user account is established, enabling you to log in to your AD account on a Mac using your Active Directory credentials.

As an IT administrator, you have the flexibility to configure these mobile accounts to be automatically generated or require AD users to confirm the creation of their respective mobile accounts. This grants users the convenience of accessing their AD account and associated resources from a Mac, regardless of their network connection status.

Supported File Systems on the Application Level

Macs support various file types for applications. Every application file has its own significance and usability. Commonly they are .app, .dmg, .pkg, .mpkg, .zip, .xip, .jar, and .dSYM. The following is a brief introduction of few of the application types. We will talk about the most commonly and frequently used application types in detail.

- **.zip**: A compressed archive file format that can contain application files. Applications packaged in a .zip file must be extracted before they can be utilized.

- **.xip**: Introduced in macOS Big Sur, this format is an extended version of .zip called XIP (extensible archive format). It enables secure distribution and installation of signed application packages.

- **.jar**: A Java Archive file that contains Java applications or applets, which can be executed on a macOS with Java Runtime Environment (JRE) installed.

- **.dSYM**: A file format used in macOS development for debugging purposes. It contains debug symbols that aid in the debugging process of applications.

- **.mpkg**: The .mpkg format is unique to macOS and represents a metapackage. It is a package file that bundles multiple installation packages together. Metapackages simplify the installation process of software that requires multiple components or dependencies.

These file types cater to various aspects of application management and deployment on macOS, providing flexibility and convenience to both developers and users.

These application file types are merely a subset of the diverse range of file formats supported by macOS. It's important to note that compatibility can vary depending on the specific version of the macOS being used and the unique requirements of each individual application. Therefore, it's advisable to consult the documentation or specifications provided by the application developer to determine the supported file types for a particular macOS version.

Now, let's talk about frequently and commonly used application file types in detail.

.pkg

The .pkg file type is an essential file format used for software installation purposes on Macs. It contains instructions and compressed files needed to install applications. See Figure 2-7.

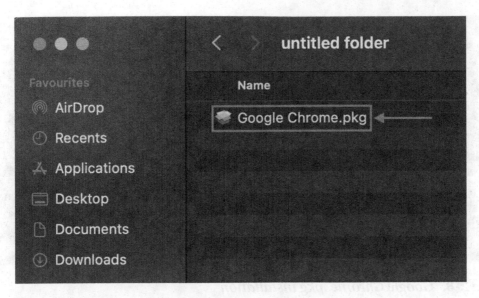

Figure 2-7. *Google Chrome Package as an example of .pkg*

When you double-click a PKG file to install a program, the macOS Installer starts working. It reads the instructions in the PKG file and guides you through the installation process. It takes the necessary files from the compressed installer and puts them in the right places on your computer's hard drive.

PKG files make the installation process consistent and simple, so it's easier for you to install programs on your Mac. They also allow developers to include extra things like libraries or frameworks that the program needs to work properly.

For example, let's consider a graphics editing software application installation. The developer gives you a PKG file to install the program on your Mac. The PKG file contains the instructions and compressed files, such as the main program file and other supporting files.

When you open the PKG file, the macOS Installer takes over. It shows you instructions and prompts to follow for the installation. As the installation goes on, the installer takes the files out of the PKG file and puts them in the right places on your computer. See Figure 2-8.

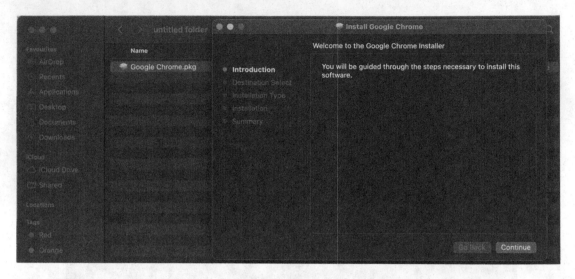

Figure 2-8. *Google Chrome .pkg installation*

By default, applications on Macs gets installed within Applications folder.

Once the installation is done, you can find and use the graphics editing program in your Applications folder. PKG files make the installation process easy and efficient, so you can quickly install and start using programs on your Mac.

.dmg

The DMG file type generally stands for Apple Disk Image file or macOS Disk Image file, which serves as a digital replica of a physical disc. When "mounted," it acts as a virtual drive that the operating system treats as if it were a genuine hard drive. This feature offers convenience in accessing and inspecting the contents of the DMG file. See Figure 2-9.

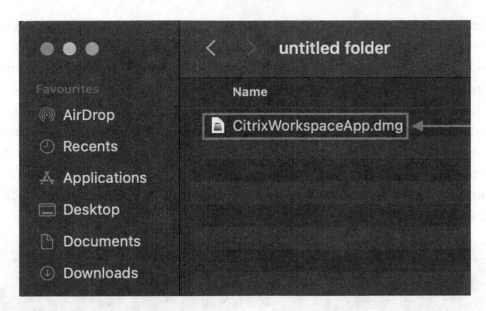

Figure 2-9. An example of .dmg

When you download software for your Mac in the form of a DMG file, you can treat it like any other file. By double-clicking the DMG file, the operating system recognizes it as a virtual drive and presents its contents through a Finder window. It simulates the experience of inserting a physical disc into your Mac. See Figure 2-10.

Figure 2-10. Mounting of a .dmg file in Finder

Once the DMG file is mounted, you can explore its contents by navigating within the Finder window. Usually, you'll find the software's installer package or application file alongside related files and resources. Additionally, you can copy files from the mounted DMG to your Mac's hard drive or directly run the software from within the DMG.

To install the software, you typically need to execute the setup program provided within the mounted DMG file. This program guides you through the installation process, allowing you to select the desired installation location and customize optional settings. Once the installation is complete, you can safely "eject" the DMG file, effectively unmounting it from your system. You can eject a mounted DMG file only when its files are not in use. See Figure 2-11.

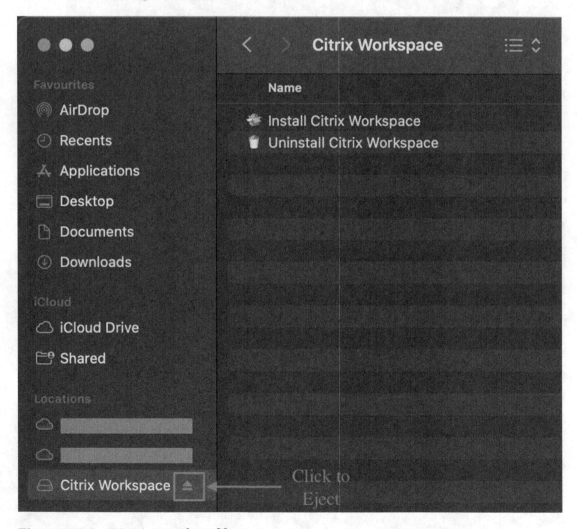

Figure 2-11. *Ejecting a .dmg file*

For instance, say you wish to install picture editing software on your Mac. You download the software from the vendor's website, and it arrives as a DMG file. By double-clicking the DMG file, it opens, and a Finder window shows the contents of the software. It will likely provide the installer package along with a Readme file or additional resources.

Next, you run the installer package by double-clicking it, triggering the launch of the setup program. This program presents a series of prompts and options, such as agreeing to the license terms, selecting the installation location, and choosing additional features. After making your selections, the installer proceeds to install the software on your Mac.

Once the installation is complete, you can launch the software from the Applications folder and begin using it. At this point, you can safely eject the DMG file by right-clicking its icon and selecting the Eject option. This action unmounts the virtual drive from the desktop.

In summary, a DMG file acts as a virtual representation of a physical disc on your Mac. It enables easy access and examination of its contents, facilitates software installation, and allows running applications without the need for physical media.

.app

An APP file is a specific file format exclusive to macOS that is used for applications. It functions as a consolidated package containing all the essential files and resources needed to run a particular application. When you double-click an APP file, it triggers the launch of the corresponding application on your Mac.

Inside an APP file, you'll encounter various directories that efficiently organize different components of the application. The most prominent directories commonly found include the following:

- **Contents**: This directory plays a vital role because it contains crucial files and subdirectories that define the overall structure and behavior of the application.

- **Resources**: This directory serves as a repository for various resources that the application relies on to function properly. These resources can include images, icons, localized files, and other types of media assets.

- **Frameworks**: This directory hosts frameworks and libraries that the application depends on to deliver enhanced functionality and features. These frameworks extend the capabilities of the application.

When you initiate the opening of an APP file by double-clicking it, macOS recognizes the file as an executable and proceeds to initiate the associated application. The operating system accesses the necessary files and resources stored within the APP file to initialize the application and present its graphical user interface (GUI) to the user.

To illustrate this concept, let's consider the well-known Google Chrome application, which is Google's web browser. The Google Chrome APP file contains several directories, including Contents, Resources, and Frameworks. The Contents directory, in turn, contains files such as Info.plist, which holds essential metadata about the application, the MacOS directory that houses the executable code responsible for the browser's functioning, and the Resources directory that stores supplementary resources like icons and localized strings.

Whenever you double-click the Google Chrome APP file, macOS acknowledges it as a valid application and launches the Safari browser accordingly. The operating system leverages the files and resources within the APP file to construct and present the Google Chrome user interface, enabling users to browse the web seamlessly.

In conclusion, an APP file is a distinctive file format specific to macOS, serving as a bundled package encompassing all the necessary files, directories, and resources required to operate a given application. By double-clicking an APP file, you initiate the execution of the associated application, resulting in the display of its graphical user interface for you to interact with. The default and recommended location for applications is the Application folder. See Figure 2-12.

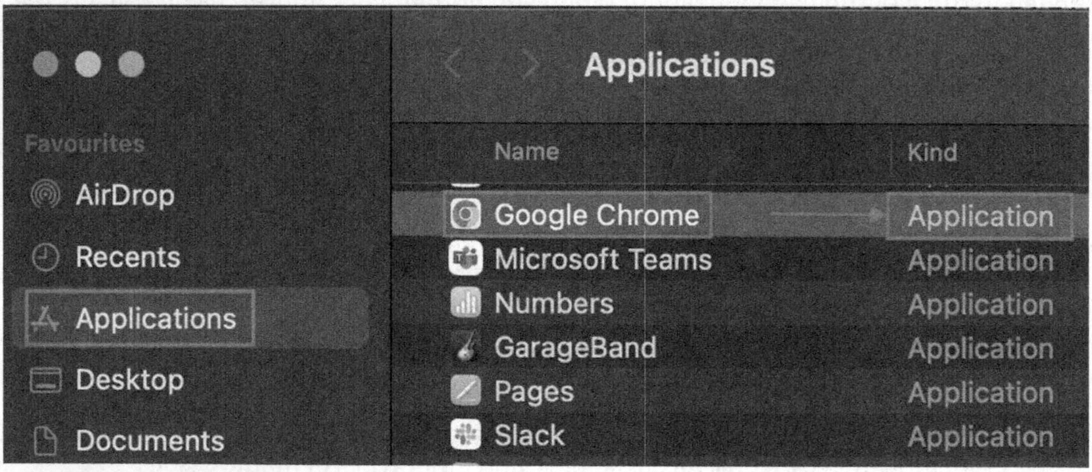

Figure 2-12. *Application with .app extension*

Overview of Built-In (Preinstalled) macOS Applications and Utilities

When you own a Mac, you have access to a diverse collection of preinstalled applications that cater to various needs. These apps enable you to engage in enjoyable activities, carry out work-related tasks, stay connected with friends, enhance your organizational skills, make online purchases, and much more.

What's great is that each app that comes with your Mac is equipped with a comprehensive help system, empowering you to become proficient in using its features and functionalities. To gain knowledge on how to make the most of an app, simply open it and navigate to the Help option in the menu bar.

The Mac operating system includes a diverse selection of preinstalled applications that offer a wide range of functionalities and features. These built-in apps provide Mac users with essential tools for productivity, creativity, communication, and entertainment. Here are several of the popular apps included on your Mac:

- **Finder**: The Finder app serves as the central hub for managing and organizing files and folders on your Mac.

- **Safari**: Safari is the default web browser that offers a fast and secure internet browsing experience.

- **Mail**: The Mail app allows you to manage multiple email accounts, send and receive messages, and organize your mailbox efficiently.

- **Calendar**: The Calendar app helps you stay organized by managing your schedule, appointments, and events.

- **Photos**: With the Photos app, you can import, edit, organize, and share your photos and videos.

- **Music**: Formerly known as iTunes, the Music app lets you access your music library, purchase songs, create playlists, and enjoy music playback.

- **Messages**: The Messages app enables you to send text messages, photos, videos, and more to other Apple users using iMessage or standard SMS.

- **FaceTime**: FaceTime allows you to make high-quality video and audio calls to other Apple users across various devices.

- **Pages, Numbers, and Keynote**: These apps are part of the iWork suite and provide powerful tools for creating documents, spreadsheets, and presentations.

- **Notes**: The Notes app allows you to create and manage digital notes, to-do lists, and important information.

These are just a few examples of the many preinstalled apps on your Mac. Additionally, you have the option to explore and download more apps from the Mac App Store to further customize and enhance your Mac experience based on your specific needs and interests.

Important Note   The availability of apps, services, features, or content may vary across different countries or regions. Go to `https://support.apple.com/HT204411` to check detailed information about the availability of Apple Media Services region-wise on Apple's support forum.

Table 2-1 shows a list of applications that come preinstalled on your Mac.

Table 2-1. *List of Preinstalled Applications in macOS*

Icon	App	Description
	App Store	Discover, purchase, install, update, and provide feedback on applications for Mac.
	Automator	Streamline and automate tasks without the need for complex programming or scripting languages.
	Books	Access and enjoy a wide selection of classic literature, bestselling books, audiobooks, and educational textbooks.
	Calculator	Easily perform a wide range of calculations, from basic to advanced or even programming-related computations.
	Calendar	Effortlessly keep track of your meetings, events, and appointments all in one convenient location.
	Chess	Engage in a game of chess with your Mac or challenge another player for an exciting and strategic gaming experience.
	Clock	Set alarms and timers, use the world clock, and take advantage of the stopwatch feature for time management and tracking purposes.
	Contacts	Store contact information such as phone numbers, addresses, birthdays, and other details of people important to you.
	Dictionary	Search for definitions and meanings of words in dictionaries and other available sources.
	FaceTime	Initiate video and audio communication with others through calls.
	Find My	View the whereabouts of your friends, devices, and belongings using location tracking.
	Font Book	Install, organize, and preview fonts with ease.
	Freeform	Collaborate with others and unleash your creativity using Freeform boards to bring ideas to life.
	GarageBand	Unleash your musical creativity with a comprehensive music creation studio built directly into your Mac.

(continued)

Table 2-1. (*continued*)

Icon	App	Description
	Home	Take full control of your HomeKit-enabled accessories and automate their functions effortlessly.
	iMovie	Explore a vast collection of video clips, effortlessly share your favorite moments, and unleash your creativity by crafting stunning trailers and movies.
	Keynote	Craft dynamic and engaging presentations with the ability to incorporate images, media, charts, animations, and much more.
	Mail	Efficiently manage all your emails in a single location.
	Maps	Easily access directions, traffic updates, and public transport information.
	Messages	Effortlessly send text and audio messages.
	Music	Enjoy your music library and explore new artists for a delightful listening experience.
	News	Stay up to date with curated news from top sources, carefully selected by editors and tailored to your personal interests.
	Notes	Quickly capture your thoughts by jotting down notes and adding multimedia elements like photos, videos, URLs, or tables for easy reference later on.
	Numbers	Create powerful spreadsheets that include formulas, functions, interactive charts, and more to effectively organize and analyze your data.
	Pages	Create professional documents that feature formatted text, images, media, tables, and other elements to effectively convey your ideas and information.
	Photo Booth	Capture enjoyable moments by taking photos or recording videos with your device.
	Photos	Effortlessly import, view, and organize your collection of photos and videos.

(*continued*)

Table 2-1. (*continued*)

Icon	App	Description
	Podcasts	Explore and subscribe to captivating audio stories that entertain, enlighten, and motivate.
	Preview	Easily view and modify PDFs and images, import images, and capture screenshots.
	Reminders	Effortlessly create lists to keep track of your to-dos, projects, groceries, and any other items you need to manage.
	Safari	Safely explore and shop online with enhanced security measures.
	Shortcuts	Effortlessly streamline your daily tasks on your Mac by utilizing pre-built shortcuts or customizing your own to automate processes and save time.
	Stickies	Easily organize your desktop by storing notes, lists, and pictures for quick and convenient access.
	Stocks	Stay up to date with the latest market news and keep track of your favorite stocks and exchanges with ease.
	TextEdit	Effortlessly create and edit various document types including plain text, rich text, HTML, and more.
	TV	Indulge in your favorite shows and movies while exploring a wealth of captivating new content to enjoy.
	Voice Memos	Effortlessly capture, play back, edit, and conveniently share your audio recordings with others.
	Weather	Stay informed about the current weather conditions in your location and around the world with real-time updates

macOS offers a diverse selection of utilities designed to enhance productivity, manage system settings, troubleshoot issues, and perform various tasks. These utilities are built-in features of the operating system and provide valuable functionality to Mac users. Here are some commonly used utilities in macOS:

- **Activity Monitor**: This application allows you to monitor and manage system processes, CPU usage, memory usage, disk activity, and network activity. It helps you identify and troubleshoot performance issues on your Mac.

- **Disk Utility**: Disk Utility provides a set of tools for managing and troubleshooting storage devices. You can use it to format, partition, repair, and erase disks, as well as to create disk images and manage RAID sets.

- **Terminal**: Terminal is a command-line interface that allows you to execute commands and perform advanced system configurations. It provides direct access to the Unix shell, enabling powerful scripting and automation capabilities.

- **Network Utility**: Network Utility offers a range of network-related tools for diagnostics and troubleshooting. It includes features such as ping, traceroute, lookup, and network port scanning.

- **Important**: Network utility was available until macOS 10.15.x (Catalina), and has been deprecated by Apple in newer macOS versions. It is no more available as a part of operating system since macOS 11 (Big Sur). It is recommended to utilise Terminal for network diagnostics. Network utility is mentioned here as a Good to Know information, if you get that downloaded and installed in your newer macOS versions by other sources and try using it. However, it is recommended to utilise only those utilities in your Macs which comes as part of it.

- **Console**: Console is an application that displays system log files, providing a way to view and analyze system events, errors, and application-specific logs. It can help identify and debug issues on your Mac.

- **Keychain Access**: Keychain Access allows you to manage passwords, encryption keys, and certificates. You can view, add, delete, and modify items stored in your keychain, which securely stores sensitive information.

- **Migration Assistant**: Migration Assistant simplifies the process of transferring data, settings, and applications from an old Mac or PC to a new Mac. It guides you through the migration process, ensuring a smooth transition.

- **System Information**: System Information provides comprehensive information about your Mac's hardware, software, and network settings. It offers detailed reports on system components, connected peripherals, network configurations, and more.

- **Bluetooth File Exchange**: Bluetooth File Exchange allows you to exchange files wirelessly between your Mac and Bluetooth-enabled devices. You can easily send and receive files such as photos, documents, and media.

These applications are just a few of the many commonly found in the Utilities folder on a Mac. The contents of the Utilities folder can vary depending on the specific version of macOS installed on your Mac and any additional software packages you have installed. Table 2-2 lists other apps and utilities that come preinstalled on your Mac.

Table 2-2. *List of Preinstalled Utilities in macOS*

Icon	App	Description
	Activity Monitor	Retrieve information on the Mac's processor, apps, disks, memory, and network activity.
	Airport Utility	Configure and maintain a Wi-Fi network and AirPort Base Station, which allows you to establish a wireless network in your premises.
	Audio MIDI Setup	Configure and manage audio and MIDI devices that are connected to your Mac, allowing you to control and customize audio input and output settings as well as MIDI functionality.
	Bluetooth File Exchange	Establish short-range wireless connections between devices using Bluetooth.
	Boot Camp Assistant	Run the Windows operating system on your Intel-based Mac using virtualization or Boot Camp.
	ColorSync Utility	Customize the color profiles on your Mac to adjust and fine-tune the display's color accuracy and appearance.

(*continued*)

Table 2-2. (*continued*)

Icon	App	Description
	Console	Inspect log messages to obtain detailed information about issues and troubleshooting on your Mac.
	Digital Color Meter	Determine the color value of any color displayed on your Mac using the built-in Digital Color Meter tool.
	Disk Utility	Manage storage and use it to format, partition, repair, and erase disks, as well as to create disk images and manage RAID sets.
	DVD Player	Play DVDs or DVD movie files using the built-in DVD player software on your Mac.
	Grapher	Visualize and analyze equations, both implicit and explicit, using dedicated software or graphing tools available on your Mac.
	Image Capture	Transfer and scan images from external devices or capture photos using your Mac's built-in camera.
	Keychain Access	Securely store and manage your passwords and account information for easy access and enhanced security.
	Migration Assistant	Transfer your information seamlessly from a Mac, PC, or disk to ensure smooth data migration and accessibility.
	QuickTime Player	Play video or audio files with ease on your Mac to enjoy your favorite media content.
	Screenshot	Capture screenshots or screen recordings effortlessly on your Mac to save and share visual information.
	Script Editor	Harness the capabilities of macOS to develop robust scripts, tools, and even full-fledged applications.
	System Information	Obtain comprehensive information about your Mac, including its specifications, warranty status, and guidance on optimizing storage capacity.
	Terminal	Access the full functionality of the UNIX operating system within macOS. Run commands and executive scripts.
	VoiceOver Utility	Personalize and tailor the settings of VoiceOver, the integrated screen reader in macOS, to suit your specific needs and preferences.

macOS File Format Systems

macOS file systems are the various methods employed by the macOS operating system to arrange and retain data on storage devices like hard drives, solid-state drives (SSDs), and external drives. These file systems dictate the organization, storage, and retrieval of data on the storage medium.

macOS file system formats are the predefined arrangements and configurations employed by the macOS operating system to store and handle data on various storage devices. These formats establish the methodology of organizing, storing, and retrieving data on the storage medium. HFS+ (Hierarchical File System Plus), APFS (Apple File System), and FAT (File Allocation Table) are some widely used file system formats in macOS.

Let's go over a little bit of history regarding the supported file systems to understand their existence. In 1984, HFS (Hierarchical File System) was introduced alongside the original Macintosh. After a span of 13 years, HFS+ emerged as a significant upgrade to the Mac's file system. Its robustness led to its widespread adoption as the primary file system on Apple devices.

However, a transformative change arrived with the introduction of APFS (Apple File System), the next-generation file system, after 19 years of HFS+. APFS had already been implemented in iOS, tvOS, and watchOS. Starting from 2017, macOS High Sierra adopted APFS as the standard file system for devices equipped with Solid State Drives (SSD).

Here are the four main types of file systems supported on macOS:

- **APFS**: It is the designated file system for macOS versions 10.13 and newer.

- **Mac OS Extended (HFS+)**: It is utilized for macOS 10.12 and earlier versions.

- **ExFAT**: It serves as a file system that ensures compatibility with Windows.

- **MS-DOS (FAT)**: It is another Windows-compatible file system.

Now let's talk about these supported macOS file systems in detail because it will help you understand their usability, benefits, functionalities and more.

APFS

With the arrival of macOS High Sierra (10.13), Apple introduced APFS, short for "Apple File System." This release corresponded with Apple's shift towards solid-state drives (SSD) as the predominant storage choice for their devices.

APFS was meticulously crafted to enhance the performance and functionality of SSD-based storage solutions, catering to their unique characteristics. Nevertheless, APFS also accommodates traditional mechanical or hybrid drives, ensuring compatibility across a range of storage mediums.APFS is the default file system used in macOS 10.13 and later versions. It brings a range of advanced features such as robust encryption, efficient space management, the ability to take snapshots for easy data recovery, improved directory sizing, and enhanced file system functionality.

While APFS is optimized for the Flash/SSD storage commonly found in modern Mac computers, it is also compatible with older systems using traditional hard disk drives (HDD) and external storage devices. Both bootable volumes and data storage can benefit from APFS in macOS 10.13 and newer.

APFS manages disk space dynamically within a container or partition. In cases where there are multiple volumes within a single APFS container, the free space in the container is shared and allocated automatically to the individual volumes as required.

It is also possible to define reserve and quota sizes for each volume if desired. Each volume occupies only a portion of the overall container, meaning that the available space is calculated by subtracting the sizes of all volumes within the container from the total size of the container.

For Mac computers running macOS 10.13 or later, you have several APFS formats to choose from:

- **APFS**: This format utilizes APFS and is recommended if you don't need encryption or a case-sensitive file system.

- **APFS (Encrypted)**: This format employs APFS and adds encryption to the volume, providing an extra layer of security.

- **APFS (Case-sensitive)**: With this format, APFS is used, enabling case sensitivity for file and folder names. This means that folders named Homework and HOMEWORK are treated as distinct entities.

- **APFS (Case-sensitive, Encrypted)**: This format combines the benefits of APFS, case-sensitive file system, and encryption. It supports case sensitivity for file and folder names while ensuring that the volume remains encrypted for heightened data protection.

Here's the article from Apple Support to understand about adding or deleting volumes in APFS containers: `https://support.apple.com/en-in/guide/disk-utility/dskua9e6a110/22.0/mac/13.0`.

Mac OS Extended (HFS+)

The Mac OS Extended file system, also referred to as HFS Plus or HFS+, serves as the default file system for all Macs from 1998 to the present with traditional or hybrid drives. Even if a Mac is operating macOS High Sierra (macOS 10.13), the default file system will be Mac OS Extended if it contains a hybrid or mechanical drive. It is ideal for mechanical (traditional) drives or drives utilized with older macOS versions

If you are formatting a drive for compatibility with older Macs or using an older Mac to format a drive, it is advisable to opt for Mac OS Extended. While APFS may function adequately, selecting Mac OS Extended provides a higher level of assurance against potential issues.

Select one of the available Mac OS Extended file system formats to ensure compatibility with Mac computers running macOS 10.12 or an earlier version:

- **Mac OS Extended (Journaled)**: This format, known as Journaled HFS Plus, safeguards the integrity of the hierarchical file system. It's suitable when encryption or case sensitivity is not necessary.

- **Mac OS Extended (Journaled, Encrypted)**: With this format, the Mac format is used along with encryption. The partition is protected by a password, ensuring the security of your data.

- **Mac OS Extended (Case-sensitive, Journaled)**: This format maintains the Mac format but adds case sensitivity to folder names. It means that folders named Homework and HOMEWORK are considered distinct entities.

- **Mac OS Extended (Case-sensitive, Journaled, Encrypted):**
  Combining case sensitivity in folder names, the Mac format, and
  encryption, this format ensures both security and differentiation
  between folder names. A password is required for access to the
  encrypted partition.

Now let's shine some light on the remaining two types of file format systems. Both
are Windows-compatible formats and both can used to format a disk that needs to be
used further with a Windows machine.

ExFAT

ExFAT is ideal for external drives shared across Mac and Windows systems. It offers
a versatile solution for seamless file sharing and editing between Mac and Windows
devices. It serves as a common ground for exchanging files between the two platforms,
making it an excellent choice for users who frequently work with both Mac and Windows
computers.

Introduced in 2006 by Microsoft, the ExFAT file system was specifically designed
to bridge the gap between the FAT32 format and Mac systems. It eliminates concerns
related to file and partition size restrictions, providing a hassle-free cross-platform
compatibility experience. It's recommended for use with Windows volumes that are
more than 32GB.

MS-DOS (FAT)

For Macs that require cooperation with Windows XP or older systems, the MS-DOS FAT
file system can be considered, although such scenarios are quite uncommon nowadays.

Windows XP is predominantly used for outdated commercial platforms that may not
integrate smoothly with the Mac environment. It's recommended to use with Windows
volumes that are less than 32GB.

These are the types of file formatting systems supported in Mac devices for an
effective management of storage drives or volumes. To conclude, newer Mac devices are
equipped with SSDs, and it is always recommended to use latest and greatest file system
on new devices (i.e., APFS), unless there is any further usage of the hard drive as per the
specific requirement.

View/Hide Hidden Files and Folders With Keyboard Shortcuts

Now you are ready to understand how to view or hide the hidden files and folders in a Mac device. Further, you will learn the keyboard shortcuts you can apply to do so.

Hidden files and folders need to be interacted with cautiously to avoid any potential risks and unwanted situations.

On a Mac, numerous files and folders are concealed for a specific purpose, mainly to safeguard the operating system from accidental harm. The hiding of files and folders in operating systems serves other beneficial purposes. Manufacturers and administrators often hide files to prevent users from unintentionally deleting or damaging crucial system-related files and folders.

Similarly, employers may hide files necessary for seamless data exchange with customers and business partners. While these hidden files carry out significant functions, they typically go unnoticed by users. However, if you need to access and view hidden folders and files on your Mac, exercising extreme caution is essential to avoid any potential damage to the operating system.

To reveal hidden files using keyboard shortcuts in Mac Finder, follow these steps:

- Open the desired location, such as Macintosh HD or the folder where you want to view hidden files, in the Finder.

- Press and hold the Command, Shift, and Period keys simultaneously: **Command + Shift + [.]**

- The hidden files and folders on your Mac will now become visible, appearing partially transparent. To hide the files again, simply use the same keyboard shortcut. See Figure 2-13.

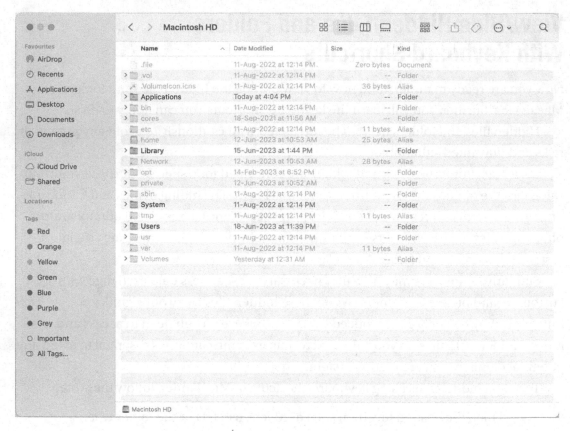

Figure 2-13. *Hidden files and the folder's view*

To reveal hidden files in Mac Finder using Terminal, type this command: `defaults write com.apple.Finder AppleShowAllFiles true`. See Figure 2-14.

Figure 2-14. *Terminal command to show hidden files in Finder*

Press the Return key to execute the command. After that, type this command:
killall Finder

Press the Return key to restart the Finder. Hidden files will now be visible in Finder.
See Figure 2-15.

Figure 2-15. *Terminal command to restart Finder*

If you want to hide the files again, you can change true to false in the command above. See Figure 2-16.

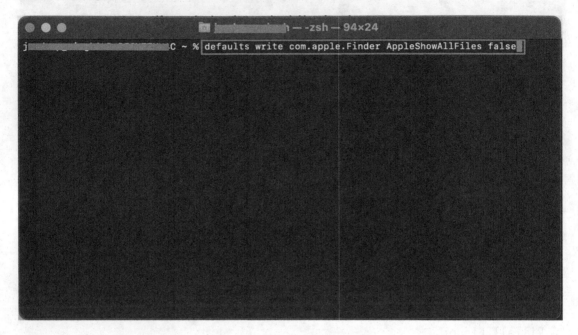

Figure 2-16. *Terminal command to hide files in Finder*

It is important to run the killall Finder command to make the changes take place. See Figure 2-17.

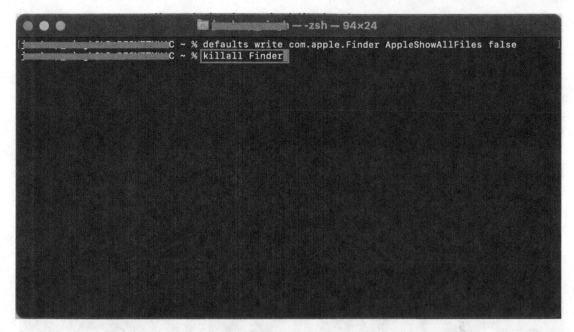

Figure 2-17.   *Terminal command to hide files in Finder*

Please note that when using Terminal, be careful while executing commands to avoid any unintended changes to your system.

For another way to hide or unhide a folder in Mac Finder using Terminal, you can follow these steps:

- Open the Terminal application on your Mac.

- Type the command `chflags hidden` in the Terminal window.

- Open a Finder window and locate the folder you want to hide.

- Drag and drop the folder from the Finder window to the Terminal window. The command is `chflags hidden folder_path`. See Figure 2-18.

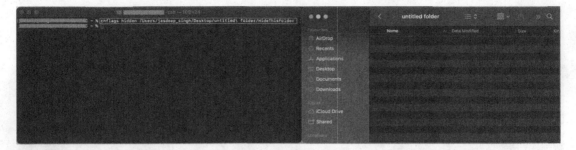

Figure 2-18. *Another Terminal command to hide files in Finder*

- Press the Return key on your keyboard.

- If you want to unhide the files again, you can change `hidden` to `nohidden` in the command above. See Figure 2-19.

Figure 2-19. *Terminal command to unhide files in Finder*

After completing these steps, the folder you dragged into the Terminal window will be hidden. Please note that the folder will no longer be visible in Finder, but it will still exist on your Mac.

Note   Unfortunately, it is not possible to hide a folder directly through the Finder on a Mac.

Overview of Important Built-In Utilities

You are already aware of the built-in utilities. However, there are few utilities that can be considered as important, so let's talk about them in detail.

Four important utilities available in Mac devices are useful to fetch important information and logs or to perform troubleshooting. They are frequently used in enterprises to get more insight into a Mac device.

- Disk Utility

- Activity Monitor

- Console

- Keychain Access

Disk Utility

Disk Utility is a preinstalled application on macOS that empowers users to control and manipulate their disk drives and storage volumes. It offers a user-friendly interface to perform a range of tasks associated with storage devices, including formatting, partitioning, erasing, repairing, and mounting or unmounting disks and volumes.

Disk Utility is widely used to manage various types of storage, such as internal and external hard drives, solid-state drives (SSDs), USB drives, optical discs, and disk images. It serves as a vital tool for effectively managing and resolving disk-related issues on Mac computers.

Disk Utility provides you with the ability to manage both internal and external storage devices. Further, using it, you can perform the following tasks:

- Format and control volumes on physical storage devices.

- Create disk images, which are single files that facilitate file transfers between computers plus backup and archiving tasks.

- Combine multiple hard disks into a RAID set, functioning as a unified disk. This can enhance performance, reliability, and storage capacity based on the chosen set type.

- Scan for and repair errors on your disks and volumes. See Figure 2-20.

Figure 2-20. *Disk Utility details*

Different partition schemes can be found in Disk Utility on macOS. When formatting and erasing a storage device in Disk Utility on Mac, you will be prompted to select a partition scheme. See Figure 2-21.

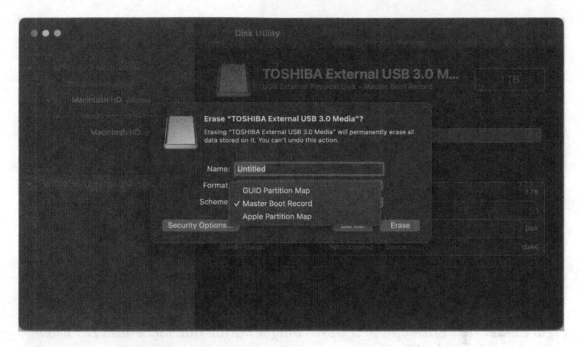

Figure 2-21. *Selection of volume schemes*

Disk Utility provides support for the following schemes:

- **GUID Partition Map**: This scheme is suitable for Intel-based and Apple Silicon Mac computers. Some newer Microsoft Windows-based computers can also use this scheme.

- **Master Boot Record**: Select this option for compatibility with all Microsoft Windows-based computers.

- **Apple Partition Map**: This scheme is compatible with older PowerPC-based Mac computers.

- When logged into a machine, you cannot format the disk in use. The Erase option will be greyed out. You can format an external disk that is mounted on the Mac. See Figure 2-22 and Figure 2-23.

Figure 2-22. *The Erase option is greyed out for the internal Macintosh HD when you're logged into the Mac*

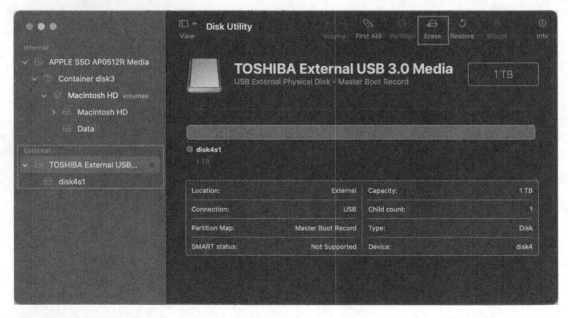

Figure 2-23. *Erase option available for external volume*

You can also manage physical disks and volumes; add, erase, or delete APFS volumes, and erase and reformat storage devices.

Encrypt and Secure Storage Devices with a Password

When formatting an internal or external storage device, you have the option to encrypt and protect it with a password. Encrypting an internal device requires entering a password to access the device and its contents. Encrypting an external device requires entering the password when connecting it to your computer. To encrypt and secure a device with a password using Disk Utility, it is necessary to erase the device first. If the device contains files you wish to keep, copy them to another storage device or volume.

Here are the tasks you can perform:

- Partition a physical disk.

- Format a disk for compatibility with Windows computers.

- Repair a storage device.

- Restore a disk.

Activity Monitor

Activity Monitor is a preinstalled utility application found on macOS that enables users to monitor and oversee a wide range of system processes and resources. It offers real-time updates on CPU usage, memory utilization, disk operations, network activity, and more.

With Activity Monitor, users gain access to detailed statistics, enabling them to track performance and pinpoint any processes that might be using excessive resources or impacting system performance. As a vital tool for system troubleshooting and performance optimization, Activity Monitor is invaluable for Mac users.

Processes on your Mac refer to the programs that are currently running. These processes can include applications, system apps utilized by macOS, and unseen background processes.

Activity Monitor provides a means to gather essential information about these processes, such as their memory usage and CPU time. By utilizing Activity Monitor, users can gain insights into the resources consumed by various processes on their Mac. See Figure 2-24.

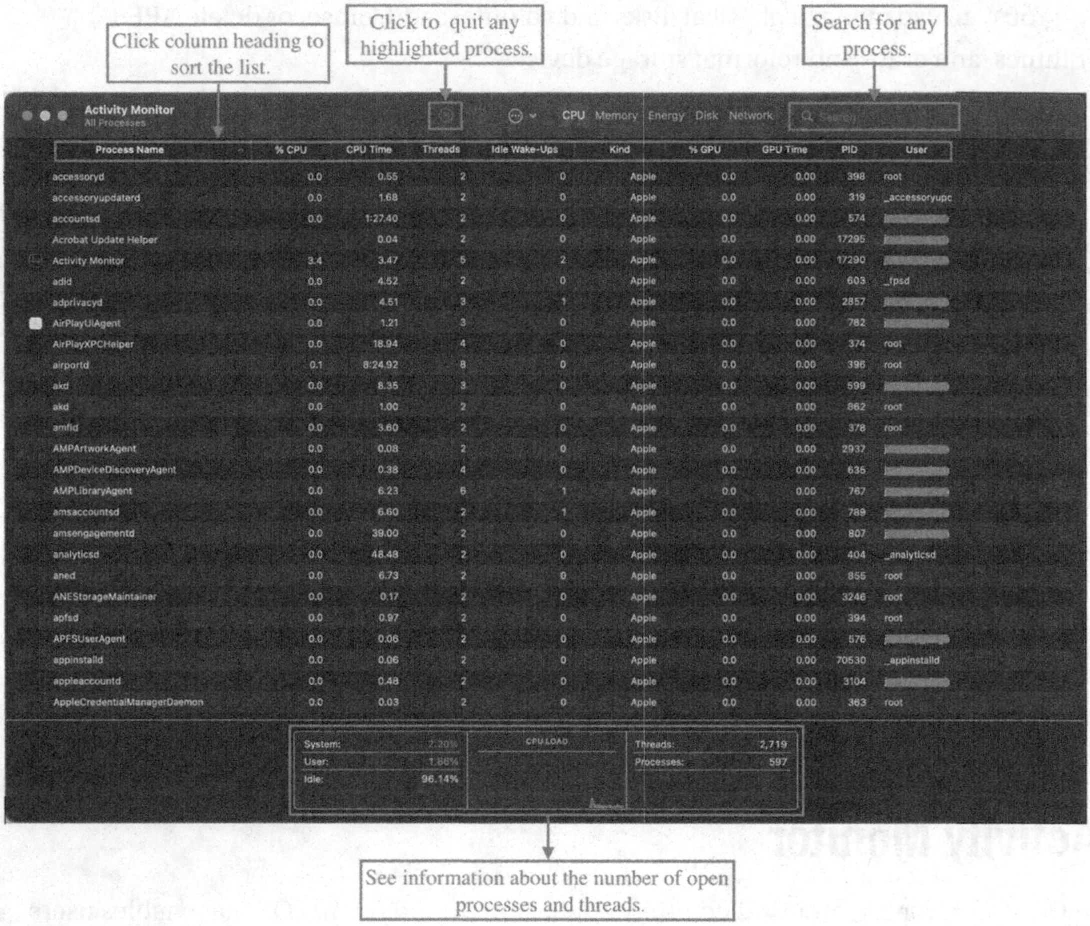

Figure 2-24. *Activity Monitor overview*

Activity Monitor is a powerful utility and offers a range of functionalities to provide valuable insights into the performance of your system. Here are some key features of Activity Monitor:

- **Process monitoring**: With Activity Monitor, you can gain real-time information about the processes running on your Mac. It displays essential details like CPU usage, memory usage, disk activity, network activity, and energy impact for each process.

- **Resource usage tracking**: Activity Monitor allows you to track the utilization of crucial system resources such as CPU, memory, disk, and network. This helps you identify processes that might be consuming excessive resources, causing performance issues, or impacting battery life.

- **Process management**: You can manage processes effectively using Activity Monitor. If you encounter unresponsive or problematic applications, you can force quit them directly from the utility, which can help resolve system freezes or crashes.

- **Detailed statistics**: Activity Monitor provides detailed statistics and graphs that allow you to analyze the performance of your Mac over time. You can examine historical data on CPU usage, memory pressure, disk usage, and network activity to identify any patterns or trends.

- **Network monitoring**: The utility features a dedicated Network tab, which provides insights into network usage by individual processes. You can monitor network connections, view data sent/received, and identify applications that are utilizing network resources.

- **Energy impact assessment**: Activity Monitor displays the energy impact of processes, enabling you to identify applications that consume significant power. This information is valuable for optimizing battery life, especially for portable Macs.

- **System monitoring**: Activity Monitor offers an overview of system-level statistics, including CPU load, memory pressure, disk usage, and network activity. This allows you to assess the overall health and performance of your Mac.

Further, you can organize processes to enhance the visibility. Within the Activity Monitor application, navigate to the View menu and select one of the following options (shown in Figure 2-25):

- **All Processes**: Displays all the processes currently running on your Mac

- **All Processes, Hierarchically**: Shows processes organized in a hierarchy, allowing you to view parent and child relationships

- **My Processes**: Displays processes owned by your user account

- **System Processes**: Shows processes owned by the macOS system

- **Other User Processes**: Displays processes that are not owned by the root or current user

- **Active Processes**: Shows processes that are currently running and not in a sleeping state

- **Inactive Processes**: Displays processes that are currently running but are in a sleeping state

- **GPU Processes**: Shows processes that are owned by the computer's GPU

- **Windowed Processes**: Displays processes that have the ability to create windows, typically referring to applications

- **Selected Processes**: Shows only the processes that you have manually selected in the Activity Monitor window

- **Applications in Last 12 Hours**: Displays only the applications that have run processes within the last 12 hours

- **Processes, by GPU**: Shows running GPU processes grouped based on the GPU they belong to

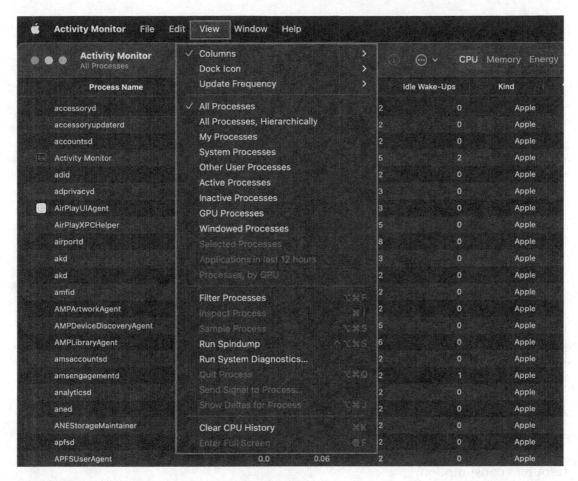

Figure 2-25. *Activity Monitor View options*

The Activity Monitor window is set to automatically update the displayed information every 5 seconds by default. However, you can also change the default time to 1 second or 2 seconds, as per the design.

To change this information, go to the View menu and click Update frequency. See Figure 2-26.

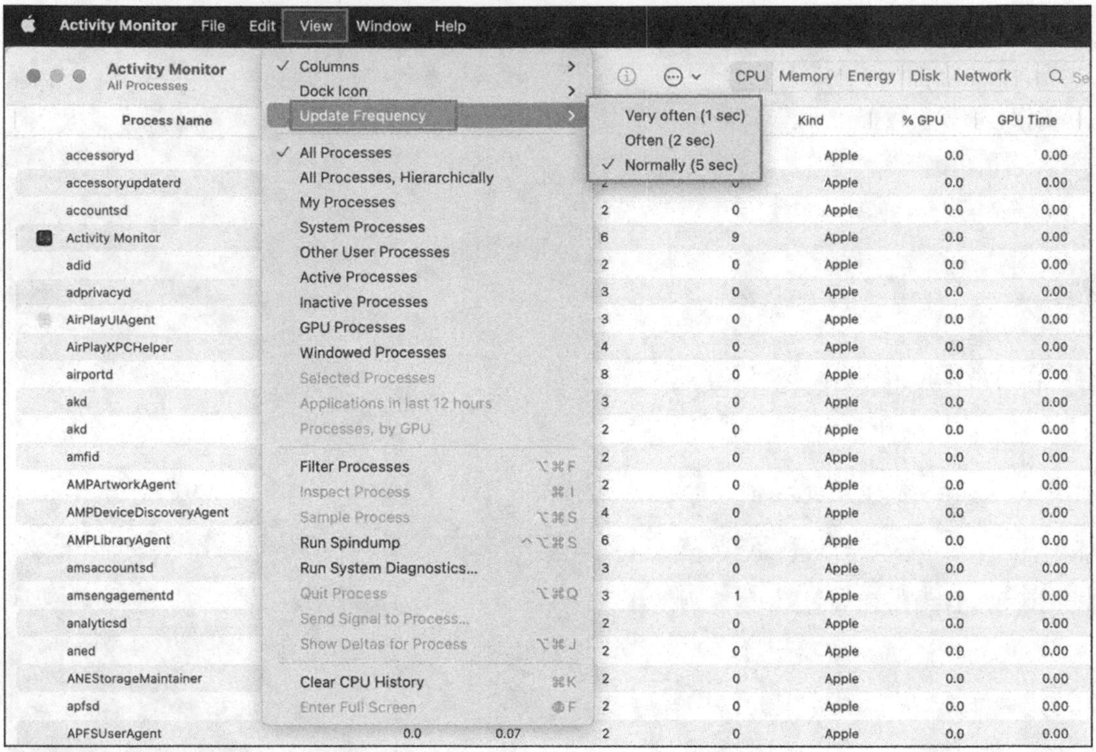

Figure 2-26. *Options to change the update frequency*

Further, Activity Monitor also provides the following capabilities for monitoring the resources consumption:

- CPU activity, to view the processor activities (Figure 2-27)

- Memory usage, to view the amount of system's memory utilization (Figure 2-28)

- Energy consumption, to view the amount of energy utilization of the Mac (Figure 2-29)

- Disk activity, to view the activities on the disk level on the Mac or Dock (Figure 2-30)

- Network activity, to view activities on the network level on the Mac or Dock (Figure 2-31)

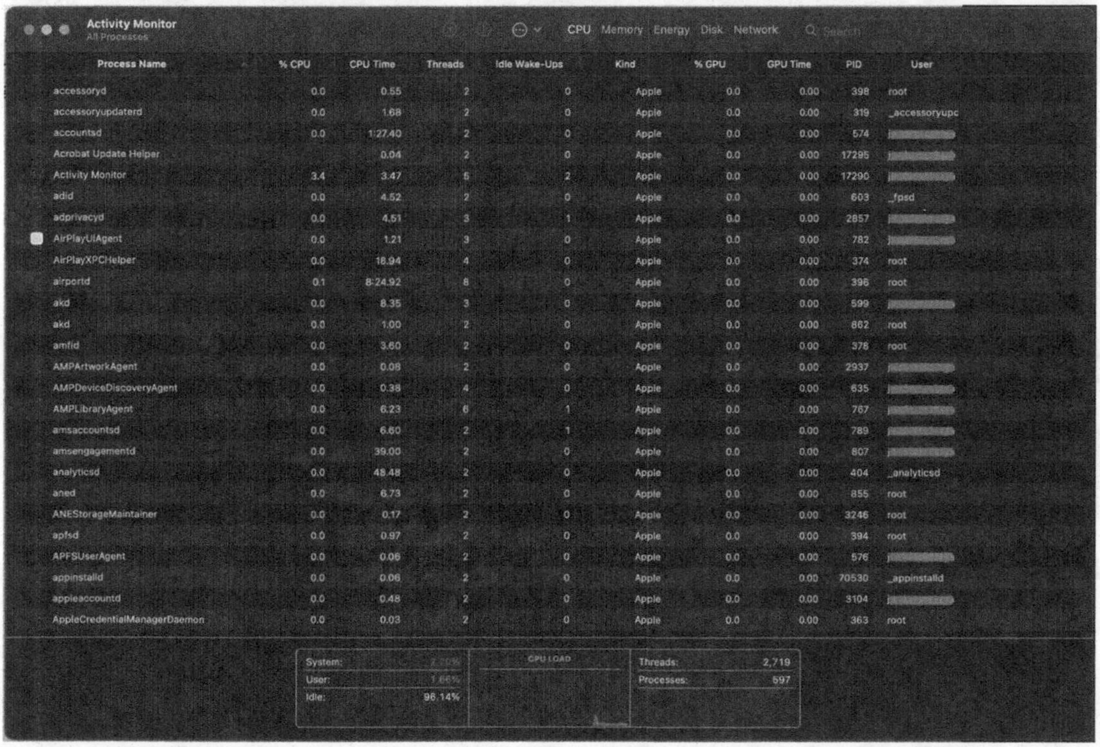

Figure 2-27. *CPU wise processors*

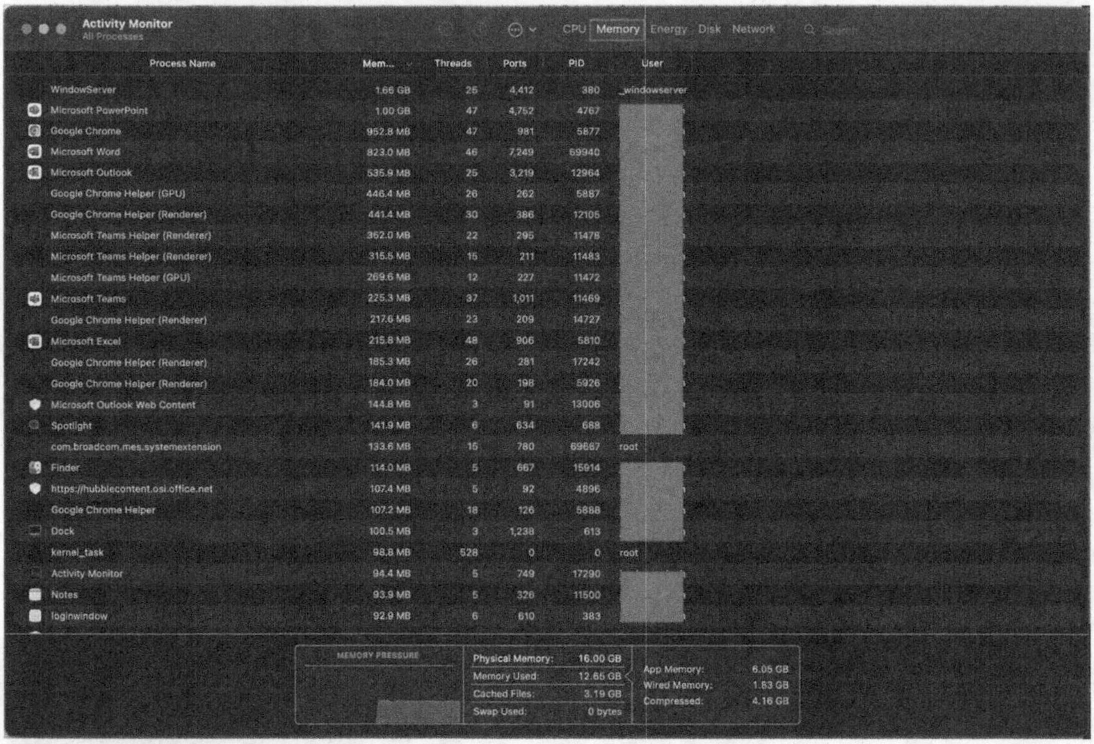

Figure 2-28. *Memory consumption*

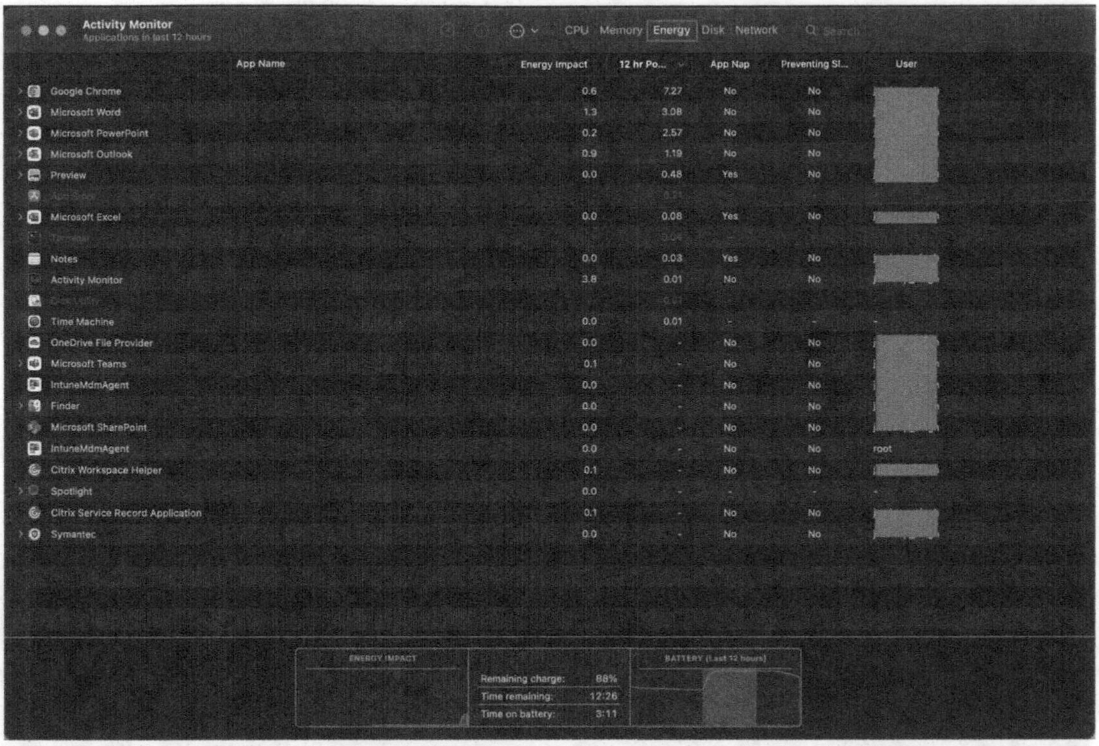

Figure 2-29. *Energy consumption*

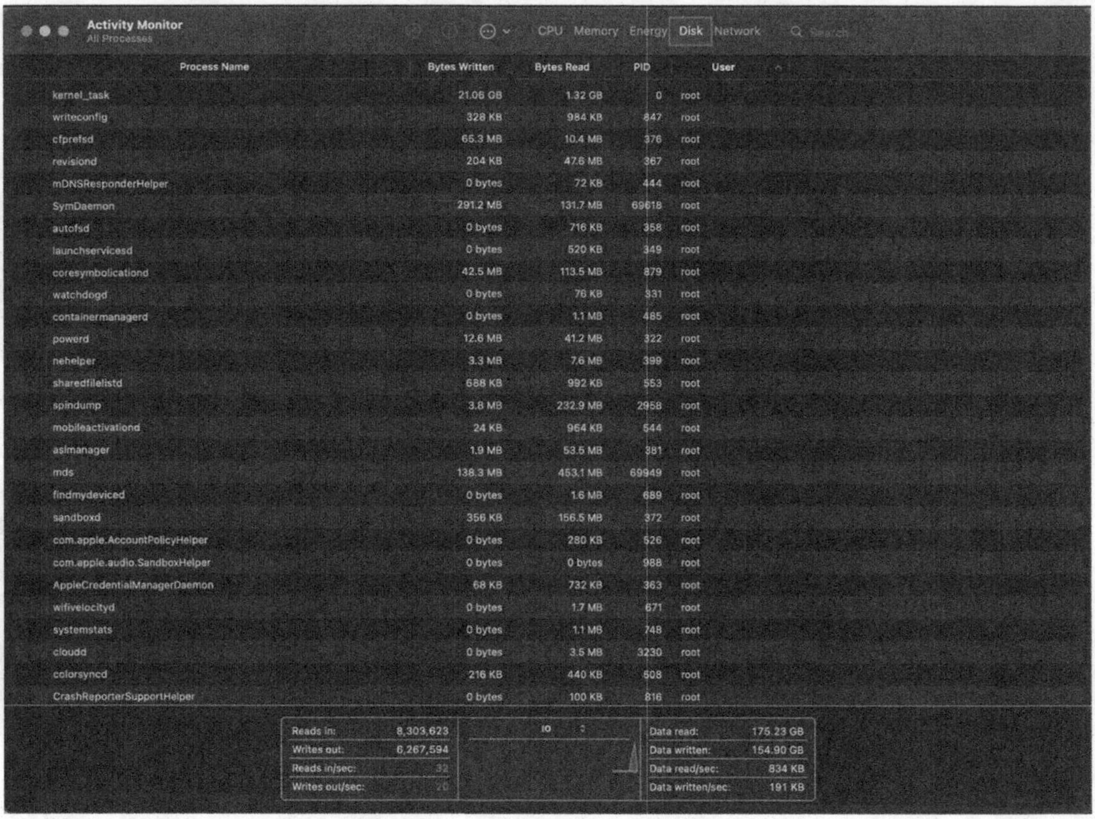

Figure 2-30. *Disk consumption*

Process Name	Sent Bytes	Rcvd Byt...	Sent Packe...	Rcvd Pack...	PID	User
kernel_task	0 bytes	0 bytes	0	0	0	root
writeconfig	0 bytes	0 bytes	0	0	847	root
cfprefsd	0 bytes	0 bytes	0	0	376	root
revisiond	0 bytes	0 bytes	0	0	367	root
mDNSResponderHelper	0 bytes	0 bytes	0	0	444	root
SymDaemon	0 bytes	0 bytes	0	0	69618	root
autofsd	0 bytes	0 bytes	0	0	358	root
launchservicesd	0 bytes	0 bytes	0	0	349	root
coresymbolicationd	0 bytes	0 bytes	0	0	879	root
watchdogd	0 bytes	0 bytes	0	0	331	root
containermanagerd	0 bytes	0 bytes	0	0	485	root
powerd	0 bytes	0 bytes	0	0	322	root
nehelper	0 bytes	0 bytes	0	0	399	root
sharedfilelistd	0 bytes	0 bytes	0	0	553	root
spindump	0 bytes	0 bytes	0	0	2958	root
mobileactivationd	0 bytes	0 bytes	0	0	544	root
asimanager	0 bytes	0 bytes	0	0	381	root
mds	0 bytes	0 bytes	0	0	69949	root
findmydeviced	0 bytes	0 bytes	0	0	689	root
sandboxd	0 bytes	0 bytes	0	0	372	root
com.apple.AccountPolicyHelper	0 bytes	0 bytes	0	0	526	root
com.apple.audio.SandboxHelper	0 bytes	0 bytes	0	0	988	root
AppleCredentialManagerDaemon	0 bytes	0 bytes	0	0	363	root
wifivelocityd	0 bytes	0 bytes	0	0	671	root
systemstats	0 bytes	0 bytes	0	0	748	root
cloudd	0 bytes	0 bytes	0	0	3230	root
colorsyncd	0 bytes	0 bytes	0	0	508	root
CrashReporterSupportHelper	0 bytes	0 bytes	0	0	816	root

Packets in:	18,401,214		Data received:	22.62 GB
Packets out:	7,755,084		Data sent:	1.20 GB
Packets in/sec:	0		Data received/sec:	55 bytes
Packets out/sec:			Data sent/sec:	102 bytes

Figure 2-31. Network activities

Performing System Diagnostics in Activity Monitor on a Mac

Activity Monitor provides the capability to generate a system diagnostics report, which contains valuable information about the state of your Mac. This report can be saved and shared with Apple Support for further analysis.

To generate a system diagnostics report, click the System diagnostics options drop-down menu, with a symbol ⊙.

Choose one of the available options:

- **Sample Process**: This option creates a report specifically for a selected process, capturing data over a period of 3 seconds.

- **Spindump**: Selecting this option generates a report for unresponsive apps that have been forcefully terminated.

- **System Diagnostics**: This option generates a comprehensive report based on various logs and system data on your Mac.

- **Spotlight Diagnostics**: By choosing this option, a report is generated based on all the processes currently running on your Mac. See Figure 2-32.

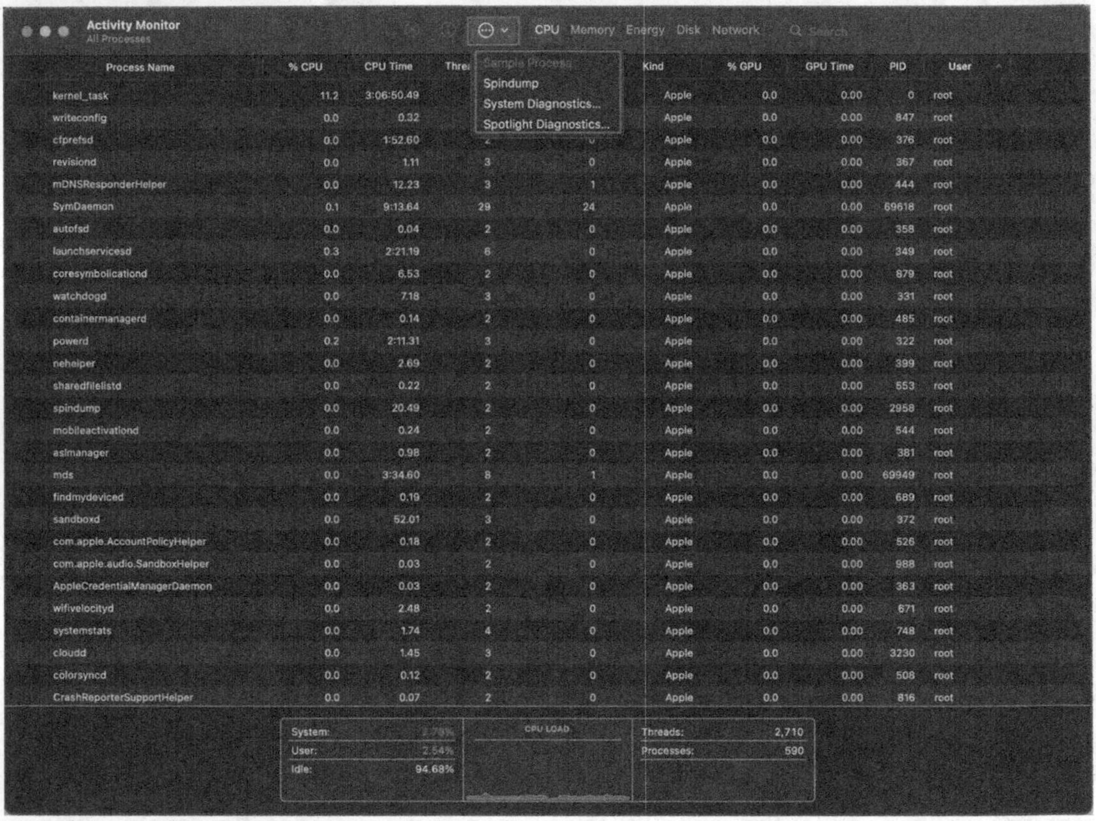

Figure 2-32. *Types of diagnostic reports*

The system diagnostics functionality in Activity Monitor can provide valuable insights for troubleshooting and resolving issues on your Mac.

Overall, Activity Monitor is a versatile tool that assists users in understanding and managing system processes and resources. It serves as a valuable resource for troubleshooting performance issues, optimizing resource allocation, and keeping an eye on the overall well-being of your Mac.

Now let's talk about another one of the important utilities on a Mac.

Console

Console is an application that enables users to view and manage log messages generated by the operating system and various applications running on their Mac. It serves as a centralized hub for accessing different types of log files, including system logs, application logs, and kernel logs. These logs contain valuable information related to system events, error messages, warnings, and diagnostic details.

With a user-friendly interface, Console allows users to browse and search through log messages, facilitating the identification and troubleshooting of issues on the Mac. It assists in locating errors, monitoring system activities, and diagnosing problems by analyzing the recorded log data.

Console is a valuable tool for both regular and advanced users who require comprehensive insights into the system's operations and performance.

Use the Console application to retrieve log messages that are logged by your Mac and connected devices. These log messages contain diverse information, covering system events, dialog text, errors, status updates, and various other types of communication. Analyzing these log messages and activities can potentially provide valuable insights into the underlying causes of any issues that may occur.

It's important to note that if you're not logged in as an administrator, you will be required to enter the administrator's username and password to gain access to and view the log messages.

Double-click a log message to find more details. See Figure 2-33.

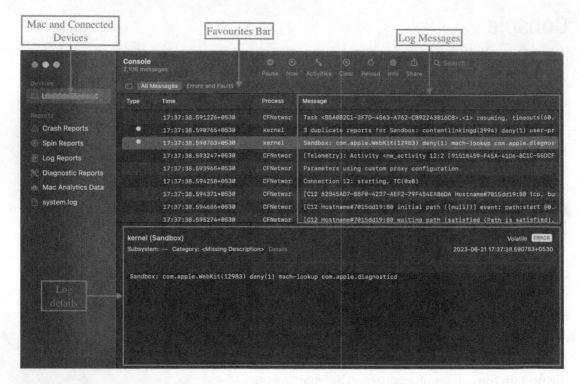

Figure 2-33. *Console overview*

The log messages for the device are showcased in the right-hand window of the Console application.

In the Console, the Type column uses colored dots to signify the nature of each log message:

Red dot: Represents faults

Yellow dot: Indicates errors

Dark grey dot: Denotes debug log messages

Light grey dot: Represents info log messages

Note   If the Type column does not contain a dot, it signifies that the log message belongs to the default type.

Console offers several advantages:

- **Log management**: Console acts as a centralized platform to conveniently access and manage various log files generated by the operating system and applications. It allows users to browse, search, and filter log messages efficiently.

- **Issue identification**: By analyzing log messages in Console, users can effectively identify and troubleshoot problems that occur on their Mac. The detailed information contained in the logs helps in understanding the root causes of errors, warnings, and system events.

- **System monitoring**: Console enables users to monitor system activities and performance by tracking log messages. It provides valuable insights into resource usage, application behavior, and other important metrics, empowering users to optimize their Mac's performance.

- **Diagnostic tool**: The recorded log data in Console is a valuable resource for diagnosing issues. Users can examine the log messages to trace the sequence of events leading to a problem and identify specific areas that require attention.

- **Developer and support tool**: Console is highly beneficial for developers and support personnel who need to analyze application or system logs for debugging purposes. It offers a comprehensive view of log data, facilitating the identification and resolution of software or hardware-related issues.

In summary, Console simplifies log management, aids in issue identification and troubleshooting, enables effective system monitoring, and serves as a valuable diagnostic tool for Mac users.

Keychain Access

Keychain Access is an application native to macOS that serves as a password and account information storage solution. It simplifies the task of managing and remembering multiple passwords.

When you interact with password-protected items like websites, email accounts, or network servers, you may be prompted to save or remember the password. Opting to save the password will store it securely in your keychain, eliminating the need to manually remember or input it each time you access the item.

A keychain is a secure and encrypted container used in Keychain Access to securely store and manage account credentials, including usernames and passwords, for various applications, servers, AirPort base stations, and websites. Additionally, keychains can be used to safeguard sensitive information such as credit card numbers or personal identification numbers (PINs) associated with bank accounts. See Figure 2-34.

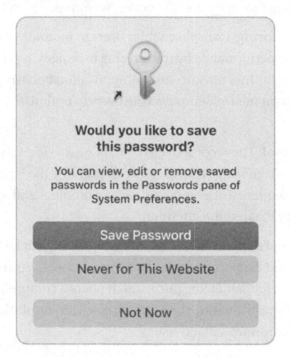

Figure 2-34. *Keychain pop-up for password storage*

Whenever you encounter a password-protected element, be it a website, email account, or network server, you may be prompted to save or remember the password. Opting to save the password allows it to be securely stored within your keychain, eliminating the need to recollect, or manually input it every time you access that particular item.

Apart from its password management functionality, Keychain Access can also handle certificates. These certificates, issued by trusted organizations, play a crucial role in verifying the authenticity and validity of websites, digital documents, and various other online materials. This additional feature further enhances the comprehensive security provisions offered by Keychain Access.

Keychain Access seamlessly combines with iCloud Keychain, providing you with the ability to sync your keychains across multiple Apple devices. Through the use of iCloud Keychain, you can effortlessly share and manage your keychain data across all your Apple devices.

To establish and manage your iCloud Keychain, all you need to do is log into your iCloud account using your Apple ID. This grants you full access to the extensive features and capabilities of iCloud Keychain, empowering you to easily create, organize, and maintain your synchronized keychain information across all your trusted Apple devices. See Figure 2-35.

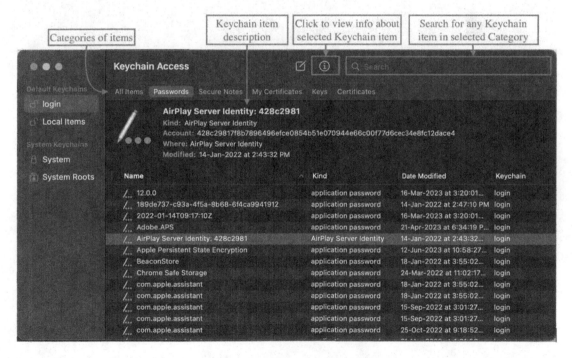

Figure 2-35. *Keychain overview*

Summary

You should now possess a comprehensive understanding of the various macOS file systems and their respective applications. Additionally, you have gained insights into the significance of different types of accounts for Mac devices and how they can be effectively used at the enterprise level for device management. Furthermore, you explored the utility of built-in tools in retrieving logs and specific information from Mac machines to aid in troubleshooting and familiarizing yourself with potential challenges. As you progress, you will delve into detailed configurations plus common issues and their troubleshooting methods to further enhance your knowledge and address any concerns that may arise.

CHAPTER 3

Configurations and Troubleshooting

In this chapter, we will delve into essential network and system tools for macOS. We will guide you through network configurations, printer and scanner management, macOS libraries, Time Machine backups, creating bootable installers, troubleshooting app installations, and system log analysis.

We will begin by exploring network configurations and basic settings, including IP address checks, DNS configuration, and proxy management. This knowledge will empower you to optimize your network connectivity and effectively troubleshoot any issues that may arise. Next, we will cover printer and scanner management, equipping you with the skills to set up new devices and troubleshoot common printing problems, ensuring a seamless workflow. We will then talk about macOS libraries, which will help you to extend your Mac system's functionality. Data backup is crucial, and we will guide you through Time Machine, enabling you to protect your important files and documents from potential loss.

Additionally, we will explain the process of creating a bootable installer for macOS, providing you with a reliable method for system reinstallation or upgrades. Troubleshooting app installations will also be covered, offering solutions to common challenges you may encounter.

Lastly, we will explore system log analysis, allowing you to view and interpret system logs to diagnose and resolve issues affecting system performance.

By the end of this chapter, you will be equipped with a comprehensive understanding of these essential configurations. You'll have the troubleshooting skills to optimize your macOS experience and effectively to tackle related issues.

© Sagar Rastogi and Jasdeep Singh 2023
S. Rastogi and J. Singh, *Exploring macOS*, https://doi.org/10.1007/978-1-4842-9882-4_3

Network Settings

Network Preferences in macOS is a system feature specifically designed for Mac computers. It serves as a centralized interface that enables users to effectively manage and configure their network connections. By accessing Network Preferences, users gain control over various network settings and services, providing them with a convenient and efficient way to handle their network-related needs.

One of the significant benefits of using Network Preferences on macOS is its capability to manage network connections seamlessly. Users can easily view available networks and then connect or disconnect from Wi-Fi, Ethernet, Bluetooth, and other network services. This feature simplifies the process of connecting to different networks, allowing users to switch between them effortlessly.

Another advantage offered by Network Preferences is its flexibility in network configuration. Users have the freedom to customize their network settings according to their specific requirements. They can modify parameters such as IP addresses, DNS servers, proxy settings, and more, allowing them to optimize network performance and ensure compatibility with different networks and devices.

Network service prioritization is another valuable feature available through Network Preferences. Users can prioritize network services based on their preferences. This allows them to define the order in which their Mac computer utilizes network interfaces, such as prioritizing Wi-Fi over Ethernet, ensuring uninterrupted internet access and seamless connectivity.

For users with advanced networking needs or troubleshooting requirements, Network Preferences provides access to advanced settings. This includes options for configuring TCP/IP parameters, managing network proxies, setting up virtual private networks (VPNs), and more. These advanced settings empower users with greater control over their network configurations, enabling them to tailor their network settings to specific needs or troubleshoot complex networking issues.

Network Preferences also includes built-in diagnostic tools that assist users in identifying and resolving network-related problems. Tools such as Network Diagnostics and Network Utility are easily accessible within the Network Preferences interface. These diagnostic tools aid in troubleshooting network issues, performing DNS lookups, checking network connectivity, and examining overall network performance.

Additionally, Network Preferences facilitates network sharing capabilities. Users can set up network sharing on their Mac computers, allowing them to share their internet connection with other devices or enable file sharing and printer sharing among devices connected to the same network. This feature enhances collaboration and convenience within a network environment.

In summary, Network Preferences in macOS offers users a comprehensive and user-friendly interface to effectively manage and customize their network connections. It provides the ability to optimize network settings, troubleshoot issues, and ensure efficient and reliable network connectivity on Mac computers.

Configuring network settings on macOS involves accessing the Network System Preferences and making necessary adjustments. Here's a guide to help you navigate through the process.

Start by clicking the Apple menu located in the top-left corner of your screen. From the drop-down menu, select System Preferences.

In the System Preferences window, locate and click the Network icon. This will open the Network settings.

On the left side of the Network settings window, you'll see a list of network services available on your Mac, such as Ethernet, Wi-Fi, and Bluetooth. Select the service for which you want to configure the settings.

If you don't find the desired service in the list, you can add it manually. Click the + button below the list. A new window will appear, allowing you to choose the interface (Ethernet, Wi-Fi, etc.) for the service. Select the interface, give the service a name, and click the Create button.

Once you've selected or created the service, you can adjust its settings. The settings you need to enter will depend on the type of network connection. Typically, you'll need to input information provided by your Internet Service Provider (ISP) or network administrator, such as IP address, subnet mask, router address, and DNS server information.

If you require more advanced settings, click the Advanced button. This will open a new window with additional options and configurations. Here, you can fine-tune settings related to TCP/IP, DNS, proxies, hardware, and other network-related parameters.

After making the necessary changes, click the Apply or OK button to save the settings.

By following these steps, you can configure network settings on macOS. It's essential to have accurate information from your ISP or network administrator to ensure proper connectivity. See Figures 3-1 and 3-2.

Figure 3-1. *Network settings access via System Preferences*

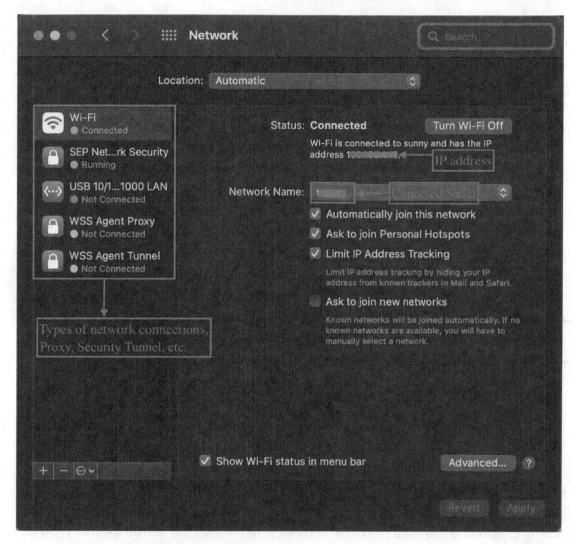

Figure 3-2. *Network types and details*

If you find yourself frequently changing network settings, macOS offers a convenient feature that allows you to save your settings as a network location. By doing so, you can easily switch between network locations and quickly adjust your network settings accordingly. This feature simplifies the process of modifying network configurations, making it more efficient and timesaving. So, if you frequently switch between different network setups, using network locations can significantly streamline the task of changing network settings on your Mac.

Please be aware that modifying your network settings can impact the communication between your computer and the network. It is recommended to use the automatic settings unless your network administrator has provided you with specific configuration details. Incorrectly entering network settings can potentially disrupt network performance, so it is crucial to exercise caution and ensure accurate settings are entered to maintain optimal network functionality.

Changing **Wi-Fi settings** on your Mac is made easy with the Network Preferences.

To change your Wi-Fi settings on a Mac, you can use the Network Preferences. This is a simple way to manage and customize your Wi-Fi connection. First, go to the Apple menu at the top-left corner of your screen and select System Preferences. Then click Network. In the Network Preferences window, you will see a list of network services. Look for Wi-Fi in the list and select it. If there is a lock icon at the bottom left of the window, click it and enter your administrator password to unlock the settings.

Within the Network Preferences, you have different options for managing your Wi-Fi connection. You can create new network services or remove existing ones. To create a new service, click the + button, choose the type of network service (such as Wi-Fi), give it a name, and click Create. To remove a service, select it and click the - button.

In the Status section, you can check the current state of your Wi-Fi connection. It will indicate whether you are connected to a network, have Wi-Fi turned on but not connected, or have Wi-Fi turned off. You can control the Wi-Fi status by using the Turn Wi-Fi On and Turn Wi-Fi Off options.

When it comes to connecting to Wi-Fi networks, you can choose a network from the available options in the Network Name section. If the network is password-protected, you will be asked to enter the password. You can also enable the "Automatically join this network" option if you want your Mac to connect to the selected network whenever it's available.

Additionally, there are options like "Ask to join Personal Hotspots" for notifications about available hotspots, "Limit IP Address Tracking" to protect your privacy, and "Ask to join new networks" for notifications about new networks. Advanced settings provide even more options for managing preferred networks, authorization requirements, TCP/IP and DNS settings, proxy servers, and hardware settings.

By utilizing the Network Preferences, you can easily modify and control your Wi-Fi settings on your Mac. It provides a user-friendly interface to manage your Wi-Fi connection according to your preferences and needs.

Network Locations on a Mac

A network location refers to a set of specific settings associated with a particular network port on your computer. This port can be your Ethernet port, modem port, or wireless networking port. The Location menu found in Network Preferences allows you to save and easily switch between different network locations.

By default, your Mac utilizes the Automatic location, which automatically provides the necessary settings for any available network ports it detects. A network port, also known as a network interface, serves as the means by which your computer connects to the Internet or a network. This can include components like a modem, Ethernet card, or Wi-Fi card.

In many cases, using the default Automatic location suffices because it adapts the appropriate settings based on the network you are connected to. For instance, if you use your Mac notebook both at work and home with a Wi-Fi connection, the Automatic location will seamlessly apply the required settings for each location.

However, if you find yourself needing to use the same network interface with different settings, you will need to establish separate locations. For example, if you manually configure your Ethernet port at work but rely on DHCP (Dynamic Host Configuration Protocol) at home, you will have to switch between locations to ensure the correct settings are in place. See Figure 3-3.

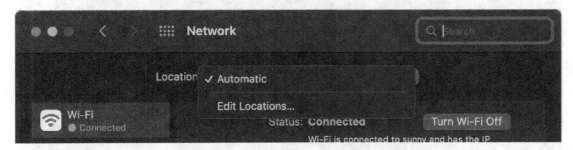

Figure 3-3. *Network locations in Network Preferences*

Creating Network Locations on a Mac

Since you now understand the network locations on a Mac, let's create a network location in a Mac machine. To adjust network settings on your Mac, you can access the Network Preferences. Here's a step-by-step guide:

Open Network Preferences on your Mac by navigating to the appropriate menu. In the Network Preferences window, locate the pop-up menu labeled Location and click it. From the options that appear, choose Edit Locations. This will allow you to manage and create different network locations. See Figure 3-4.

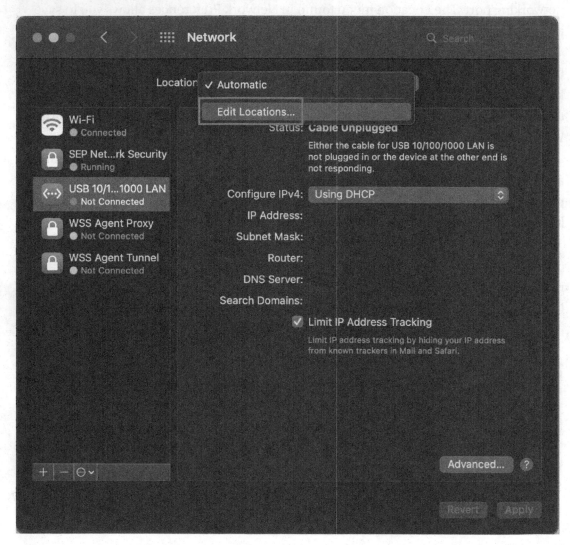

Figure 3-4. *Edit network locations*

To add a new location, click the Add button. A dialog box will appear where you can enter a name for the location you are creating. See Figure 3-5.

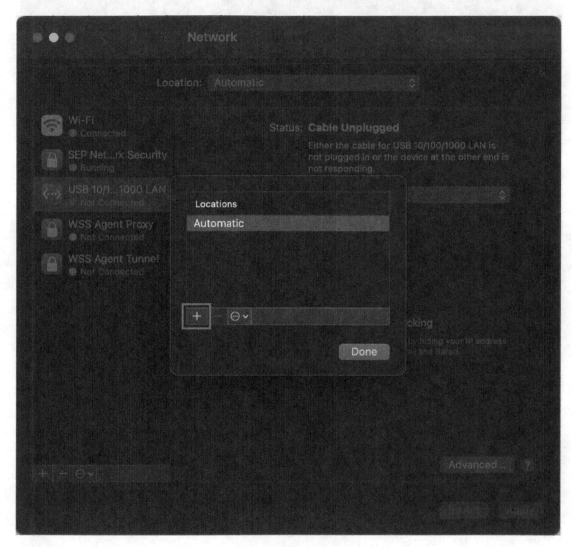

Figure 3-5. *Adding more network locations*

Once you've provided a suitable name, click the Done button. See Figure 3-6.

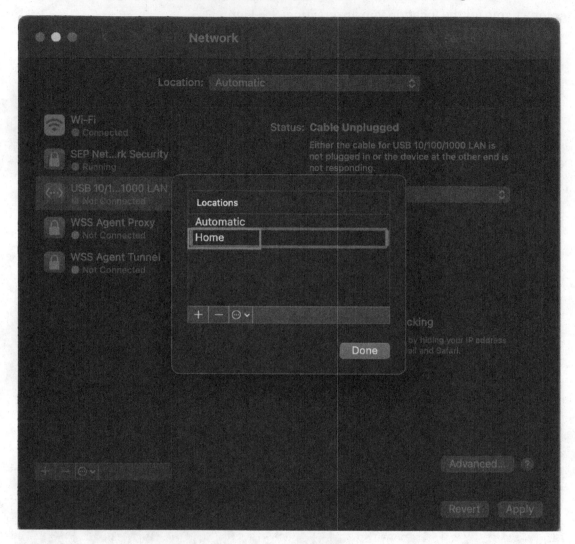

Figure 3-6. *Done adding more network locations*

Now, you can customize the settings for each network port within that specific location. This enables you to define the network configurations that will be applied when using those ports.

After you've made the desired changes to the network settings for the selected location and network ports, click the Apply button to save the modifications. See Figure 3-7.

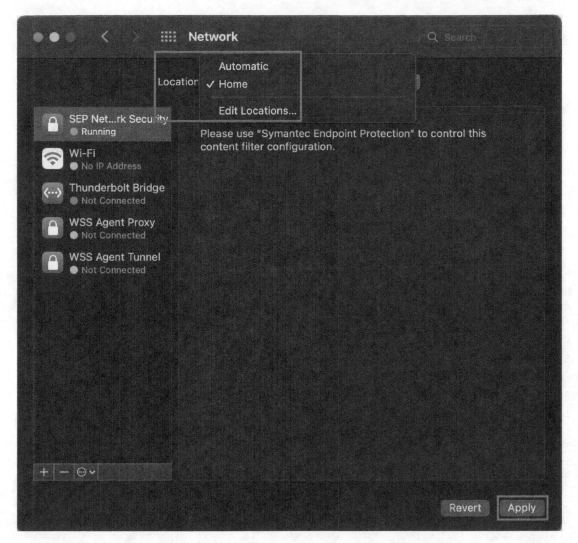

Figure 3-7. Multiple network locations

By following these steps, you can easily open Network Preferences, create new locations, assign specific settings to network ports, and ensure that your Mac's network configurations are tailored to your preferences.

Switching to a Different Network Location

Post creating network locations, you can switch to different locations swiftly to apply the defined settings as per specific location. To switch network locations on your Mac, you have two simple methods at your disposal.

The Apple menu approach: Begin by clicking the Apple menu, located in the top-left corner of your screen. From the menu options presented, select Location. This will reveal a list of available network locations that you have previously created. Choose the specific location you wish to switch to, and let your Mac handle the rest. See Figure 3-8.

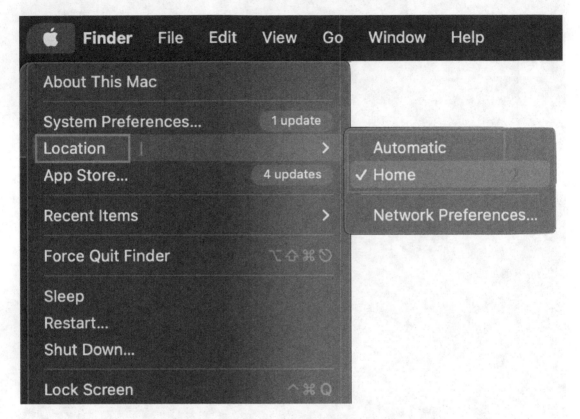

Figure 3-8. *Switching network locations from the Apple menu*

Network Preferences method: Commence by clicking the Apple menu once again, but this time choose System Preferences from the list. Inside the System Preferences window, locate and click the Network icon. Within the Network Preferences, keep an eye out for the Location pop-up menu. Click it and behold a selection of network locations at your disposal. Simply pick the desired location you want to switch to, and then solidify your choice by clicking the Apply button. See Figure 3-9.

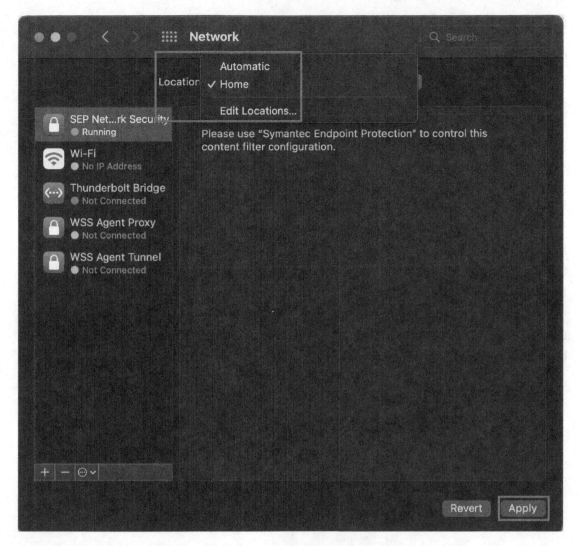

Figure 3-9. *Switching network locations from Network Preferences*

By employing either of these methods, you gain the ability to effortlessly transition between various network locations on your Mac. This grants you the flexibility to tailor your network settings according to your unique requirements and preferences.

Connecting a Mac to the Internet via Ethernet

Connecting to the Internet using Ethernet on your Mac involves a few straightforward steps. First, ensure that your modem/router is powered on and securely attached to a wall jack via the provided cable/wire. This step is crucial.

As a next step, procure an Ethernet cable and employ it to create a link between your computer and either the modem or another network device, such as a switch or router. If your Mac is devoid of an Ethernet port, there is no cause for concern! There are alternative solutions, such as a USB-to-Ethernet adapter or a Thunderbolt-to-Gigabit Ethernet adapter, which can be used to establish the desired connection.

Normally, your Mac will automatically establish an internet connection. However, if it doesn't, you'll need to manually enter the network settings. If you're unsure about the required settings, it's recommended to reach out to your network administrator or ISP for assistance.

To configure the network settings, open Network Preferences on your Mac and select the Ethernet option. This will grant you access to advanced settings. Click the Advanced button to proceed. See Figure 3-10.

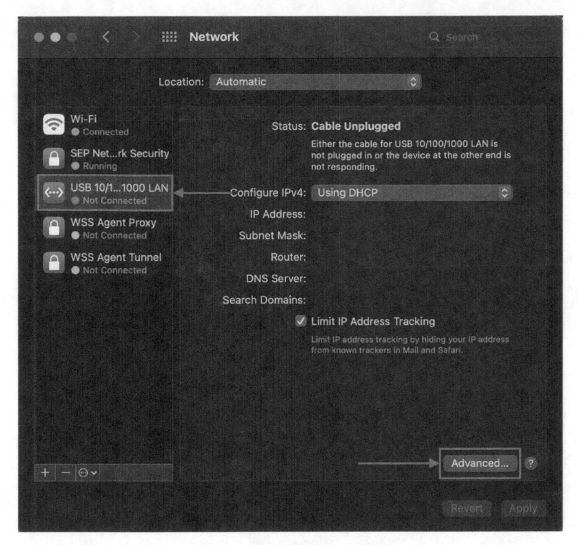

Figure 3-10. *Advanced options for wired network connections*

Within the Advanced settings, locate the pop-up menu named Configure IPv4. The option you should select will be determined by the configuration method recommended by your ISP. See Figure 3-11.

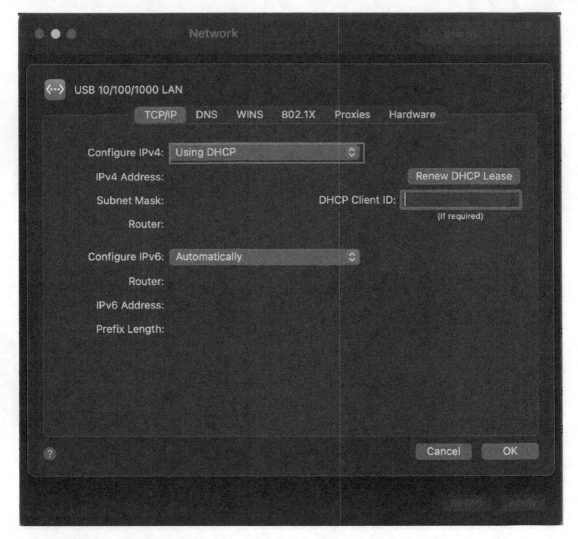

Figure 3-11. *Configuration of advanced options for wired network connections*

There are several possibilities.

DHCP: Select this if your ISP assigns IP addresses automatically.

DHCP with manual address: Opt for this option if your ISP has provided you with specific IP address details alongside DHCP or other network settings.

BootP: Use this option if your ISP uses BootP.

Manually: Select this option when your ISP has provided you with a designated IP address, subnet mask, and router address. See Figure 3-12.

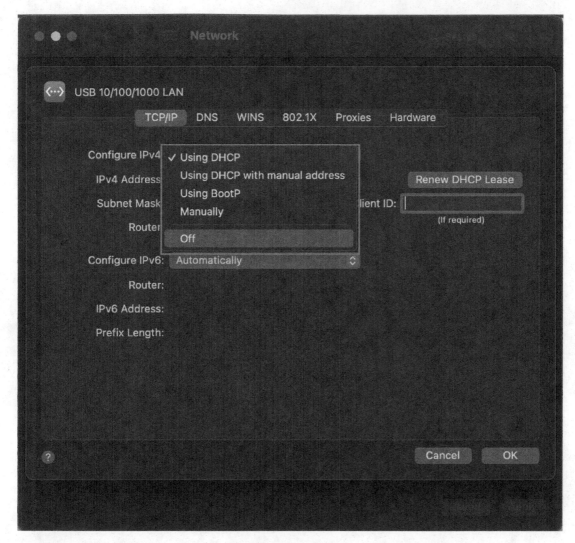

Figure 3-12. *Configuration of advanced options for wired network connections*

After choosing the suitable configuration method, proceed to the DNS tab. In this section, you have an opportunity to include your ISP's DNS server IP address by simply clicking the Add button located below DNS Servers. If your ISP has supplied any search domain addresses, you are welcome to enter them as well. It is important to note that these entries may not be required if you have already configured your IP settings to employ DHCP. See Figure 3-13.

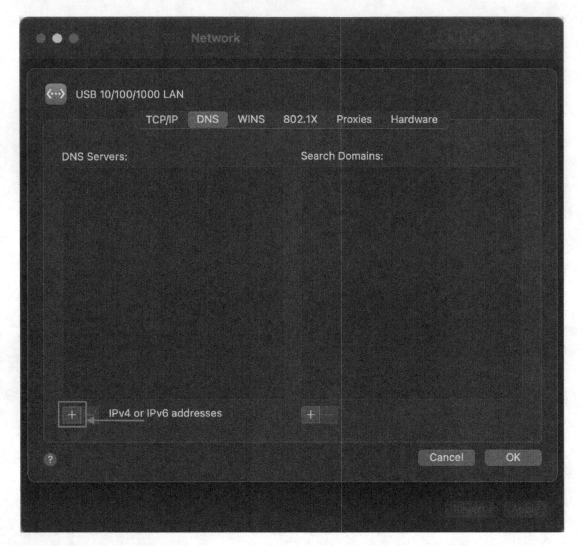

Figure 3-13. *Configuration of a DNS Server*

After entering the required information, click OK to activate the settings for the
Ethernet service. Your Mac will then initiate the process of establishing an internet
connection using the configured Ethernet settings. See Figure 3-14.

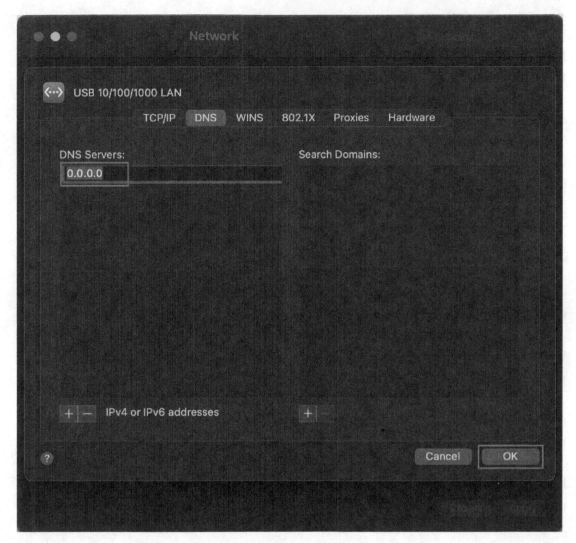

Figure 3-14. *Configuration of DNS Server*

By following these steps, you'll be able to successfully set up and configure an Ethernet connection on your Mac. This will grant you access to the Internet via Ethernet networks or your DSL/cable modem. Enjoy the benefits of a reliable and speedy wired connection on your Mac computer.

Sharing a Wi-Fi Password on a Mac

In the digital age, sharing a Wi-Fi password with someone has become a hassle-free task. If you find yourself in a situation where you need to provide access to your Wi-Fi network to another person's nearby Mac, iPhone, or iPad, fear not! Your Mac is equipped with a convenient feature that allows you to effortlessly share the password.

To begin, ensure that your Mac is both unlocked and connected to the Wi-Fi network in question. Additionally, make sure you are signed into your Apple ID, as this will enable the seamless sharing process.

Next, ensure that the Apple ID of the individual you wish to share the password with is saved in your Contacts app. This ensures that your Mac can readily identify the recipient's device.

Now comes the exciting part. Move the other person's device close to your Mac, ensuring that they are within the vicinity of your Wi-Fi network's range. This proximity is essential for the successful sharing of the password.

On the recipient's device, have them navigate to the Wi-Fi settings and select the Wi-Fi network that belongs to you from the available options. As they do so, your Mac will spring into action.

Within a moment, a notification will appear on your Mac. This notification, aptly named the Wi-Fi password notification, carries the crucial information that the other person requires to join your network. It's a digital key that unlocks the virtual doors of your Wi-Fi realm.

With the notification in sight, it's time to finalize the process. Simply click the Share button, initiating the transfer of the Wi-Fi password to the awaiting device. In an instant, the password is conveyed, granting the other person immediate access to your Wi-Fi network.

Through this seamless process, your Mac acts as a conduit, effortlessly transmitting the vital Wi-Fi password from your device to another. No more tedious manual entries or scribbling passwords on scraps of paper. The power to share access to your Wi-Fi network lies at your fingertips, all thanks to the intelligent capabilities of your Mac.

Terminal Commands for Networks

Using network terminal commands in macOS offers several benefits.

Control and customization: Terminal commands provide granular control and customization options for network configurations. You can modify settings like IP addresses, subnet masks, gateways, and DNS servers to tailor your network setup to specific requirements.

Troubleshooting: Network terminal commands allow you to diagnose and resolve network-related issues. You can use commands like ping to test connectivity, view routing tables to analyze network paths, flush DNS cache to resolve DNS-related problems, and renew DHCP leases to troubleshoot IP assignment issues.

Automation and scripting: Terminal commands can be used in scripts or automated workflows to streamline network management tasks. This allows you to automate repetitive processes, configure network settings in bulk, or integrate network management with other system operations.

Efficiency and speed: Using terminal commands can be quicker and more efficient than navigating through graphical user interfaces (GUIs) for certain network tasks. With a few command inputs, you can perform actions like enabling or disabling network interfaces, changing network configurations, or connecting to Wi-Fi networks without the need for GUI interactions.

Remote administration: Network terminal commands can be executed remotely via SSH (Secure Shell) or other remote access protocols. This enables network administrators to manage and troubleshoot networks on macOS systems from a central location, even if they are physically located elsewhere.

Learning and skill development: Familiarity with network terminal commands enhances your knowledge and proficiency in network administration. It allows you to gain a deeper understanding of network concepts, protocols, and configurations, empowering you to efficiently manage and troubleshoot networks across various platforms.

While network terminal commands offer powerful capabilities, it is important that you have the necessary knowledge and permissions to use them effectively. Incorrectly executed commands can disrupt network connectivity or lead to unintended consequences.

Here are some commonly used terminal commands for network-related tasks in macOS.

Check Network Connectivity

ping [IP or domain]: Sends ICMP echo requests to test network connectivity.

View Network Information

`ifconfig`: Displays information about network interfaces.

`ipconfig getifaddr [interface]`: Retrieves the IP address of a specific network interface.

Get IP address: `ipconfig getifaddr en0`

Get subnet mask: `ipconfig getoption en0 subnet_mask`

Get DNS server: `ipconfig getoption en0 domain_name_server`

Get information about how en0 obtained its DHCP: `ipconfig getpacket en0`

Display Routing Table

`netstat -nr`: Shows the routing table, including the destination, gateway, and interface

Flush DNS Cache

`dscacheutil -flushcache`: Clears the DNS cache on your Mac

Renew DHCP Lease

`sudo ipconfig set [interface] DHCP`: Renews the DHCP lease for a specific network interface

Enable/Disable Network Interfaces

`networksetup -setnetworkserviceenabled [service] [on/off]`: Enables or disables a network service

Change Network Configuration

`networksetup -setmanual [interface] [IP] [subnet mask] [gateway]`: Sets a manual IP configuration for a network interface

`networksetup -setdhcp [interface]`: Switches a network interface to DHCP configuration

Manage Wi-Fi Connections

networksetup -setairportpower [airport] [on/off]: Turns the Wi-Fi interface on or off

networksetup -setairportnetwork [airport] [SSID] [password]: Connects to a specific Wi-Fi network

Network Setup

Get a list of locations on the computer: networksetup -listlocations

Get the active location: networksetup -getcurrentlocation

Configure a manual static IP address: networksetup -setmanual Wi-Fi 192.168.1.xxx

255.255.255.0 192.168.1.xxx

Configure a DNS server: networksetup -setdnsservers Wi-Fi 192.168.1.xxx 192.168.1.xxx Get DNS server: networksetup -getdnsservers Wi-Fi

Please note that some commands may require administrator privileges (use sudo) and you should replace the [interface], [IP], [subnet mask], [gateway], [airport], [SSID], and [password] placeholders with the appropriate values specific to your network configuration.

Printers and Scanners

The Printers & Scanners preferences in macOS provide a centralized location to manage and customize your printing and scanning settings. By accessing this feature, you can add, remove, and configure printers and scanners connected to your Mac. Here are some key aspects of Printer & Scanners preferences. See Figure 3-15.

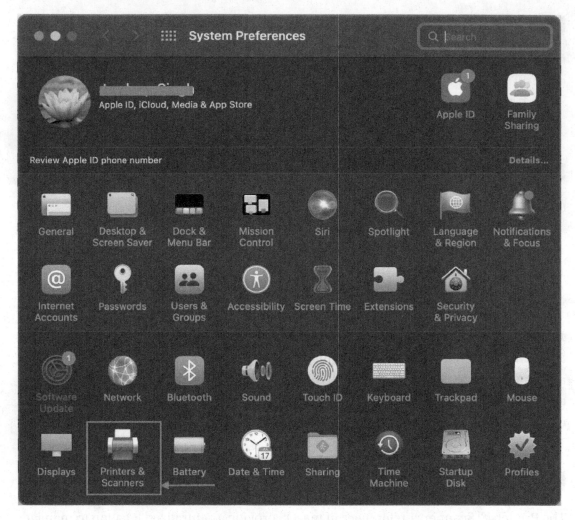

Figure 3-15. *Printers & Scanners preferences via System Preferences*

Adding a printer or scanner: To start using a printer or scanner with your Mac, you need to add it to the list of available devices. Simply select the + symbol in Printers & Scanners preferences and macOS will start searching for compatible devices connected to your computer or network. In most cases, macOS will automatically detect and configure the printer or scanner using Air Print technology.

Printer and scanner settings: Once a printer or scanner is added, you can access its settings to customize its behavior. For printers, you can adjust options like paper size, print quality, and default printing preferences. Scanners offer settings for resolution, file format, and destination folder for scanned documents. These settings allow you to optimize the printing and scanning experience according to your needs. See Figure 3-16.

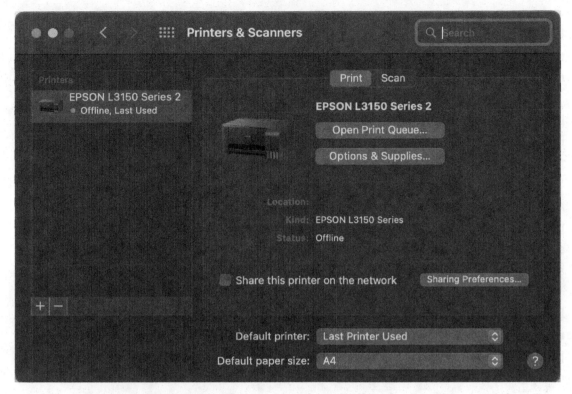

Figure 3-16. *Printers & Scanners*

Managing printers and scanners: The Printers & Scanners preferences provide a
convenient way to manage your devices. You can rearrange the order in which printers
are listed, set a default printer, and choose whether to display printer status in the menu
bar. Additionally, you can remove printers or scanners that are no longer in use or
update their settings as needed.

Printer and scanner options: macOS offers various options for advanced printer
and scanner configuration. You can access features like duplex printing (double-sided),
color management, printer sharing, and printer driver selection. For scanners, you
can specify OCR (Optical Character Recognition) settings, image correction, and other
advanced scanning options.

Troubleshooting and maintenance: If you encounter any issues with printing or
scanning, the Printers & Scanners preferences can assist in troubleshooting. You can use
features like Reset printing system to reset printer settings, Open Print Queue to manage
print jobs, and Scanner to test and diagnose scanning functionality.

Overall, the Printers & Scanners preferences in macOS provide a user-friendly interface to manage and customize your printing and scanning experience. Whether you need to add a new printer, adjust settings, or troubleshoot issues, this feature streamlines the process, ensuring efficient and reliable printing and scanning on your Mac.

To enable printing functionality on your Mac, you need to add your printer to the list of available printers in the Printers & Scanners settings/preferences. If you have recently transitioned from a Windows computer to a Mac, you will find that this process resembles utilizing the Printing control panel on a Windows machine.

When you add a printer, macOS uses a technology called AirPrint in most cases. AirPrint allows seamless communication between your Mac and the printer without the need for additional software or drivers. However, if your printer requires specific software to function correctly, macOS will automatically download and install the appropriate printer driver for you.

Exercise caution and refrain from manually installing any printer software that may have been included with the printer or downloaded from the manufacturer's website. macOS takes care of this for you by providing instructions during the printer setup process in the Printers & Scanners preferences. This ensures that you have the latest and compatible software specifically tailored for your printer.

By relying on macOS to handle the printer installation process, you can be confident that your printer will be properly configured and ready for use. If there are any required software updates, macOS will notify you and guide you through the process of downloading them, ensuring optimal compatibility and performance between your Mac and the printer.

Taking advantage of the built-in printer setup features in macOS simplifies the process of adding and configuring printers, allowing you to focus on your printing tasks without the hassle of manual software installations.

AirPrint

AirPrint is a remarkable technology developed by Apple that revolutionizes the way we print our documents and photos. With AirPrint, you no longer need to go through the hassle of downloading or installing drivers to achieve high-quality printed output. It simplifies the printing process, allowing you to effortlessly produce stunning prints from your Mac, iPhone, iPad, or iPod touch.

Gone are the days of tedious driver installations. AirPrint makes printing a breeze by providing seamless integration between your Apple devices and compatible printers. Discovering available printers on your network becomes a hassle-free experience, as AirPrint automatically detects and presents them to you.

One of the key advantages of AirPrint is its ability to intelligently select the appropriate media for your print job. Whether you need to print a vibrant photograph or a crisp document, AirPrint ensures that the right paper type and size are chosen, saving you the trouble of manually configuring these settings.

Moreover, AirPrint goes beyond basic printing capabilities by offering enterprise-class finishing options. You can easily accomplish professional touches like stapling, hole punching, and collating without the need for additional software or complex setups. AirPrint empowers you to create polished, high-quality prints with just a few clicks.

The beauty of AirPrint lies in its seamless integration and intuitive functionality. It eliminates the complexities associated with traditional printing processes, allowing you to focus on the content you wish to print rather than the technicalities of printer drivers. Whether you're a casual user or a business professional, AirPrint offers a convenient and reliable solution for your printing needs.

So, enjoy the convenience of AirPrint and experience the joy of effortless printing. Let your Mac, iPhone, iPad, or iPod touch collaborate harmoniously with AirPrint-enabled printers to bring your digital creations to life on paper. With its easy discovery, automatic media selection, and enterprise-class finishing options, AirPrint sets a new standard for hassle-free, high-quality printing.

More details related to AirPrint and list of compatible printers can be found on Apple's support article at `https://support.apple.com/en-gb/HT201311`.

USB Printer Configuration

Setting up your USB printer with your Mac is a breeze, requiring just a few straightforward steps. For most USB printers, the process is as straightforward as updating your software and plugging in the printer. Whether you need to print documents or bring your cherished memories to life on paper, let's explore the process together.

Let's start by ensuring that your Mac's software is current. Begin by clicking the Apple menu located in the top-left corner of your screen. From the menu options, select System Preferences to access various settings. Within System Preferences, locate the

Software Update section and navigate to it. Here, you will find a list of available software updates. It is recommended to install all updates, even if none are visibly indicated. This practice ensures that your Mac possesses the most recent printer software information provided by Apple, which in turn prevents any potential complications when connecting your printer due to software unavailability.

Now it's time to prepare your printer for action. Unpack your printer using the instructions provided, carefully install the ink or toner cartridges, and load it with paper. Power on the printer, ensuring there are no error messages or complications hindering its functionality. A smooth setup experience starts with a well-prepared printer.

With the preliminary preparations complete, it's time to establish the connection between your Mac and the printer. Take the USB cable provided with your printer and connect it to an available USB port on your Mac. As you make the connection, pay attention to any prompts or messages that may appear on your screen. If prompted to download additional software specific to your printer model, proceed with the download and installation. This guarantees that your Mac possesses all the necessary drivers and software components to communicate seamlessly with your printer.

Remember, if your Mac has a single USB-C port, then you will need to use a multiport adapter to connect your printer. This adapter expands the capabilities of your USB-C port, allowing for hassle-free connection of the USB printer cable.

By following these straightforward instructions, you will effortlessly integrate your USB printer with your Mac. From important documents to cherished photographs, printing becomes a convenient and efficient process. So, ensure your software is updated, prepare your printer meticulously, connect the USB cable, and embark on a seamless printing journey.

Wi-Fi or Network Printer Configuration

In the realm of wireless printing, the seamless connection between your Mac and printer on the same Wi-Fi network can be a reality, requiring little to no setup. Let's embark on the journey of discovery and see if your printer is readily available for use.

Begin by opening a file on your Mac that you wish to print. Navigate to the File menu and select the Print option. A window will emerge, presenting various printing settings. Locate the Printer pop-up menu and click it. You will be presented with two options: Nearby Printers or Printers & Scanners Preferences. Choose the latter to delve deeper into printer availability. If your desired printer is already listed, you're in luck—it's ready to serve your printing needs. However, if your printer is absent from the list, fret not, for we shall add it together.

To ensure a smooth printing experience, it is advisable to update your Mac's software if you do not possess an AirPrint-compatible printer. For those who do own an AirPrint printer, worry not, as you need not undertake this step.

Now, let's prepare your printer for its upcoming duties. Refer to the instructions that accompanied your printer, providing guidance on unpacking it, installing ink/toner cartridges, and loading paper into the appropriate tray. Once these preparations are complete, power on the printer and ensure it exhibits no error messages or malfunctions. A pristine printer sets the stage for flawless printing endeavors.

The time has come to establish a connection between your printer and your Wi-Fi network. Adhere to the instructions provided by the printer's manufacturer, guiding you through the network connection process. For Wi-Fi printers, it may be necessary to establish a temporary connection between the printer and your Mac using a USB cable in an order to initiate the Wi-Fi setup process. Once the connection is established, proceed to install the accompanying Mac software for your printer, which will activate the printer's setup assistant. This assistant will facilitate the connection of your printer to the designated Wi-Fi network. Upon successful setup, you may disconnect the USB cable, freeing your printer to remain connected to the Wi-Fi network independently.

Now that your printer is primed and connected, let's ensure it appears on your list of available printers. Access the Apple menu situated at the top-left corner of your screen. From the menu options, choose System Preferences. Within the System Preferences window, locate and click the Printers & Scanners option, which grants you access to a collection of printer-related settings. Look for the Add button and give it a click. This action will prompt a dialogue box to appear, revealing a list of printers detected on your local network. Please exercise patience, as it may take a moment or two for your printer to populate the list. Once your printer is visible, select it from the list and click the Add button to finalize the setup process. If you encounter a message urging you to download new software, it is crucial to proceed with the download and installation to ensure optimal performance of your printer.

With the successful installation and activation of printer, you can print your documents, pictures and more with an ease of wireless printing functionality. This really provides the convenience of usability.

Network Printer Configuration by IP Address

In the world of printing, there may be instances where the printer you wish to use on your network isn't readily available in the list of printers. Rest assured; there is a solution to add your printer as an IP printer. This method necessitates that the printer is compatible with certain printing protocols such as AirPrint, HP Jet direct (Socket), Line Printer Daemon (LPD), or Internet Printing Protocol (IPP).

Before we dive into the steps, it's essential to ensure that your Mac's software is up to date, unless you're already using an AirPrint-compatible printer. Keeping your software current is crucial for a seamless printing experience.

Once you've confirmed your software is updated, let's prepare the printer for its integration. Unpack the printer according to the instructions provided, install ink or toner, and load paper into the tray. Power on the printer and ensure it displays no errors or issues.

Now, it's time to establish a connection between your printer and the network. You may follow the directions provided printer manufacturer to complete this step successfully.

With the printer connected to the network, you can move forward and include it in the roster of available printers on your Mac. To accomplish this, go to the Apple menu and choose System Preferences. Once inside the System Preferences window, search for and click Printers & Scanners. Here, you'll discover an array of settings specifically related to printers.

To add the printer, click the Add button. A new window will appear, presenting several options. Look for and select the IP button, which will lead you to a dialogue box where you can enter the necessary printer information. Refer to Table 3-1 for the specific details required. See Figure 3-17.

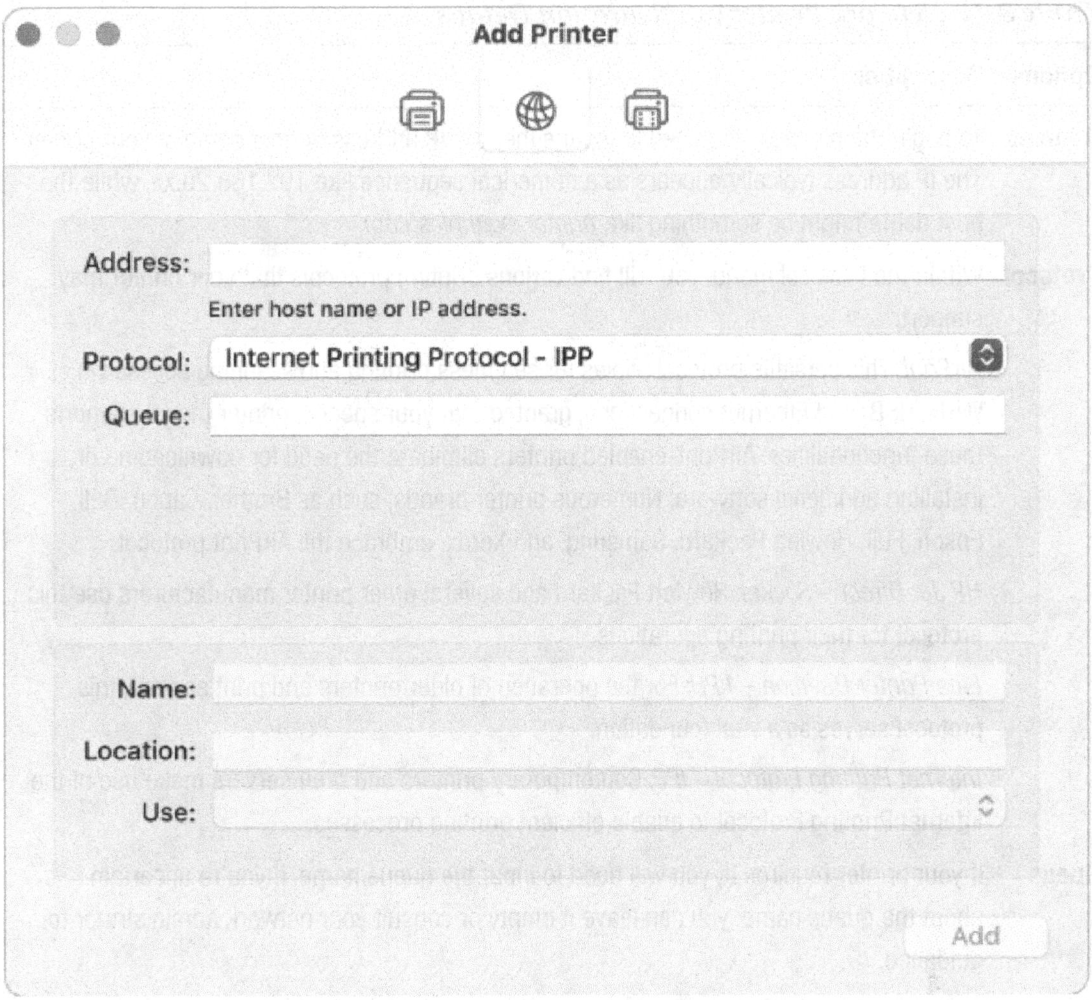

Figure 3-17. *Network printer configuration*

Table 3-1. *Network Printer Configuration Details*

Options	Description
Address	To begin the process, you need to input either the IP address or host name of your printer. The IP address typically appears as a numerical sequence like 192.168.20.xx, while the host name might be something like *printer.examples.com*.
Protocol	Within the Protocol menu, you will find various printing protocols that your printer may support: *AirPrint:* This versatile protocol allows for seamless printing and scanning access via Wi-Fi, USB, and Ethernet connections, granted that your specific printer model supports these functionalities. AirPrint-enabled printers eliminate the need for downloading or installing additional software. Numerous printer brands, such as Brother, Canon, Dell, Epson, Fuji, Hewlett Packard, Samsung, and Xerox, embrace the AirPrint protocol. *HP Jet Direct – Socket:* Hewlett Packard and several other printer manufacturers use this protocol for their printing operations. *Line Printer Daemon – LPD:* For the operation of older printers and print servers, this protocol serves as a vital foundation. *Internet Printing Protocol – IPP:* Contemporary printers and print servers make use of the Internet Printing Protocol to enable efficient printing processes.
Queue	If your printer requires it, you will need to input the queue name. If you're uncertain about the queue name, you can leave it empty or consult your network administrator for guidance.
Name	Assign a descriptive name to the printer (such as Color Laser Printer) to enable easy identification in the printer pop-up menu.
Location	Specify the location of the printer (e.g., outside my office) to facilitate its identification in the printer pop-up menu.
Use	If the software options presented in the pop-up menu do not correspond to your printer model, you can opt for Select Printer Software and manually search for your printer in the provided list. If your specific printer is not listed, you might consider visiting the manufacturer's website to download and install the appropriate printer software, commonly referred to as a printer driver. Alternatively, you can explore generic printer software available in the pop-up menu as an alternative.

By following these steps, you'll successfully add the network printer as an IP printer. This expansion of your printing capabilities allows for more convenience and versatility. Whether it's documents, photos, or other print-worthy materials, your Mac is now equipped to handle a broader range of printing tasks. Embrace the seamless integration and make the most of your enhanced printing capabilities.

Bluetooth Printer Configuration

To print wirelessly from a Mac to a Bluetooth-enabled printer, you will need to make sure your Mac has Bluetooth capability. Follow these steps to set up and add a Bluetooth printer to your Mac.

Firstly, ensure that your Mac's software is up to date. If you do not have an AirPrint printer, it is recommended to check for any available software updates. Keeping your software updated ensures compatibility and the latest features.

Now, establish the Bluetooth connection between your printer and Mac. Consult the printer's documentation for precise instructions on how to pair the printer with your Mac using Bluetooth. This process may involve entering a passkey or following specific on-screen prompts.

After successfully connecting the printer to your Mac via Bluetooth, you need to add it to the list of available printers. Begin by clicking the Apple menu located in the top-left corner of the screen. From the dropdown menu, select System Preferences to access the settings.

Within the System Preferences window, locate and click Printers & Scanners. This will open a panel where you can manage your printer settings. To add your Bluetooth printer, click the + button, typically found at the bottom left or top left of the panel.

A new window will appear, presenting different options for adding a printer. Click the IP button and then select the Default option. This will allow your Mac to search for available printers on the network.

Scan the list of printers displayed and look for your Bluetooth printer. If it does not appear in the list, you can enter its name in the search field provided and press the Return key. This may help locate the printer and add it to the available printers on your Mac.

Finally, after successfully connecting your Bluetooth printer and adding it to the list, you may receive a notification to download and install new software. It is crucial to follow this prompt and download any recommended software updates for optimal performance and compatibility with your printer.

With these steps completed, your Bluetooth printer is now set up and ready for wireless printing from your Mac. You can choose the printer as your default option or select it whenever you wish to print documents or files. Enjoy the convenience of wireless printing with your Mac and Bluetooth-enabled printer.

Wi-Fi/Mobile Printer Configuration via a Configuration Profile

In certain cases, specific network printers mandate the installation of a configuration profile to facilitate their detection on your network through AirPrint. If you have been provided with a printer profile for installation, it is crucial to download or transfer it to your Mac prior to commencing the installation procedure.

To install the printer profile, begin by locating the downloaded or copied profile file on your Mac. Once located, simply double-click the profile file to open it. This action will initiate the installation process, and the profile will be installed in the Profiles pane of System Preferences.

To include the printer in your list of available printers, start by accessing the Apple menu situated at the top-left corner of your screen. From the dropdown menu, select System Preferences. Inside the System Preferences window, locate and click Printers & Scanners to gain access to the printer settings where you can proceed with the addition process.

In the Printers & Scanners panel, click the + button, typically found at the bottom left or top left of the window. A new window will appear, providing options for adding a printer. Click the IP button and then select the Default option.

Next, scan through the Printers list to find the printer you want to add. In this list, the printer will be identified as an AirPrint Profile. Once you have located the printer, select it and click the Add button to include it in your printer list.

If your printer is not visible in the list, it is crucial to confirm that you have installed the most recent profile dedicated to that specific printer. Furthermore, ensure that there is a functional network connection established between your computer and the printer. If you encounter any challenges, it is advisable to seek guidance from your network administrator. They can assist you in obtaining the latest profile and resolving any potential network connectivity problems.

By following these steps, you can successfully install a printer configuration profile on your Mac, add the printer to your printer list, and ensure its proper functionality with AirPrint. Enjoy the convenience of wireless printing from your Mac to the network printer with ease and efficiency.

In conclusion, the Printers & Scanners preferences in macOS provide a user-friendly and efficient way to manage and set up printers on your Mac. Whether you are connecting a USB printer, configuring a network printer, or using a Bluetooth-enabled printer, macOS offers seamless integration and easy setup processes.

By updating your software, preparing your printer, and following the step-by-step instructions within the Printers & Scanners preferences, you can quickly add printers to your list of available devices. macOS supports various printing protocols, such as AirPrint, HP Jet Direct, Line Printer Daemon, and Internet Printing Protocol, ensuring compatibility with a wide range of printer models.

Additionally, the option to add printers using IP addresses or host names, along with the flexibility to customize printer names and locations, enhances the overall user experience. The inclusion of Bluetooth printer support further expands the wireless printing capabilities of your Mac.

If a printer requires a configuration profile, macOS simplifies the installation process, allowing for easy discovery and integration of network printers using AirPrint.

Overall, the Printers & Scanners preferences in macOS provide a comprehensive and user-centric approach to managing printers. With its intuitive interface and robust features, macOS ensures that setting up and using printers on your Mac is a hassle-free experience, enabling you to effortlessly print your documents and files with convenience and efficiency.

Libraries in a Mac

In macOS, there are several important library folders that contain essential files and resources used by the system and applications. These library folders help organize and manage various components of the operating system and installed software. macOS includes two main libraries for organizing files and resources.

System Library: The System Library is not hidden and can be found at the Macintosh HD - Library path. It contains essential system-level components and frameworks used by macOS. The System Library includes system preferences, drivers, kernel extensions, and other important files that are required for the proper functioning of the operating system.

User Library: The User Library is a hidden library that resides in the Macintosh HD /Users/Username/Library directory. It is specific to each user and contains user-specific preferences, settings, caches, and other files related to applications installed on the user's account. The User Library also holds individual user preferences for various applications, such as browser settings, application support files, and user-specific data.

These libraries serve important roles in macOS by providing a structured organization of files and resources, separating system-level components from user-specific data. While the System Library is easily accessible, the User Library is hidden by default to prevent accidental modification or deletion of critical files. However, users can access the User Library by using the Go menu in the Finder and holding down the Option key.

Library Folders on Macs

The Library folder on macOS is a vital system directory that houses various critical support files essential for the proper functioning of your Mac and its applications. It serves as a repository for a wide range of files, including user account settings, preference files, application scripts, caches, cookies, fonts, and other service-related files.

These files play a crucial role in enabling your Mac and its applications to operate smoothly and efficiently. User account settings and preferences stored in the Library folder ensure that your personalized configurations and preferences are maintained across different applications. Additionally, containers help isolate application data and files, ensuring proper organization and data management.

Caches and cookies stored in the Library folder enhance application performance by storing temporary data that can be quickly accessed when needed. Fonts stored in this folder are available system-wide, allowing applications to access and utilize different font styles and characters.

Overall, the Library folder is an integral part of macOS, serving as a centralized location for important support files that contribute to the optimal functioning of your Mac and its applications. It ensures that your system runs smoothly and efficiently, providing you with a seamless computing experience.

Hidden Library Folder

The Library folder in macOS is intentionally hidden by Apple to safeguard users from inadvertently deleting or altering critical files stored within it. This hidden status helps prevent accidental modifications that could disrupt the functioning of applications and the complete system.

The Library folder contains essential files, such as application preferences, caches, and various system files required for the proper operation of programs. Removing or tampering with these files can potentially harm your system's stability or impair the performance of specific applications. Therefore, it is strongly advised not to remove files from the Library folder unless you have a clear understanding of their purpose and the potential consequences.

By keeping the Library folder hidden, Apple aims to maintain the integrity and reliability of your macOS environment, ensuring that crucial system components and application support files remain intact. It serves as a protective measure to prevent inadvertent actions that could negatively impact your system's functionality. It is important to exercise caution and seek appropriate guidance before making any changes within the Library folder.

Accessing Library Folders

Accessing the Library folders in macOS can be done using various methods. Here are a few approaches.

Using Finder

Open a Finder window.

Select the Go option in the menu bar at the top.

While holding the Option key on your keyboard, the Library option will appear in the drop-down menu.

Click Library to directly access the User Library folder for the logged-in user.

Using the Go to Folder Option

Open a Finder window.

Click the Go option in the menu bar.

Select Go to Folder from the drop-down menu or use the Command+Shift+G shortcut. Enter the path to the desired library folder:

System Library: /Library

User Library: ~/Library

Click Go to access the specified library folder.

Using Terminal

Initiate the Terminal application by navigating to the Utilities folder, which can be found within the Applications folder. In the Terminal window, type the command to navigate to the desired library folder:

System Library: cd /Library

User Library: cd ~/Library

Press Enter to execute the command and access the specified library folder.

These methods provide flexibility in accessing both the System Library and User Library folders in macOS, allowing you to manage important system files and user-specific resources as needed.

What Files or Folders Can Be Removed from a Library?

Here is a compilation of folders on your Mac that can be removed safely without incurring any adverse consequences:

Mail attachments: Located at ~/Library/Mail, you can remove old email attachments that are no longer needed.

Unneeded iTunes/Music backups: Found at ~/Library/Application Support/ MobileSync/Backup, you can delete unnecessary backups created by iTunes.

Leftovers of uninstalled programs: You can safely remove the following folders related to uninstalled programs:

```
~/Library/Preferences
~/Library/Containers/[App name]/Data/Library/Preferences ~/Library/
Application Support/[App or Developer name] /Library/Application Support/
[App or Developer name]
~/Library/Application Support/[App or Developer name] /Library/Application
Support/[App or Developer name] ~/Library/Containers/[App Name]/Data/
Library/Caches/[App Name] ~/Library/Saved Application State ~/Library/
Cookies ~/Library/LaunchAgents ~/Library/Screen Savers
```

Deleting these folders will help free up storage space on your Mac by removing unnecessary files. However, please ensure that you only delete files from these specific locations and exercise caution to avoid deleting any important files or folders that are still in use.

Is It Safe to Remove Caches From the Library Folder?

Deleting caches from the Library folder is generally considered safe, if you have a clear understanding of the files you are removing. However, it is important to exercise caution and avoid deleting files from the Cache folder unless you have a specific reason to do so.

Time Machine

Time Machine is a powerful backup solution built into macOS and available by default within the Applications folder, designed to protect and preserve your valuable data. It offers several key features and functionalities that ensure your files are securely backed up and easily restorable. There are several benefits of Time Machine.

One of the standout features of Time Machine is its ability to perform automatic backups. It creates incremental backups, capturing changes made to your files on an hourly, daily, and weekly basis. This ensures that you have multiple versions of your files available, allowing you to restore them to a specific point in time.

Setting up Time Machine is hassle-free. You connect an external hard drive or a network storage device to your Mac and select it as the backup destination. From there, Time Machine takes care of the rest, seamlessly backing up your data in the background.

Time Machine operates continuously, monitoring your files for any modifications. As soon as you connect the backup drive to your Mac, Time Machine initiates the backup process, ensuring that your data is always up to date and protected.

Restoring files from Time Machine is a straightforward process. With its intuitive interface, you can easily browse through the backup timeline and retrieve specific versions of files or even entire folders. Additionally, Time Machine offers the option for a full system restore, allowing you to revert your Mac to a previous state in case of critical failures or data loss.

If you are migrating to a new Mac, Time Machine provides invaluable assistance. By connecting the backup drive to your new Mac, you can seamlessly transfer your files, applications, and settings, making the transition smooth and efficient.

Time Machine also excels in space management. It intelligently manages storage space by retaining only the latest version of each file and removing older backups as the backup drive fills up. This ensures that you have sufficient space for new backups while still having access to older versions when needed.

Time Machine simplifies the backup process by automating it for you. Once set up, it works silently in the background, continuously capturing changes made to your files. This means that you don't have to worry about manually initiating backups or keeping track of individual files.

With Time Machine, retrieving files from your backups is a breeze. You can easily browse through the backup timeline and access previous versions of your files, allowing you to recover specific documents or even restore entire folders. This flexibility ensures that you can retrieve important data whenever you need it.

By using Time Machine, you create a reliable safety net for your personal data. In the event of accidental deletions, system failures, or hardware issues, you can restore your files from a recent backup, minimizing the risk of permanent data loss.

Overall, Time Machine provides a user-friendly and efficient way to protect and restore your personal data on your Mac. By taking advantage of this built-in feature, you can enjoy the peace of mind that comes with having a reliable backup system in place, ensuring the safety and recoverability of your important files.

To create a Time Machine backup on your Mac, follow these simple steps.

Establish a connection between your Mac and an external storage device, such as an external hard drive. Ensure that the device has enough storage capacity to accommodate your backups.

To access Time Machine preferences, you have a couple of options. You can either click the Time Machine icon in the menu bar and choose "Open Time Machine Preferences," or you can navigate to System Preferences and select the Time Machine icon from there. See Figure 3-18.

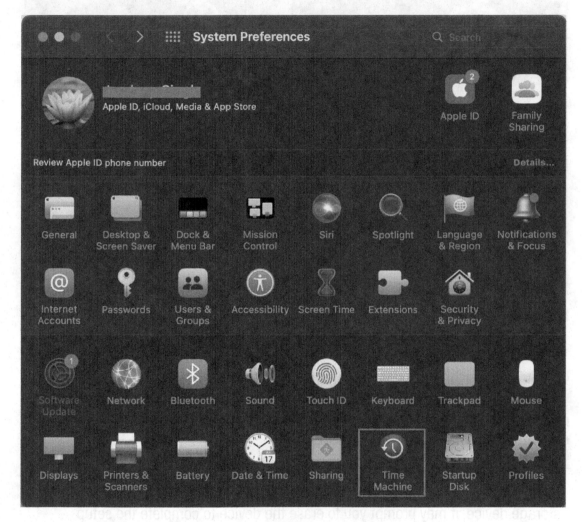

Figure 3-18. *Time Machine access via System Preferences*

Once in Time Machine preferences, click the Select Backup Disk option. This will display a list of available external storage devices. See Figure 3-19.

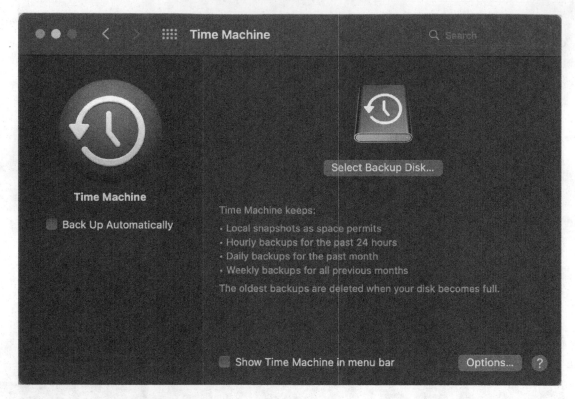

Figure 3-19. *Time Machine configuration*

Choose the name of your external storage device from the list and click the Use Disk button. Time Machine will then prompt you to confirm your selection.

After confirming your selection, Time Machine will immediately begin creating periodic backups of your Mac. These backups will be generated automatically, without requiring any further action on your part.

Note   If you are setting up Time Machine for the first time on the external storage device, it may prompt you to erase the device to complete the setup process. Ensure that you have backed up any important data on the device before proceeding with the erasure.

By following these steps, you can create a Time Machine backup on your Mac, allowing you to protect your important files and easily restore them in the event of data loss or system issues.

If you wish to manually initiate a backup using Time Machine on your Mac, there's a simple process to follow. Start by accessing the Time Machine menu located in the menu bar. From there, select the option called Back Up Now. By choosing this option, you can immediately trigger a backup, without having to wait for the next scheduled backup.

To keep track of the progress of an ongoing backup, you can rely on the Time Machine menu. It will provide you with real-time updates, indicating how much of the backup has been completed. This way, you can have a clear idea of the status and progress of your backup. See Figure 3-20.

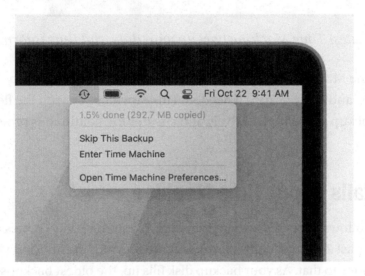

Figure 3-20. *Time Machine backup is underway*

If you find yourself in a situation where you need to skip a backup that is currently in progress, the Time Machine menu offers a convenient option to do so. Simply select Skip This Backup from the menu, and the ongoing backup will be skipped accordingly.

When there is no backup in progress, the Time Machine menu will display the date and time of the most recently completed backup. This serves as a helpful reference point, allowing you to easily determine when your files were last backed up. See Figure 3-21.

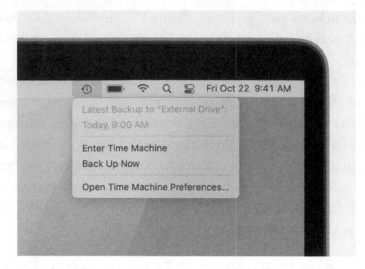

Figure 3-21. *Latest Time Machine backup with date and time information*

With the Time Machine menu, you can manually start a backup, keep track of backup progress, and skip backups if needed. This provides you with the flexibility to manage your backup schedule effectively and ensures the continuous protection of your valuable data.

Useful Details About Time Machine

Time Machine follows a specific backup schedule. It automatically creates hourly backups for the past 24 hours, daily backups for the previous month, and weekly backups for all months prior to that. As your backup disk fills up, the oldest backups are removed to make space for new ones. This ensures that you have a comprehensive backup history while managing storage efficiently.

During the initial backup process, it is normal for it to take a significant amount of time. However, the great thing is that you can continue using your Mac as usual while the backup is in progress. Time Machine only backs up the files that have changed since the last backup, which means that future backups will be faster and more efficient.

If there are specific files or folders that you want to exclude from your backups, you can easily customize this in Time Machine preferences. By clicking the Options button, you can add items to be excluded from the backup. Conversely, if you want to stop excluding an item that was previously excluded, simply select it and click the remove (-) button.

If you have set up multiple backup disks for Time Machine, there is a convenient option to browse through them. By pressing and holding the Option key, you can access the Time Machine menu and choose Browse Other Backup Disks. This allows you to explore and restore files from different backup destinations.

Time Machine provides a reliable and flexible backup solution, ensuring that your important files are protected. By understanding its backup schedule, customization options, and the ability to browse different backup disks, you can effectively manage and utilize Time Machine to safeguard your data.

Restoring Files via Time Machine

Restoring files with Time Machine is a straightforward process that allows you to retrieve specific versions of files or even reinstate your complete system from a previous backup. Here are the steps to restore files using Time Machine.

Make sure that your Time Machine backup disk is properly connected to your computer. To access the Time Machine preferences, click the Apple logo positioned in the top-left corner of your screen and choose System Preferences from the menu options. Look for the Time Machine icon, which resembles a curving arrow surrounding a clock face, and click it to open the Time Machine preferences.

Within the Time Machine preferences, tick the box adjacent to "Show Time Machine in menu bar." By doing so, the Time Machine icon will be added to your menu bar, providing convenient access. See Figure 3-22.

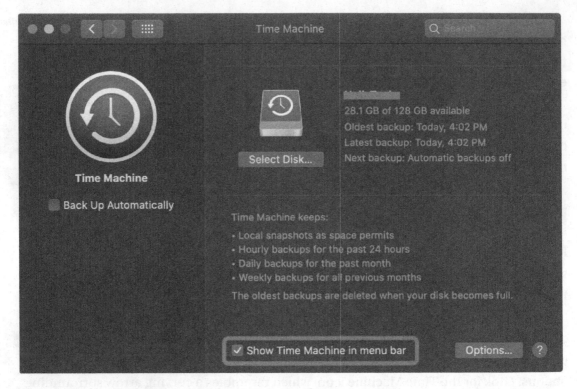

Figure 3-22. *Show Time Machine in menu bar*

To enter the Time Machine interface, simply click the Time Machine icon in the menu bar and choose Enter Time Machine. See Figure 3-23.

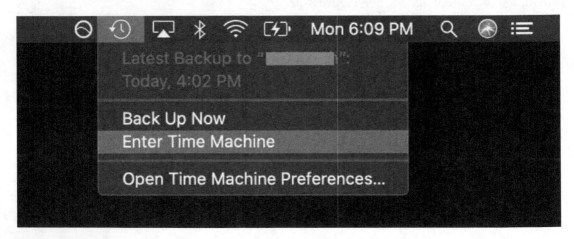

Figure 3-23. *Enter Time Machine via the menu bar*

Once inside Time Machine, you will be presented with a screen displaying all the previous backups in a stacked format. The backups are organized by date, with the most recent ones appearing on top. You can use the timeline located in the bottom-right corner to navigate through the backups and see when they were created. To preview a file, you can press the space bar to ensure it is the correct one you wish to restore.

Locate the file or folder you want to restore and select it. Then, click the Restore button to initiate the restoration process. Time Machine will copy the selected item from the backup and place it back into its original location on your computer. See Figure 3-24.

Figure 3-24. *Time Machine Backup Restore*

It's important to note that Time Machine gives you the ability to restore individual files or folders, allowing you to retrieve specific items you may have accidentally deleted or modified. By accessing previous backups, Time Machine ensures that your important files are recoverable, giving you peace of mind in case of data loss or other unforeseen events.

Restoring a Mac from a Time Machine Backup

If you have a Time Machine backup for your Mac, you can employ the Migration Assistant tool to transfer your personal files, applications, and user account data from the backup to your Macintosh computer.

Migration Assistant is compatible with Time Machine backups and allows for a seamless restoration process, ensuring that all your important files and settings are transferred to your Mac effortlessly.

Prior to initiating the file transfer from your Time Machine backup to your Mac through Migration Assistant, it is important to verify that your Time Machine backup disk is connected and powered on. This ensures that the backup remains accessible throughout the entirety of the transfer process.

Next, open the Migration Assistant application which can be found in the Applications/Utilities folder or by using Spotlight search. See Figure 3-25.

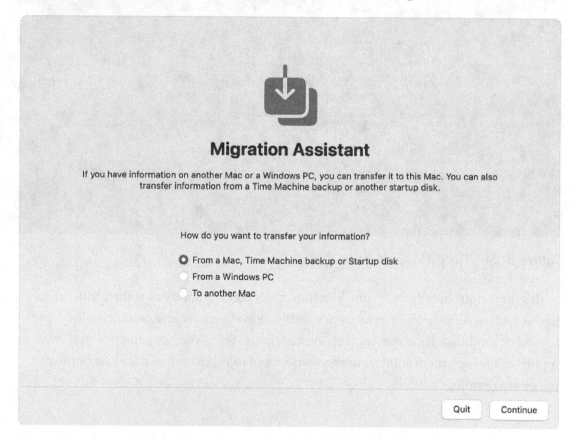

Figure 3-25. *Time Machine backup restore via Migration Assistant*

When prompted to select your preferred method for transferring information, opt for the option that enables you to transfer from a Mac, Time Machine backup, or startup disk. This ensures that Migration Assistant correctly identifies and utilizes your Time Machine backup as the source for the transfer. Click Continue to proceed further. See Figure 3-26.

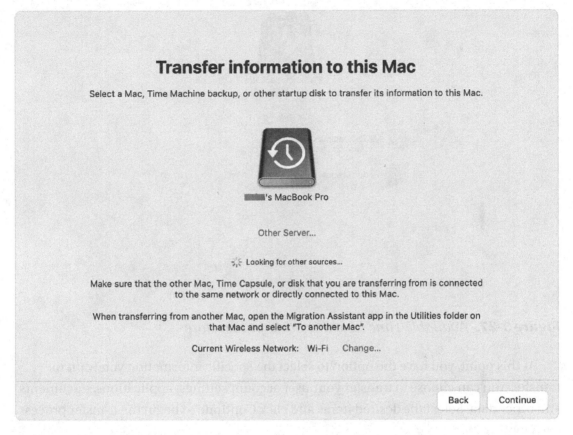

Figure 3-26. *Time Machine backup restore via Migration Assistant*

From the available options, select the Time Machine backup that you wish to restore from. This will display a list of available backups. Choose the specific backup that contains the files and data you want to transfer. Once selected, click Continue to proceed. See Figure 3-27.

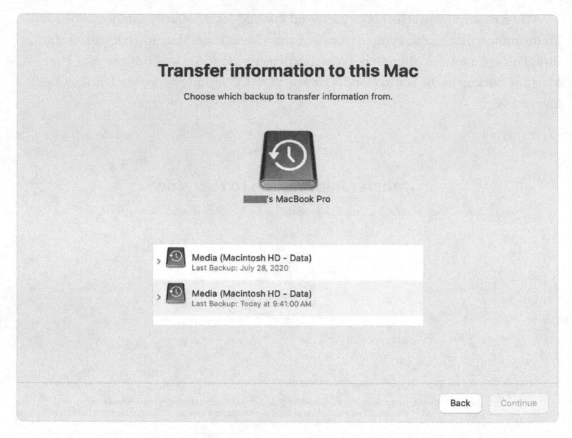

Figure 3-27. *Available Time Machine backups to restore*

At this point, you have the option to select the specific information you want to transfer. You can choose to transfer your user account settings, applications, documents, and other data. Select the desired items and click Continue to begin the transfer process. See Figure 3-28.

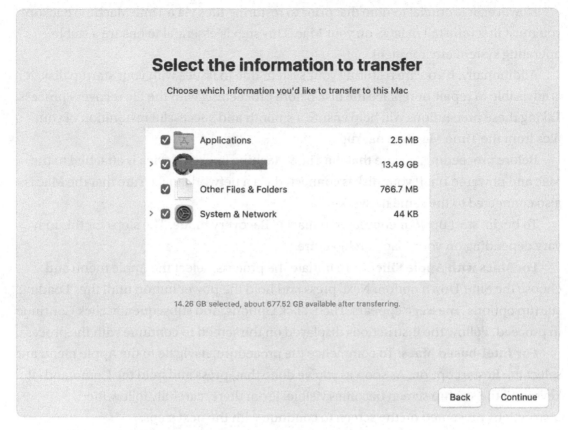

Select the information to transfer

Choose which information you'd like to transfer to this Mac

☑	Applications	2.5 MB
☑		13.49 GB
☑	Other Files & Folders	766.7 MB
☑	System & Network	44 KB

14.26 GB selected, about 677.52 GB available after transferring.

Back   Continue

Figure 3-28. *Selecting specific information to restore*

Please note that larger transfers may take a significant amount of time to complete. Be prepared for the process to potentially take several hours, depending on the size of the backup and the amount of data being transferred.

Once the transfer is complete, you will have successfully transferred files from your Time Machine backup to your Mac using Migration Assistant. Your Mac will now contain your personal files, applications, and other data that were backed up in your Time Machine backup.

Restoring All Files via a Time Machine Backup

If you have been using Time Machine to regularly back up your Mac, you have the option to recover your files in case of damage to your system or startup disk.

However, it is crucial to note that prior to restoring files via a Time Machine backup, you must first reinstall macOS on your Mac. This step is essential to ensure a stable operating system environment.

Additionally, if you are restoring your system due to issues with your startup disk, it is advisable to repair or replace the disk before proceeding with the file recovery process. Taking these precautions will help ensure a smooth and successful restoration of your files from the Time Machine backup.

Before proceeding, ensure that the Time Machine backup device is attached to the Mac and powered on. If your disk is connected via a network, make sure that the Mac is also connected to the same network.

To begin, start up your computer in macOS Recovery mode. The steps for this may vary depending on your Mac's architecture.

For Macs with Apple Silicon: To initiate the process, select the Apple menu and choose the Shut Down option. Next, press and hold the power button until the "Loading startup options" message appears. Then, click Options, and subsequently click Continue to proceed. Follow the instructions displayed on the screen to continue with the process.

For Intel-based Macs: To commence the procedure, navigate to the Apple menu and select the Restart option. As soon as you've done that, press and hold the Command+R keys until the startup screen becomes visible. From there, carefully follow the instructions presented on the screen to continue with the next steps.

In the Recovery window, locate and choose the option Reinstall macOS Monterey to initiate the reinstallation process. This will reinstall the version of macOS stored on your computer's built-in recovery disk, inclusive of any installed updates. Proceed by clicking Continue.

After macOS has completed the installation of the new system files, Migration Assistant will prompt you to transfer information from another Mac or a Time Machine backup. Opt for the choice called "Transfer from a Time Machine Backup" and click Continue.

If necessary, provide the name and password associated with your backup disk connection. Additionally, you may be prompted to enter the password used to encrypt the backup.

Next, select the specific date and time corresponding to the desired backup you wish to restore. Follow the instructions presented on the screen to finalize the restoration process.

Once you have successfully restored your system, it is normal for Time Machine to initiate a full back up during the next scheduled backup time. This full backup is part of the regular process, and once it is completed, Time Machine will resume its incremental backup approach.

Creating a Bootable Installer for a Mac

Creating a bootable installer for macOS may offer several benefits.

Easy installation: A bootable installer allows for a convenient and straightforward installation of macOS on multiple Mac computers. It eliminates the need to download the installation files individually for each device, saving time and effort.

Offline installation: With a bootable installer, you can perform a clean installation of macOS even when you don't have a stable internet connection. This is particularly useful in situations where internet access is limited or unreliable.

System recovery: A bootable installer serves as a valuable tool for system recovery. If your Mac encounters critical issues or fails to start up properly, you can use the bootable installer to troubleshoot and repair the system, reinstall macOS, or restore your data from a backup.

Upgrading multiple devices: If you have multiple Mac computers that need to be upgraded to a newer version of macOS, a bootable installer simplifies the process. You can use the same installer on each device, ensuring consistency and efficiency in the upgrade process.

Customization and troubleshooting: Creating a bootable installer allows for customization options and advanced troubleshooting. You can include additional tools or utilities in the installer, enabling you to diagnose and fix issues, perform disk repairs, or recover data from unbootable systems.

Accessibility and convenience: Having a bootable installer readily available provides peace of mind and ensures that you can quickly respond to any unexpected situations or emergencies that require macOS reinstallation or recovery.

Overall, creating a bootable installer for macOS enhances flexibility, convenience, and reliability when it comes to installing, upgrading, recovering, and maintaining your Mac systems.

However, it is important to note that, in today's time and as per Apple's recommendation, macOS should be reinstalled via the internet recovery method, which confirms the authentic download of the operating system from Apple's server and further install firmware updates as a part of macOS, if any.

Still, an external media can be used inclusive of bootable files to install macOS, as a part of troubleshooting. Jamf and similar Mobile Device Management suites provide the capability to avoid this manual effort and manage the macOS upgrade and update activities efficiently.

Here are the steps to create bootable installer media.

Using an external drive or a secondary volume as a startup disk for installing the macOS provides additional flexibility and convenience, especially for advanced users familiar with the command line.

While a bootable installer is not mandatory for upgrading or reinstalling macOS, it offers notable advantages in scenarios where multiple computers require installation without the need to download the installer repeatedly. This process is particularly beneficial for system administrators and individuals with expertise in command line operations, allowing them to streamline the installation process and efficiently manage macOS installations across multiple devices.

Prerequisites

To create a bootable installer for macOS, you will need a USB flash drive, or another secondary volume formatted as Mac OS Extended with a minimum of 14GB of storage space available.

Additionally, you will require a downloaded installer for the specific version of macOS you intend to create the bootable installer for, such as Monterey, Big Sur, Catalina, or Mojave.

There are certain steps to complete the process.

Step 1: Downloading macOS

Upon successfully downloading the appropriate installer for macOS Monterey, macOS Big Sur, macOS Catalina, macOS Mojave, or any other specific version, you will find it located in your Applications folder. The installer will be listed as an application named Install macOS [version name]. See Figure 3-29.

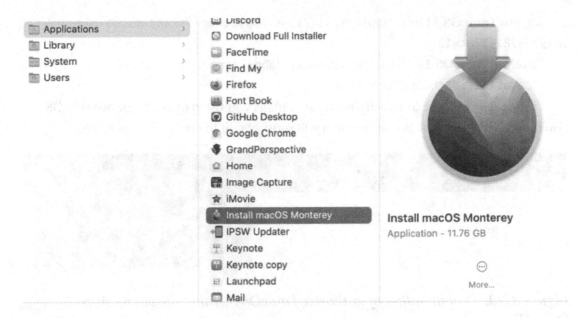

Figure 3-29. *macOS installer file in the Applications folder*

If the installer automatically opens upon completion of the download, make sure to quit the installer without proceeding with the installation process.

Obtaining the Appropriate Installer

Before proceeding, it is essential to confirm that you have obtained the installer on a Mac device that is compatible with the specific version of macOS you need.

Download the installer on a Mac running macOS Sierra 10.12.5 or a more recent version, or on a Mac using OS X El Capitan 10.11.6.

For system admins in an enterprise, it is recommended to download the installer directly from Apple rather than using a locally hosted software-update server. This ensures that you have the most up-to-date and reliable version of the installer.

Recommended and Authentic Download Weblinks from Apple

Monterey (macOS 12): `macappstores://apps.apple.com/us/app/macosmonterey/id1576738294?mt=12`

Big Sur (macOS 11): `macappstores://apps.apple.com/us/app/macos-bigsur/id1526878132?mt=12`

Catalina (macOS 10.15): `macappstores://apps.apple.com/us/app/macoscatalina/id1466841314?mt=12`

The image in Figure 3-30 will display as soon as you try to open the above macOS download URL via a web browser, and it will prompt you to open the App Store.

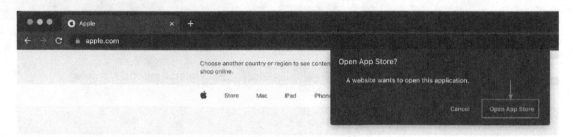

Figure 3-30. *Downloading of authorized macOS installer file via an App Store URL*

When you click Open App Store, it will automagically open the App Store with the requested macOS. Once you click Get, it will initiate the process of downloading macOS in your Mac and placing it in the Applications folder. See Figure 3-31.

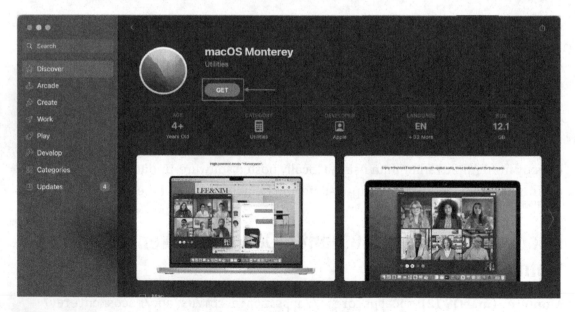

Figure 3-31. *Downloading the authorized macOS installer file via an App Store URL*

However, as mentioned earlier, if the installer automatically opens upon completion of the download, make sure to quit the installer without proceeding with the installation process.

Step 2: Formatting an External Drive (USB Flash Drive/External HDD)

Before proceeding, it is crucial to note that if you are using a flash drive that already contains data, it will be completely erased during this process. Make sure to back up any important files before continuing.

To prepare the flash drive for creating a bootable installer, follow these steps.

First, open Finder on your Mac. From there, navigate to the Applications folder and then proceed to the Utilities folder. Within the Utilities folder, locate and open Disk Utility.

In Disk Utility, you will find the flash drive listed under the External section in the left pane. Select the flash drive by clicking it. Once selected, you will see various options at the top of the Disk Utility window. Look for the Erase button and click it. See Figure 3-32.

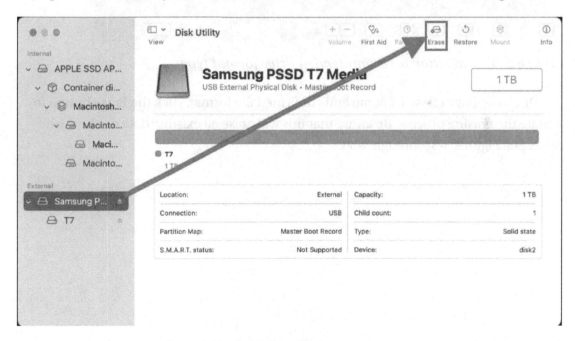

Figure 3-32. *Erasing the external storage device*

A dialog box will appear where you can choose a name for the flash drive. Select a user-friendly name that you can easily identify later. Additionally, ensure that the format is set to Mac OS Extended (Journaled), as this is the recommended format for creating a bootable installer. See Figure 3-33.

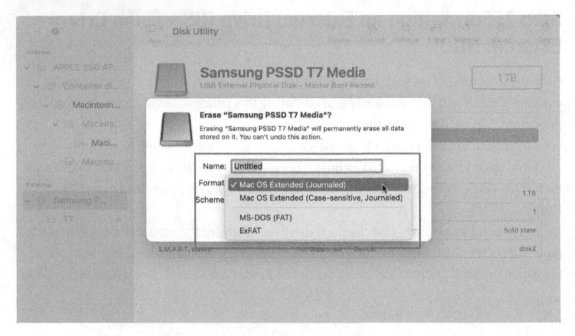

Figure 3-33. *Selection of recommended drive format type*

Once you have chosen a name and confirmed the format, click the Erase button to initiate the erasing process. Be aware that this will erase all existing data on the flash drive. See Figures 3-34 through 3-36.

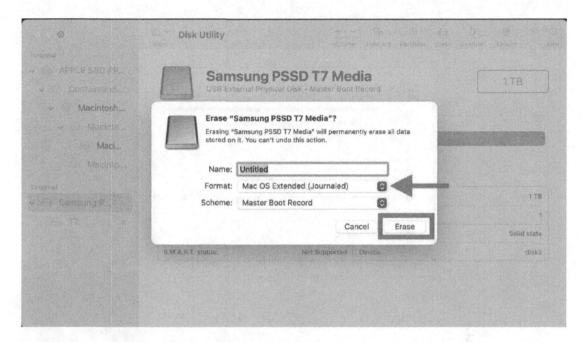

Figure 3-34. *Click the Erase button to proceed*

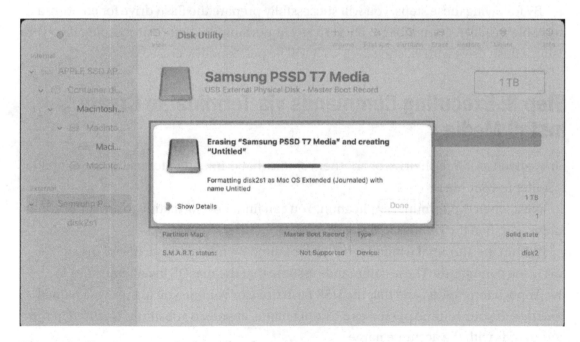

Figure 3-35. *Erasing of selected volume in process*

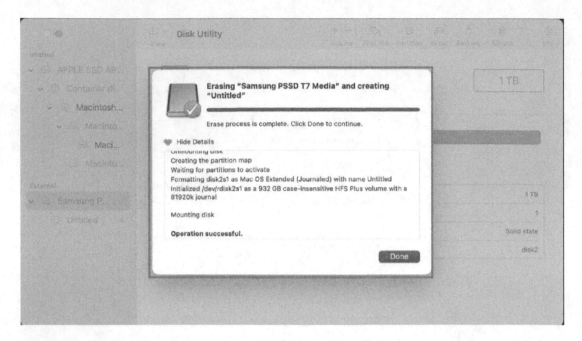

Figure 3-36. *Erasing process successfully completed*

By following these steps, you will successfully prepare the flash drive for creating a bootable installer. Remember to back up any important files before proceeding if you are using a flash drive with existing data, as it will be permanently erased.

Step 3: Executing Commands via Terminal to Create Install Media

First, attach a USB flash drive or another volume that is intended for use as the bootable installer to your Mac.

Next, open the Terminal application. You can find it by navigating to an Applications folder and then the Utilities folder.

Within the Terminal window, you'll be required to input or paste one of the following commands. These commands assume that the macOS installer resides in the Applications folder, and that the USB flash drive or volume you are using is named ***Untitled***. If your volume possesses a distinct name, ensure to substitute ***Untitled*** in the commands with the accurate name.

At this point, you can choose the appropriate command based on the version of macOS you are installing.

For macOS Monterey: `sudo /Applications/Install\ macOS\ Monterey.app/Contents/Resources/createinstallmedia -volume /Volumes/ Untitled`

For macOS Big Sur: `sudo /Applications/Install\ macOS\ Big\ Sur.app/Contents/Resources/createinstallmedia -volume /Volumes/Untitled`

For macOS Catalina: `sudo /Applications/Install\ macOS\ Catalina.app/Contents/Resources/createinstallmedia -volume /Volumes/Untitled`

For macOS Mojave: `sudo /Applications/Install\ macOS\ Mojave.app/Contents/Resources/createinstallmedia -volume /Volumes/Untitled`

After typing the appropriate command in Terminal, press the Return key on your keyboard to execute the command.

You will receive a prompt to enter your administrator password. Type your password and press the Return key. It's important to note that Terminal doesn't display any characters as you type your password.

When asked, type Y to confirm and erase the volume. Press the Return key to proceed. Terminal will provide progress updates as the volume is being erased.

Once the volume has been successfully erased, you may encounter an alert requesting Terminal's access to files on a removable volume. Click OK to authorize the copying process to proceed.

The creation of the bootable installer will take some time to complete. Once it finishes, you will see a message indicating that the process was successful. See Figure 3-37.

```
Last login: Fri Oct 29 22:16:00 on ttys000
                    8 ~ % sudo /Applications/Install\ macOS\ Monterey.app/Contents/Resources/create
installmedia --volume /Volumes/Untitled
Password:
Ready to start.
To continue we need to erase the volume at /Volumes/Untitled.
If you wish to continue type (Y) then press return: Y
Erasing disk: 0%... 10%... 20%... 30%... 100%
Making disk bootable...
Copying to disk: 0%... 10%... 20%... 30%... 40%... 50%... 60%... 70%... 80%... 90%... 100%
Install media now available at "/Volumes/Install macOS Monterey"
                    8 ~ %
```

Figure 3-37. *Execution of a command via Terminal to create bootable installer media*

Upon completion of the process, as indicated by Terminal, you will observe that the volume now bears the identical name as the installer you previously downloaded, such as Install macOS Monterey. At this point, you can exit the Terminal application and volume can be ejected safely.

By following these steps, you can successfully create a bootable installer using Terminal. Remember to enter your administrator password when prompted and confirm any actions necessary to complete the process.

Using a Bootable Installer

Prior to proceeding further, it is crucial to ascertain whether your Mac is equipped with Apple Silicon or Intel architecture. Once you have identified the specific type of Mac you possess, you can proceed with the subsequent steps that are relevant to your system.

Apple Silicon-based Mac

To initiate the installation procedure, verify that you have inserted the bootable installer into a Mac that is both connected to the Internet and compatible with the target macOS version you intend to install. Keep in mind that the macOS version that initially shipped with the Mac determines the earliest version it can support. Although the bootable installer doesn't download macOS directly from the Internet, it does necessitate an Internet connection to obtain firmware and other pertinent information specific to the Mac model.

After successfully connecting the bootable installer and confirming an active internet connection, power on the Mac and persist in holding the power button until the startup options window emerges. Within this window, you will observe the various bootable volumes listed, including the one housing the bootable installer that you previously inserted. Proceed by selecting the volume associated with the bootable installer and click the Continue to proceed.

An installer for macOS will open, presenting you with onscreen instructions to guide you through the installation process. Simply follow these instructions to proceed with the installation of macOS on your Mac.

Intel Processor-Based Mac

To initiate the installation process, insert the bootable installer into a Mac that is connected to the Internet and meets the compatibility requirements for the desired macOS version. It is essential to note that the Mac's compatibility is limited to the earliest macOS version that was originally bundled with it. Although the bootable installer itself does not download macOS from the Internet, it does require an internet connection to access firmware and other critical information specific to the Mac model.

After connecting the bootable installer and confirming the internet connection, power on or restart the Mac, and immediately press and hold the Option (Alt) ⌥ key. Continue holding the Option key until a dark screen emerges, presenting the available bootable volumes for selection.

Once the screen appears, release the Option key, and select the volume that contains the bootable installer. To confirm your selection, click the upward arrow or press the Return key. *Please note that if you encounter any difficulties starting up from the bootable installer, ensure that the Start-up Security Utility is configured to permit booting from external or removable media.*

Upon selecting the appropriate volume, you will be prompted to choose your preferred language. Choose your desired option from the available bootable volumes and proceed by selecting Install macOS (or Install OS X) from the Utilities window. Click Continue and carefully follow the instructions displayed on the screen to proceed with the macOS installation.

Using the Start-up Security Utility

To ensure the secure and reliable startup of your Mac, you can use the Startup Security Utility. This utility enables you to establish your preferred startup disk as the default choice, ensuring that your Mac consistently boots from the designated disk. Additionally, it provides the means to safeguard your system by ensuring that only legitimate and trusted operating systems are used during the startup process. By leveraging the Startup Security Utility, you can enhance the security and integrity of your Mac's startup procedure.

For Mac users who have Apple's T2 Security Chip, the Startup Security Utility presents a range of powerful features designed to enhance the security of their devices and protect against unauthorized access. These features include firmware password protection, which adds an additional layer of security by requiring a password to be entered before accessing certain system settings. Secure Boot ensures that only trusted and verified operating systems are allowed to run on the Mac, guarding against the execution of unauthorized software.

Additionally, users can set specific boot media that are allowed to be used, providing greater control over the startup process, and further fortifying the Mac against potential threats. With the comprehensive functionality provided by the Startup Security Utility, Mac users can enjoy enhanced security measures to safeguard their systems and data.

What If My Mac Doesn't Boot Using a USB Drive?

In certain situations, Intel Macs equipped with a T2 chip, typically those released after 2018, may encounter difficulties when attempting to boot from an external drive containing a macOS installer. This issue arises from a configuration within the Security Start-up Utility that requires adjustment. To address this, follow these steps.

Begin by booting the Mac into macOS Recovery mode. This can be achieved by pressing the combination of Command (⌘) and R keys simultaneously during startup.

A list of user accounts will appear on the screen. Choose and log into the administrator account.

Once the Mac has successfully booted, navigate to the Utilities menu, and select Start-up Security Utility.

If prompted, provide the necessary authentication by entering the macOS password. Select an administrator account and provide its corresponding password.

Upon launching the utility, locate the option labeled "Allow booting from external media" within the External Boot section located at the bottom of the window. See Figure 3-38.

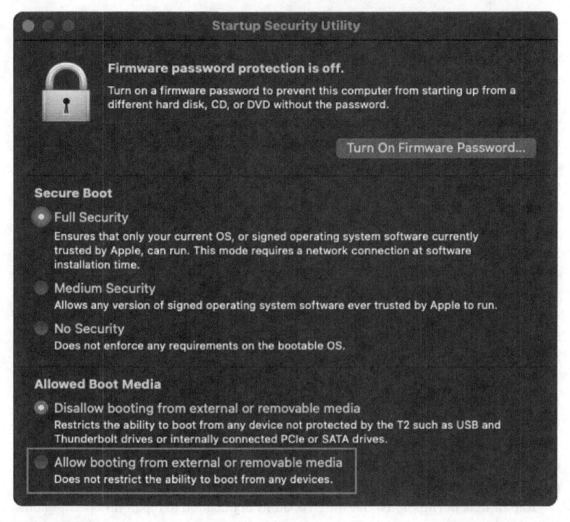

Figure 3-38. *Startup Security Utility options*

After enabling this option, exit the utility and proceed to restart the Mac.

Following these steps should resolve the issue, allowing the Mac to boot successfully from the USB device.

Troubleshooting App Installation

App installation on macOS is typically a hassle-free process that doesn't require much concern. When you do encounter issues with app installation on macOS, there are several troubleshooting steps you can follow to resolve the problem.

Check the system's prerequisites: Confirm that your Mac fulfills the app's specified minimum system requirements. Verify the required macOS version, available disk space, and any other prerequisites.

Internet connection: Ensure that you have a stable internet connection. Some apps may require an internet connection during installation or download additional files.

Restart the Mac: Restarting your Mac can help resolve temporary software glitches that may be interfering with the installation process.

Software updates: Make sure your macOS is up to date. Check for any available software updates by going to the Apple menu ➤ System Preferences ➤ Software Update. Install any pending updates and try installing the app again.

App Store issues: If you're installing the app from the Mac App Store, sign out of your App Store account and then sign back in. Go to the App Store menu ➤ Sign Out. After signing back in, try installing the app again.

Gatekeeper blocking the app: To install a program that macOS Gatekeeper identifies as coming from an unidentified developer, you may need to bypass the security feature. Go to System Preferences ➤ Security and Privacy ➤ General ➤ Click Open to allow the program

Free up disk space: Check if your Mac has sufficient free disk space. Insufficient space can prevent app installations. Delete any unnecessary files or applications to free up space.

Package installer is damaged: You can attempt to resolve the problem by downloading the application installer file once more and initiating the installation process again.

Repair disk permissions: Use the Disk Utility application to repair disk permissions. Open Finder ➤ Applications ➤ Utilities ➤ Disk Utility. Select your startup disk, click the First Aid tab, and choose Repair Disk Permissions.

Clear app cache: If you're experiencing issues with a specific app, try clearing its cache. Open Finder ➤ Go menu ➤ Go to Folder. Enter ~/Library/Caches and locate the folder related to the problematic app. Delete the folder or its contents and then attempt to reinstall the app.

Disable antivirus/firewall: Temporarily disable any antivirus or firewall software on your Mac, as they may interfere with the installation process. After installation, you can reenable them.

Conflicts with other software: You can try installing the application in Safe Mode. Safe Mode allows you to start your Mac with a minimal set of software and disables certain components that may be causing conflicts. By entering Safe Mode, you can determine if the issue is related to software that loads during startup. During Safe Mode, login items, non-system fonts, and system extensions are disabled, and a First Aid check is performed on your startup disk to ensure its integrity. This can help identify and resolve any potential conflicts that may be hindering the application installation process.

Contact the app developer: If none of the above steps resolve the issue, reach out to the app developer's support for further assistance. They may provide specific troubleshooting steps or offer guidance tailored to the app you're trying to install.

By following these troubleshooting steps, you should be able to address common issues with app installation on macOS and successfully install the desired applications on your Mac.

Safe Mode in a Mac

Safe Mode is a troubleshooting mode in macOS that allows you to start your Mac with a minimal set of software and system extensions. It can be helpful when you're experiencing issues such as application crashes, startup problems, or unusual system behavior. In Safe Mode, your Mac performs a series of checks and disables certain components that may be causing conflicts.

Apple Silicon

On Mac computers with Apple Silicon, such as those equipped with M1 and M2 chips, the process to access Safe Mode is slightly different. Follow these steps to enter Safe Mode on an Apple Silicon Mac.

To initiate the process, select the Apple menu and choose the Shut Down option to power off your Mac. Next, press and hold the power button on your Mac until the startup options window appears. Finally, click the Options button to proceed further.

Select your startup disk labeled Macintosh HD or the name of your disk. Click the Continue in Safe Mode option. Enter your administrator password if prompted.

Your Mac will now start up in Safe Mode, indicated by Safe Boot in the upper-right corner of the screen.

In Safe Mode, your Apple Silicon Mac will load only essential system files and software, disabling login items, non-system fonts, and system extensions. This helps isolate and troubleshoot software-related issues.

Intel Processor

On Mac computers with Intel processors, the process to access Safe Mode is different compared to the one for the Apple Silicon chipset.

Commence by shutting down your Mac through the Apple menu and selecting the Shut Down option. Once the shutdown process is complete, press the power button to power on your Mac.

Upon starting up your Mac, promptly press and hold the Shift key. Continue holding the Shift key until you see the Apple logo and a progress bar, and then release the Shift key.

Your Mac will now boot into Safe Mode. You will see Safe Boot in the upper-right corner of the screen.

You can use your Mac in Safe Mode to diagnose and resolve problems, such as app crashes and installation issues, startup issues, or performance problems. Once in Safe Mode, you can perform troubleshooting steps like removing recently installed software, running disk utility for disk repairs, or disabling problematic login items.

To exit Safe Mode, proceed to restart your Mac in the usual manner, without the need to press any keys during the restart process.

Remember, Safe Mode is a valuable tool for troubleshooting software issues on your Mac, allowing you to pinpoint and resolve problems that may be affecting its normal operation.

Viewing System Logs in a Mac

Your Mac keeps various types of reports that can provide valuable insights into system and app issues. These reports are stored as text files on your Mac's storage drive and can be accessed easily for troubleshooting purposes. By examining these reports, you can diagnose and resolve common Mac problems, ensuring optimal performance and stability.

There are several types of reports that your Mac generates.

Crash reports: These reports contain information about app or process crashes. They are saved with a .crash extension.

Spin reports: These reports provide details about app or process issues. They are saved with a .spin extension.

Log reports: These reports contain information about system and app events. They help track the processing of specific apps or the overall system. Log reports have file extensions such as .log, ._log, or .its.

Diagnostic reports: These reports offer insights into hardware resources, system response times, and other diagnostic information. Diagnostic reports have file extensions such as .diag or .dpsub.

Mac analytics data: This refers to the contents of the Message Tracer Store data, which can be found at /var/log/DiagnosticMessages.

system.log: This contains the contents of the legacy system log file located at /private/var/log/system.log.

By examining these reports, you can gather important information about crashes, performance issues, and system events, which can assist in identifying and resolving problems on your Mac. Accessing and analyzing these reports can be valuable in troubleshooting and maintaining the health of your Mac.

Reading Logs in Console

In the Console application, you can access a collection of reports that offer general diagnostic data and detailed information about your computer's operating system and apps. These reports can be accessed conveniently from the sidebar and provide valuable insights for troubleshooting and analysis. See Figure 3-39.

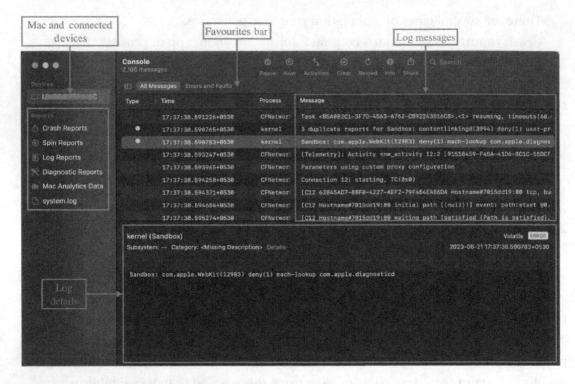

Figure 3-39. *Access reports via Console*

Reading Logs in Folders via Finder

In macOS, apart from Console, you can also access log files stored in specific folders using Finder. By navigating to these log folders, you can read the log files directly in Finder.

~/Library/Logs to access application logs of a Mac user.

~/Library/Logs/DiagnosticReports to access diagnostic reports of a Mac user

/Library/Logs to access application logs of a system

/Library/Logs/DiagnosticReports to access reports of a system

/var/log to access the system log folder

/var/log/system.log to access the system log

/var/log/DiagnosticMessages to access Mac analytics data

Summary

In this chapter, you explored essential network and system tools for macOS, including network configurations, printer and scanner management, macOS libraries, Time Machine backups, creating bootable installers, troubleshooting app installations, and system log analysis.

By gaining knowledge and skills in these areas, you are now equipped to optimize your macOS experience, troubleshoot issues, protect your data, and enhance system performance. Whether it's fine-tuning network settings, efficiently managing printers and scanners, leveraging macOS libraries, safeguarding your files with Time Machine, creating bootable installers, resolving app installation problems, or analyzing system logs, you have the tools and understanding to ensure a smooth and effective operation of your Mac system.

With this comprehensive understanding and skill set, you are well prepared to overcome related challenges and ensure the smooth and optimal operation of your Mac system.

## CHAPTER 4

Troubleshooting in macOS and Ventura OS Overview

In this chapter, we will discuss specific Mac issues and how to troubleshoot those issues. Basically, we will cover startup, network, and printer issues along with detailed troubleshooting steps. We will also discuss macOS Ventura operating system settings in detail along with required screenshots. Additionally, we will cover important features and improvements in Ventura OS.

Recommendations for Resolving Various Mac Issues

In this section, you will explore various Mac issues and how to troubleshoot those issues. It is not possible to include every kind of problem and solution, but all major issues and solutions are covered here.

Your computer can experience issues due to a variety of factors. Troubleshooting is usually a process of experimentation and failure, regardless of what's causing the problem. In some situations, you may need to attempt several different solutions before you find the one that works; in other cases, the issue may be simple to resolve.

We offer the following advice, regardless of the problem you're seeking to address:

- Note the steps you take.

- Make a note of any errors.

- Check cables constantly.

- Computer restart is one of the best solutions to do always.

© Sagar Rastogi and Jasdeep Singh 2023
S. Rastogi and J. Singh, *Exploring macOS*, https://doi.org/10.1007/978-1-4842-9882-4_4

Troubleshooting Specific Mac Issues

Here are the best steps to follow for a Mac startup issue:

- Check the power and connections.

- Check that your Mac is correctly connected to a power source.

- Examine the power cable and adapter for signs of wear and tear.

- Check that the battery on your laptop is fully charged.

- Reset the System Management Controller (SMC). Refer to `https://support.apple.com/en-us/HT201295`,

- Do a NVRAM or PRAM reset. Refer to `https://support.apple.com/en-us/HT204063`,

- Start your Mac in Safe Mode: Refer to `https://support.apple.com/guide/mac-help/start-up-your-mac-in-safe-mode-mh21245/mac#:~:text=1%20Start%20up%20a%20Mac%20with%20Apple%20silicon,in%20Safe%20Mode%2C%20then%20release%20the%20Shift%20key`.

First Aid Using Disk Utility

Here's how to use Disk Utility:

- Restart your Mac and hold down Command (⌘) + R until the Apple logo appears to enter Recovery Mode.

- Select Disk Utility and click Continue in the macOS Utilities window.

- In the left sidebar, select your startup disk and press the First Aid button.

- Allow Disk Utility to check and fix any disc errors.

- Restart your Mac normally if Disk Utility resolves any difficulties.

Problems with Third-Party Hardware or Software

Disconnect all external devices from your Mac (excluding the keyboard and mouse) and check to see whether it boots up properly.

If you have recently installed software or drivers, consider deleting or updating them. Look for expert assistance: After trying the solutions, if your Mac still won't boot, it can be beneficial to call Apple Support or go to an Apple Approved Service Provider for more help.

Reboot Network Devices

To reboot network devices, follow these steps:

- Turn off your router and modem.

- Remove the power supply from both devices.

- Wait approximately 30 to 60 seconds.

- Reconnect the modem's power supply and wait for it to fully boot up.

- After that, reconnect the Wi-Fi router's power supply and give it time to fully boot up. Connecting your Mac to the Wi-Fi network once more might help.

Verify Your Wi-Fi Connection

To verify your Wi-Fi connection, follow these steps:

- Make that your Wi-Fi router is turned on and operating normally.

- Verify that other devices can connect to the same Wi-Fi network.

- To ensure a solid signal, try to get closer to the Wi-Fi router if possible.

Examine Connections to the Printer

Here are the best steps to follow for printer management issues on a Mac:

- Make sure your Mac and the printer are correctly connected.

- Make sure the USB cable is firmly inserted into the printer and the Mac if it is a USB printer.

- Make sure the printer is linked to the same network as your Mac if it is an Ethernet or network-connected printer.

- Ensure that your wireless printer is linked to your Wi-Fi network if it is a wireless printer.

- Examine the printer for any error messages or blinking lights that may point to a connectivity issue.

Check the Compatibility of the Printer

Verify that the printer and the Mac's operating system are compatible. Check whether your printer is Mac compatible by going to the printer manufacturer's website and searching for your printer model. For the version of Mac operating system that your computer uses, get the most recent drivers and software.

Software Update

Updating the applications on your Mac can frequently fix compatibility problems. Select System Preferences (before Ventura) or System Settings (Ventura onwards) from the Apple menu by clicking it in the top left corner of the screen.

Install any macOS updates by selecting Software Update from the menu. This ensures that your Mac has the most recent system updates and printer drivers.

Add a Printer Manually

You can manually add a printer if your Mac does not automatically recognize it. From the Apple menu, open System Preferences/System Settings and choose Printers & Scanners. To add a new printer, click the + button. Your Mac will look through the network for any available printers. Select your printer if it has been recognized and click Add. To finish the installation, heed any further instructions.

Restart the Printer

The printing system can be reset to fix persistent printer problems. In System Preferences/System Settings, select Printers & Scanners. Right-click (or use the Control key) on the printer list on the left and choose the Reset printing system option. If prompted, confirm the action and provide your administrator password.

All printers will be removed from the list as a result, so follow the previous instructions to add them again.

Examine the Print Queue and Start Printing Again

Issues can arise from print tasks getting stuck in the print queue. Select the printer from the list in System Preferences/System Settings by opening Printers & Scanners.

Select the Open Print Queue button. Any failed or pending print jobs can be cancelled in the print queue box by selecting them and using the x key.

To see if the problem has been fixed after clearing the print queue, try printing a test page or a fresh document.

Clearing the print queue and resetting any temporary difficulties can also be accomplished by restarting your Mac.

Add the Printer Again After Removing It

You can try uninstalling the printer and adding it back in again if the previous methods don't fix the issue.

Select the printer from the list in System Preferences/System Settings by opening Printers & Scanners.

To remove the printer, click the - button. If asked, confirm the removal.

After that, add the printer once more by clicking the + button and install it by following the on-screen directions.

Get in Touch with the Printer's Manufacturer

If you've tried all the troubleshooting procedures above and the problem persists, you should contact the printer manufacturer for assistance. Look for support or contact information on the manufacturer's website. Contact customer service for specific troubleshooting methods or more help based on your printer model and Mac configuration.

macOS Ventura Overview

macOS Ventura (macOS 13) is Apple's latest significant update to its operating system for Mac computers. Following macOS Monterey, Ventura was officially announced at the Worldwide Developers Conference (WWDC) on June 6, 2022 and subsequently released on October 24, 2022.

The name "Ventura" is a tribute to Ventura County, and it is the tenth macOS version to adopt a name inspired by the company's home state of California. This release brings forth a range of new features and improvements, enhancing the Mac user experience and productivity.

This macOS version introduces a host of updates, primarily centered around boosting productivity. Among the notable additions are that two apps originally from iOS and iPadOS, Weather and Clock, are now integrated into the macOS ecosystem. Additionally, a feature called Freeform has been introduced through an update across all three operating systems. These enhancements are geared towards providing users with a more seamless and efficient computing experience on Mac devices.

It also brings a set of fresh system features, including Stage Manager, an alternative multitasking interface that complements the existing Mission Control. With Stage Manager, users can enjoy an enhanced way of managing and organizing their tasks, offering a more intuitive and flexible approach to multitasking on Mac devices. This addition aims to optimize productivity and streamline the user experience, allowing for seamless navigation and control over various open windows and applications.

Further, macOS Ventura introduces a collection of exciting new apps that enrich the user experience.

The Weather app offers detailed weather forecasts at your fingertips. By simply clicking the Weather widget, users are sent to this app directly, bypassing external websites like The Weather Channel.

The Clock app is a convenient tool for managing world time, alarms, stopwatches, and timers. A quick click on the Clock widget grants immediate access to this versatile app, eliminating the need to navigate through the Date & Time section of System Preferences.

With version 13.1, macOS Ventura introduces the Freeform app, a dynamic whiteboard tool that supports real-time collaboration. Perfect for brainstorming and sharing ideas, this app empowers users to collaborate seamlessly and enhances productivity in creative endeavors.

With strong new methods to accomplish more, macOS Ventura enhances the tasks you perform frequently on your Mac computer. macOS Ventura provides plenty of new tricks for Apple computer users, from multitasking capabilities and security changes to faster Spotlight searching and iPhone camera sharing. But which features are worthwhile investing your time on, and which ones are just frills? Here are the following features in detail.

System Settings: System Preferences was renamed to System Settings in macOS Ventura, making it closer to iPhone and iPad Settings. The list of settings on the left side has replaced the grid of icons. When you initially open it, a sidebar on the left will display all of the customized options. To access the relevant setting, click any icon. When System Settings is opened, the Appearance setting is already selected. See Figure 4-1.

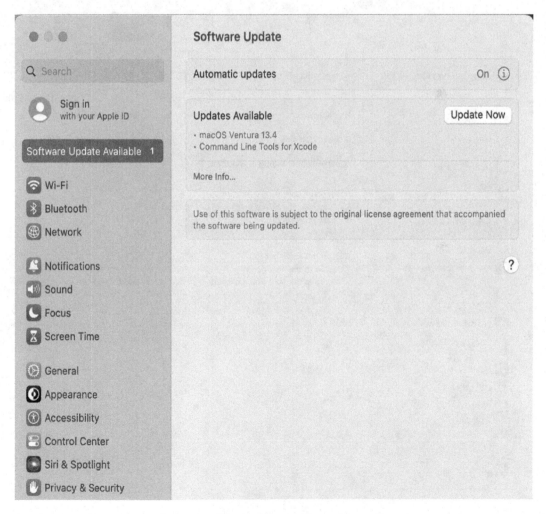

Figure 4-1. *Overview of System Settings*

Look in System Settings: Use the built-in search in the top-left corner if you're unsure of what you're looking for. Type something into the search box by clicking it. The number of topics in the results list will be filtered as you input to match your search phrase and provide possibly related settings that might provide what you need.

You may also access a setting by clicking and holding System Settings in the Dock to open the contextual menu.

Appearance: You can modify how macOS appears by using the appearance options. For highlight selections, you can set a custom color or pick one that has already been created. See Figure 4-2.

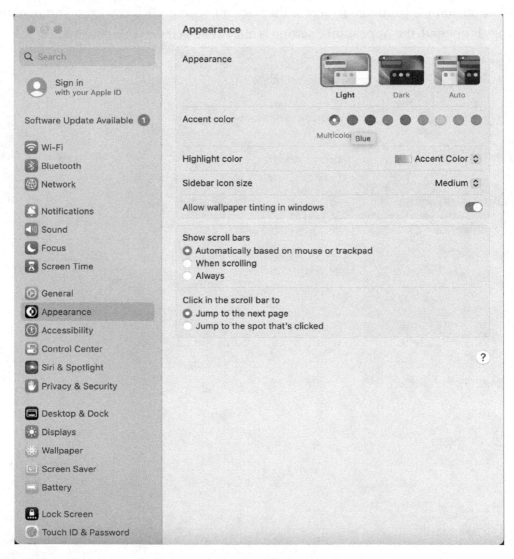

Figure 4-2. *Appearance pane in System Settings*

Accent color: Select the color to be used for controls such as buttons and pop-up menus.

Highlight color: With this, you can modify the color of highlighted text or other content in documents. Apple offers a selection of colors, but by selecting Other and using the built-in macOS color picker, you can set your own colors.

Sidebar icon size: You can now choose the icon size for the Finder's sidebar. Medium is the default, Large is appropriate if you have trouble clicking the icons already there, and Small is the best option if your display is small.

Allow wallpaper tinting in windows: Give some window sections, including toolbars or status bars, a subtle tint using colors from the desktop picture.

Show scroll bars:L In macOS, the scroll bars' behavior can be modified. They are hidden by default but become visible when you move your pointer over them. You can change this so that, regardless of the input device, they only appear while scrolling, or whenever the content is too large for the viewport.

Click in the scroll bar to: By altering this setting, macOS will no longer skip to content when you click inside a scroll bar. When Jump to the Next Page is selected, content advances by screen heights or pages in the direction of your click; when Jump to the Spot is selected, the scroll bar advances to the document's point relative to the spot on the scroll bar that was clicked.

Apple ID: Everything that your Apple ID controls, including your Password & Security settings, Payment Settings, Family Sharing, iCloud, and Devices, is included in this setting. See Figure 4-3.

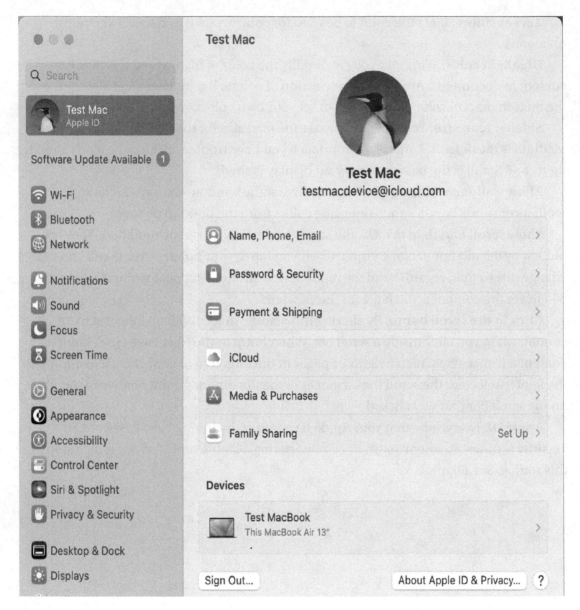

Figure 4-3. *System Settings options*

Apple ID-Family Sharing: You may view the subscriptions and services you're sharing with others if you use Family Sharing, as well as who in your family has the Ask to Apple ID - Family Sharing Buy option turned on. You can share access to great Apple services with up to five other family members thanks to Family Sharing.

Wi-Fi: To control your Wi-Fi connections, use this setting. You can validate your Wi-Fi's name and toggle Wi-Fi on or off. See Figure 4-4.

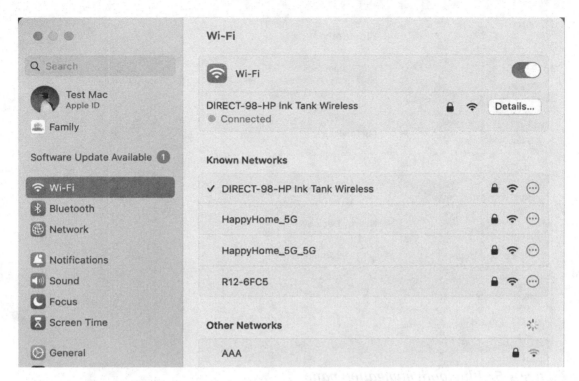

Figure 4-4. *Wi-Fi navigation pane*

Bluetooth: Any Bluetooth devices that your Mac has associated with can be controlled via the Bluetooth option. You can enable or disable Bluetooth with this setting. Services like Airplay, Airdrop, Find My, and Location services will not function if Bluetooth is turned off. The name of the Mac is shown, and it can be found when Bluetooth is enabled. See Figure 4-5.

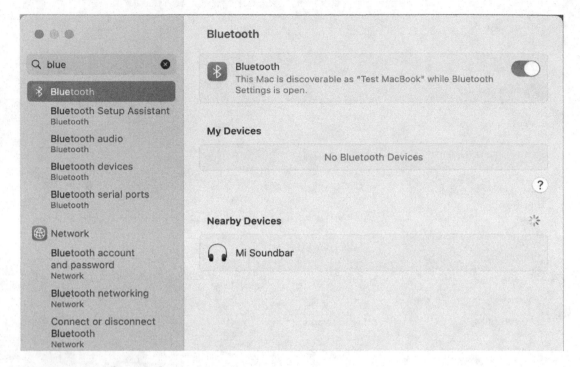

Figure 4-5. *Bluetooth navigation pane*

Network: The Network setting allows you to customize your Ethernet, firewall, and network service management. Although you can also access Wi-Fi and VPN settings from here, System Settings' sidebar makes it simpler to do so. See Figure 4-6.

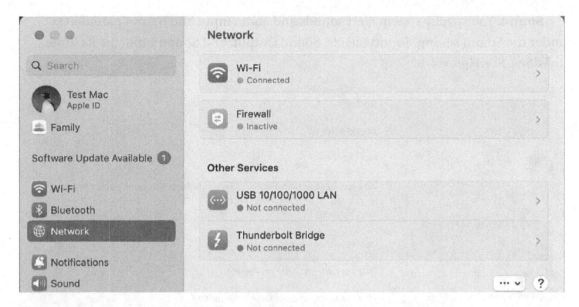

Figure 4-6. *Overview of network settings*

Notifications: In the Notification Center, which is in the upper-right corner of your Mac display, you may set preferences for when you don't want to be bothered by alerts, how apps display notifications, and how notifications are grouped. See Figure 4-7.

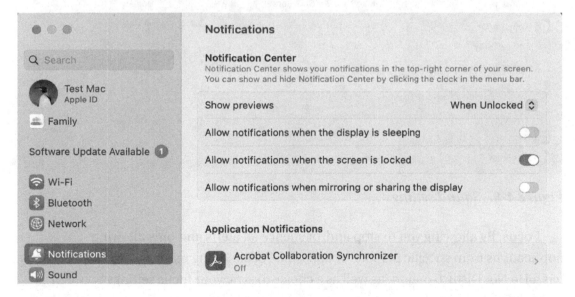

Figure 4-7. *Notifications navigation pane*

Sound: You specify system alert sounds and audio input and output parameters under the Sound setting. Sound Effects, Sound Output, and Sound Input are its three divisions. See Figure 4-8.

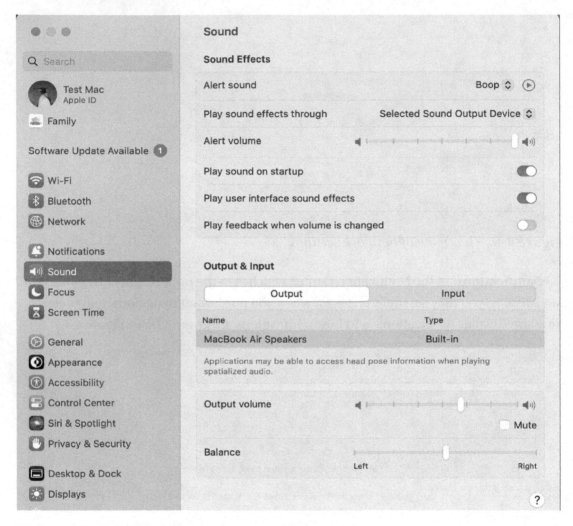

Figure 4-8. *Sound settings*

Focus: By allowing you to stop and/or silence all alerts and only allowing notifications from specific persons or apps, the Focus setting reduces distractions. Focus has a Do Not Disturb option, as well as a choice to sync your focus settings between devices. See Figure 4-9.

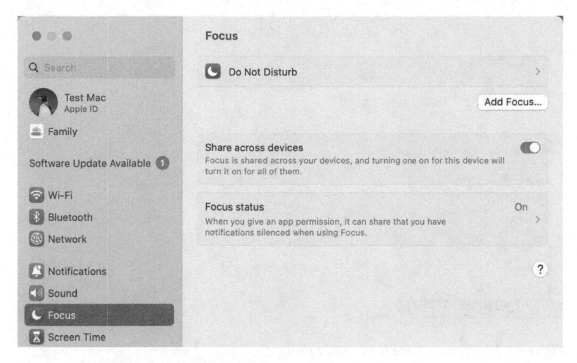

Figure 4-9. *Focus navigation pane*

Screen Time: You can switch Screen Time on or off, view and manage each family member's Screen Time preferences, and establish a Screen Time passcode. Depending on how you signed in with your Apple ID and whether you are the parent or legal guardian of a kid included in a Family Sharing group, different options may be available to you. See Figure 4-10.

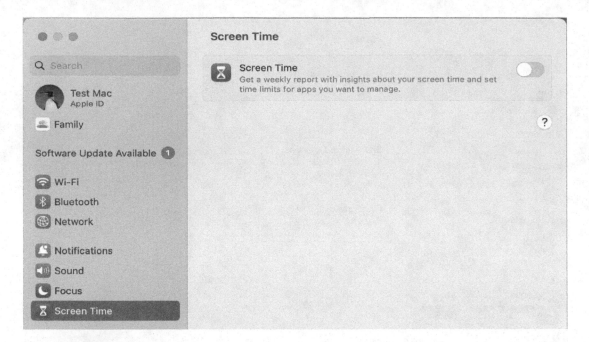

Figure 4-10. *Screen Time navigation pane*

General: You may find information about your Mac in the General setting. It includes information like the serial number, how much storage is being used, or the language that is configured on your Mac. With Time Machine, backups can also be set up. See Figure 4-11.

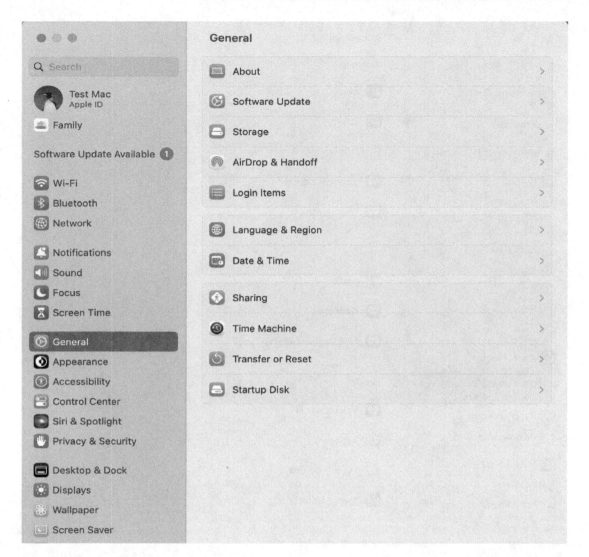

Figure 4-11. *General settings*

Accessibility: A Mac comes with accessibility as standard. Whether you struggle with vision, hearing, or physical mobility, macOS has several tools to support alternative methods of working for you. Press Option+Command+F5 or, if your Mac or Magic Keyboard has Touch ID, press Touch ID three times quickly to enable or disable Accessibility options. See Figure 4-12.

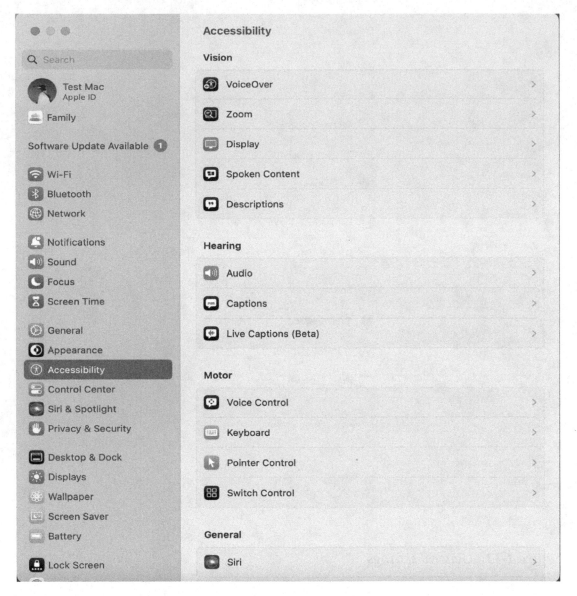

Figure 4-12. *Accessibility navigation pane*

Control Center: The things that you can select to present in Control Center, the Menu Bar, or both are displayed in the Control Center settings. Click an item in the list, such as Wi-Fi or Focus, to see a preview on the right where you can adjust choices. Click the pull-down menu and choose Show in the Menu Bar to display an item in the menu bar. See Figure 4-13.

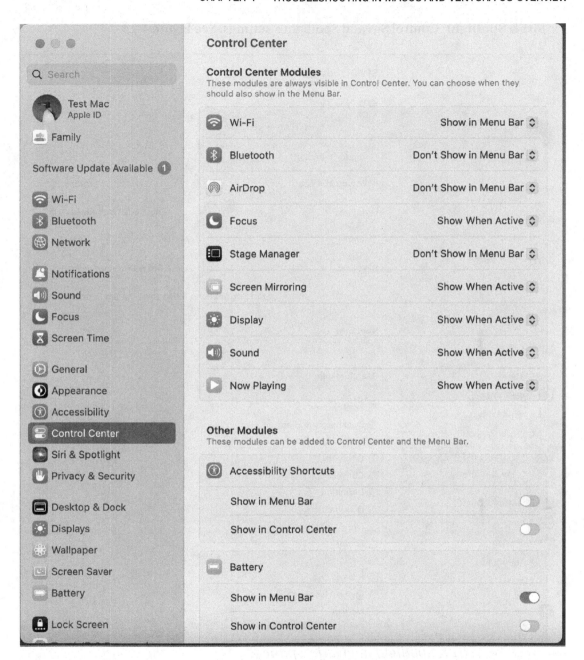

Figure 4-13. *Control Center navigation pane*

Siri & Spotlight: Control Siri and Spotlight's settings. See Figure 4-14.

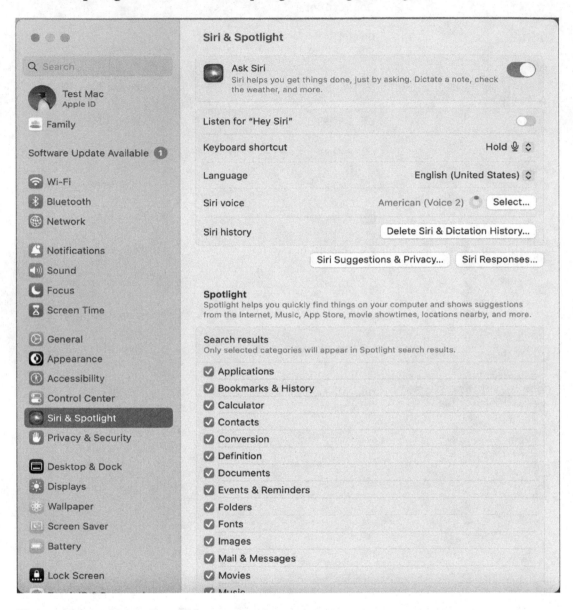

Figure 4-14.   *Siri & Spotlight navigation pane*

Privacy & Security: Your Mac can be protected from malware and tampering by using the Privacy & Security settings to control the information that is made available to others on a network or over the Internet. See Figure 4-15.

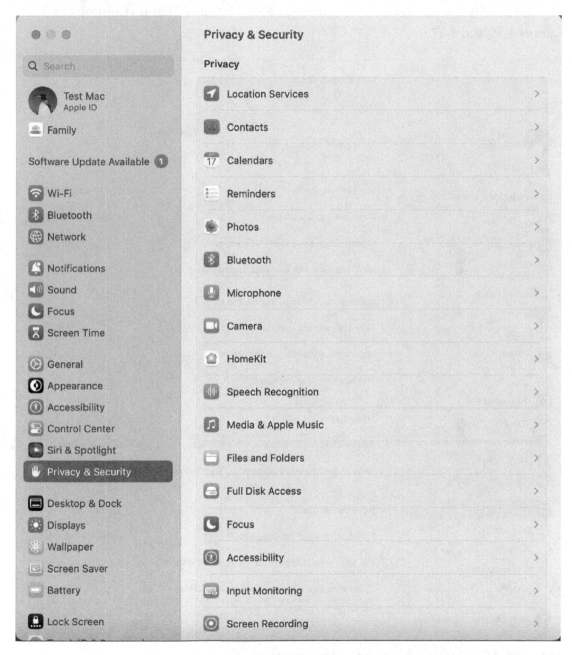

Figure 4-15. *Privacy & Security navigation pane*

Desktop & Dock: By control-clicking the thin line between apps and folders, many of the Dock's settings can be changed. Since it gives you a comprehensive view of all your Dock's settings, the System Settings section for Dock settings is interesting to view. You can modify the settings for Stage Manager, Menu Bar, and Mission Control. See Figures 4-16 and 4-17.

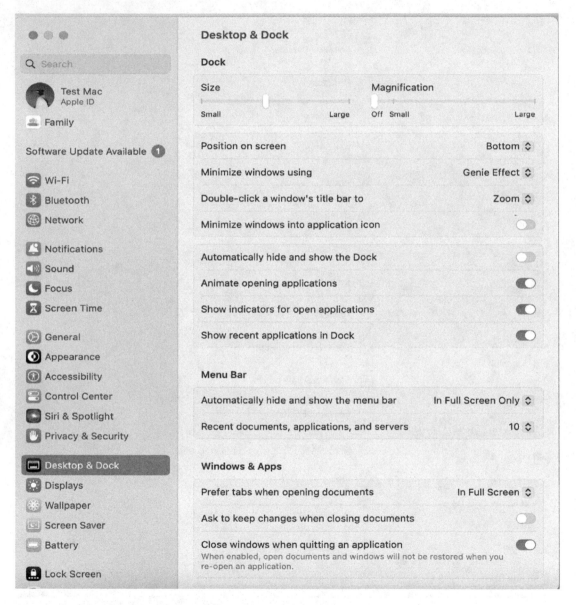

Figure 4-16. *Desktop & Dock navigation pane*

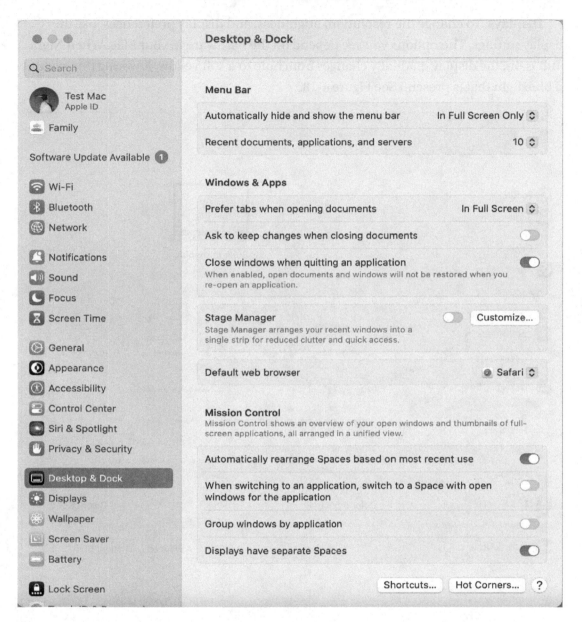

Figure 4-17. *Desktop & Dock settings*

Displays: To change the resolution, brightness, and display preferences, use the display settings. The options you see depend on the hardware in your Mac. When Night Shift is on, the display gradually changes from blue to a soft yellow, lowering the amount of blue light that is present. See Figure 4-18.

Figure 4-18. *Displays navigation pane*

Wallpaper: Change and control the image or color that appears as your desktop's backdrop as shown in Figure 4-19.

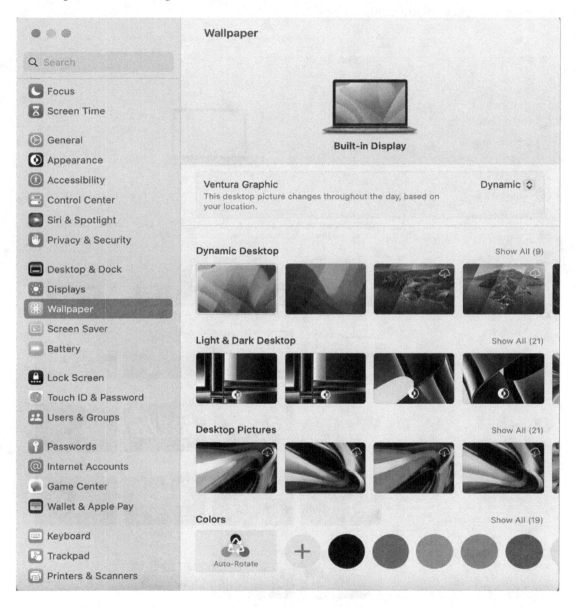

Figure 4-19. *Wallpaper navigation pane*

Screen Saver: Using this, you may configure your screen saver to conceal your desktop while you are away. If you want the screen saver to start right away, you can set up a hot corner. See Figure 4-20.

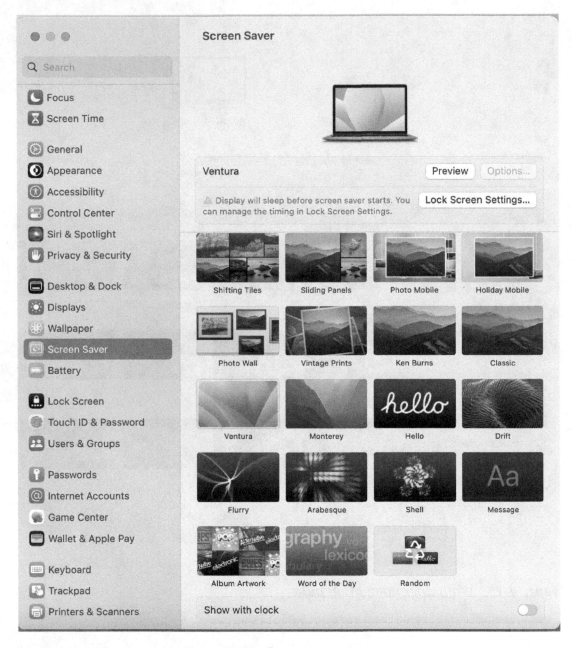

Figure 4-20. *Screen Saver navigation pane*

Battery: This configuration is exclusive to mobile Macs like the MacBook Air or MacBook Pro. To adjust parameters that manage how much energy your computer uses, use the Battery settings. You can extend the life of your battery by using these choices. See Figure 4-21.

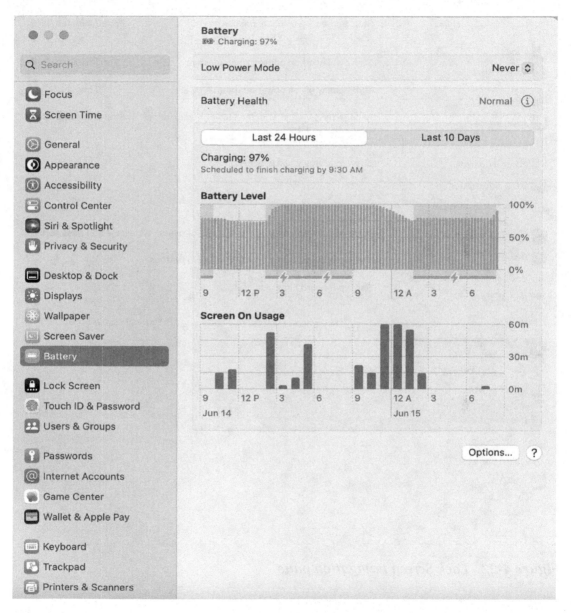

Figure 4-21. *Battery navigation pane*

Lock Screen: Your Mac can be secured with Lock Screen to prevent tampering and unauthorized access. See Figure 4-22.

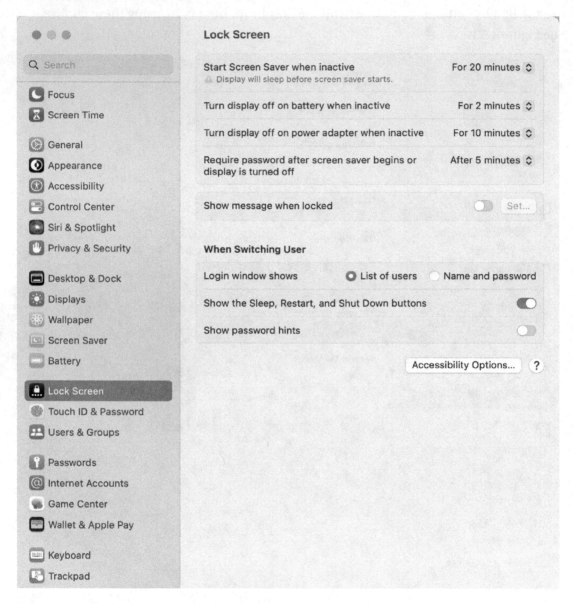

Figure 4-22. *Lock Screen navigation pane*

Touch ID & Password: For Macs with Touch ID, you can set fingerprints to unlock your computer and perform other tasks that need Touch ID and a password for authorization here. You can also simply update your password. See Figure 4-23.

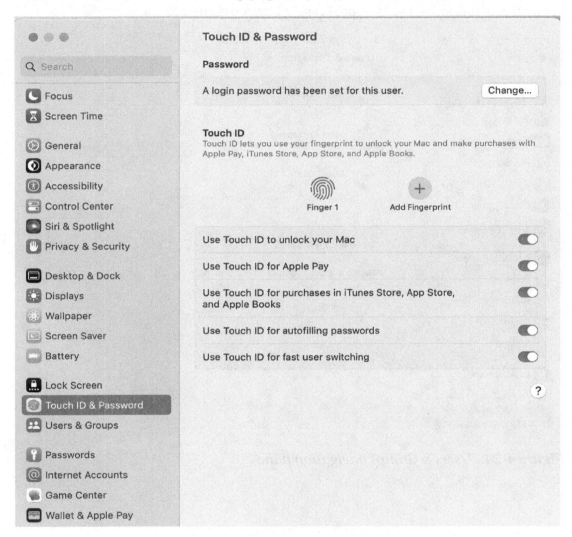

Figure 4-23. *Touch ID & Password navigation pane*

Users & Groups: Create individual accounts for each user who will need access to your Mac so they can customize settings and features without affecting other users. See Figure 4-24.

Source of image: `https://support.apple.com/en-in/HT201548`.

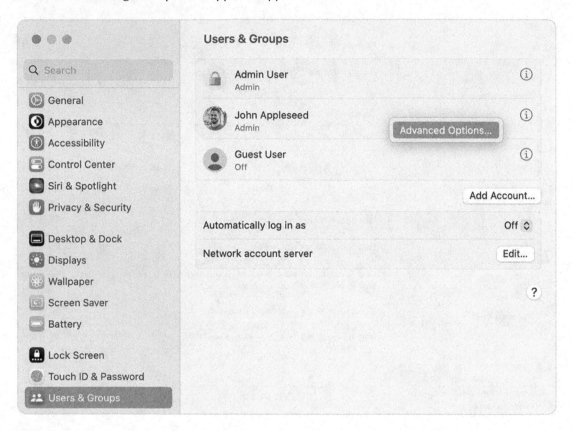

Figure 4-24. *Users & Groups navigation pane*

Passwords: To view, add, or update the usernames, passwords, or passkeys you saved for websites on your Mac, use the Passwords settings. See Figure 4-25.

Source of image: `https://support.apple.com/en-ca/HT211145`.

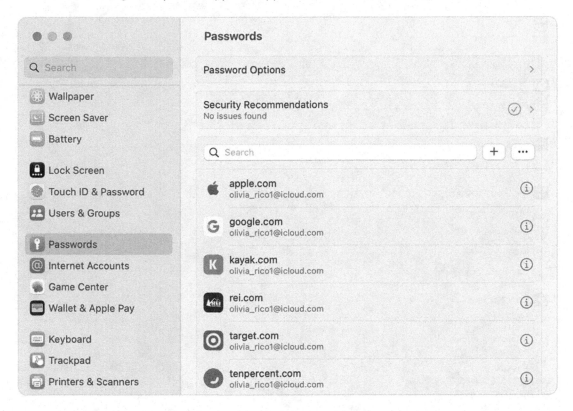

Figure 4-25. *Passwords navigation pane*

Internet Accounts: To rapidly set up your Internet accounts from Google, LinkedIn, Yahoo!, and other providers for several Mac apps, including Mail, Contacts, Calendar, Notes, Reminders, and Messages, use the Internet Accounts settings. See Figure 4-26.

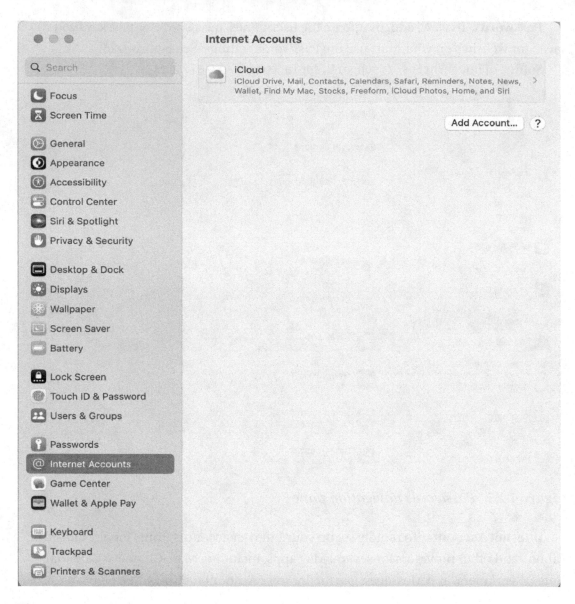

Figure 4-26. *Internet Accounts navigation pane*

Game Center: On your Mac, you can play single-player or multiplayer games. You are given a Game Center account when you log in using your Apple ID. Additionally, if you want to download and play a variety of ground-breaking games on all your supported devices, you can subscribe to Apple Arcade. See Figure 4-27.

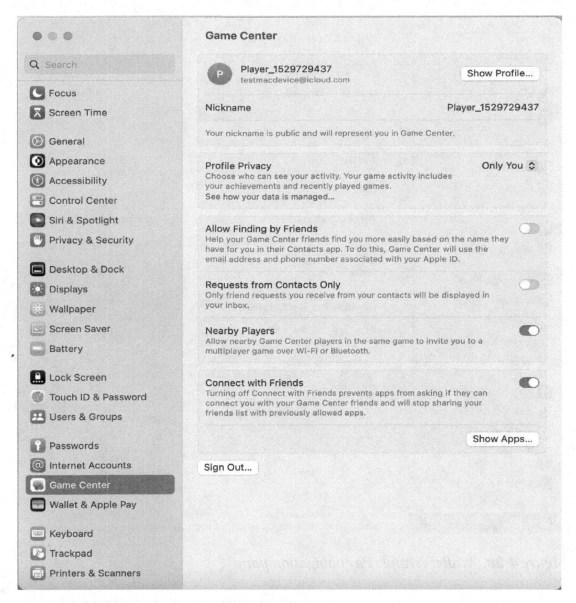

Figure 4-27. *Game Center navigation pane*

Wallet & Apple Pay: Use the Wallet & Apple Pay settings on your Mac or Magic Keyboard if it has Touch ID to add your credit cards, debit cards, prepaid cards, store cards, and Apple Card so you may use them to make purchases on websites that accept Apple Pay. See Figure 4-28.

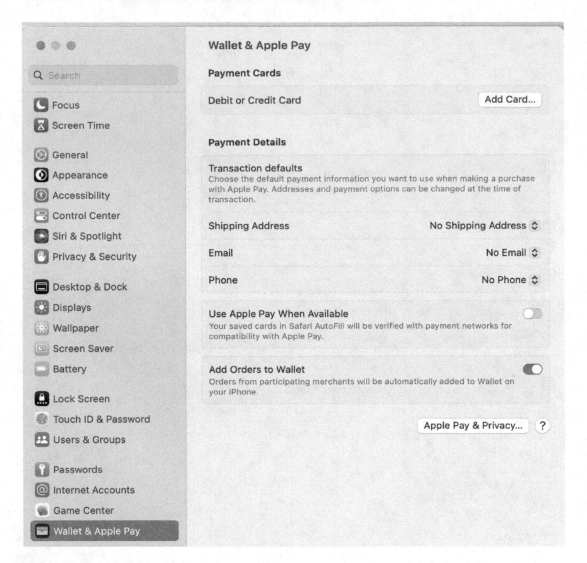

Figure 4-28. *Wallet & Apple Pay navigation pane*

Keyboard: The keyboard setting allows you to manage dictation and keyboard input. Keyboard function keys, keyboard backlighting, and keyboard shortcuts can all be customized. The settings on your Mac can be changed if it has a Touch Bar. See Figure 4-29.

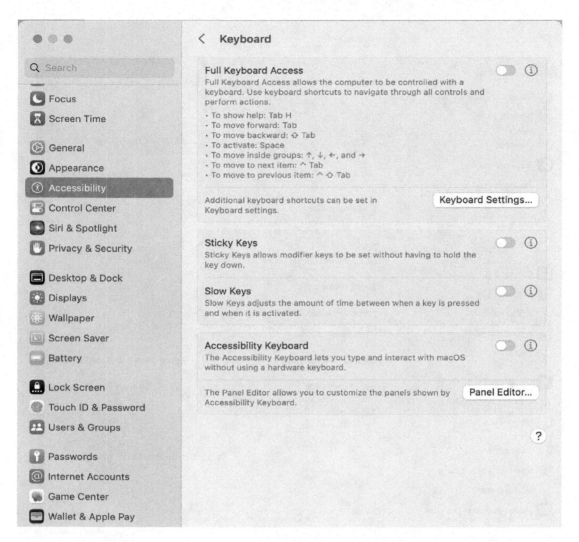

Figure 4-29. *Keyboard settings*

Trackpad: You can configure functionality for the built-in trackpad on your laptop or for a Magic Trackpad that is Bluetooth-connected to a desktop computer using the Trackpad Settings. Three tabs are available under the Trackpad Setting: More Gestures, Scroll & Zoom, and Point & Click. See Figure 4-30.

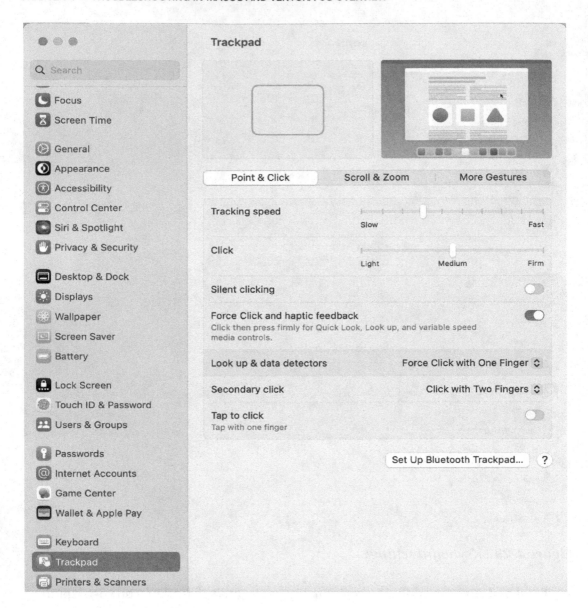

Figure 4-30. *Trackpad settings*

Printers & Scanners: You can control your printers, scanners, and fax machines by using the Printers & Scanners settings. See Figure 4-31.

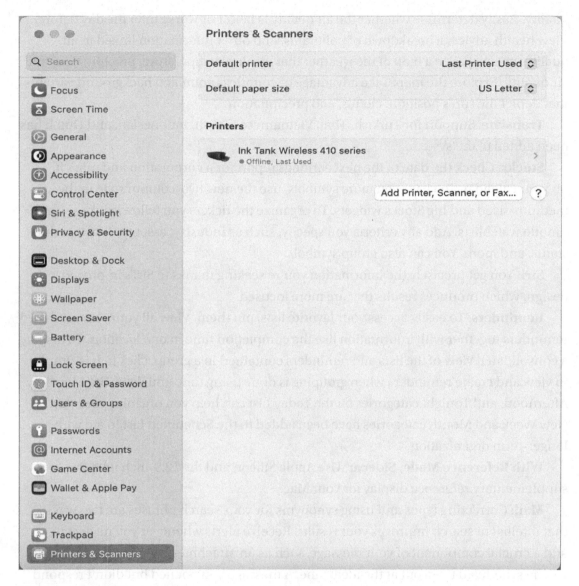

Figure 4-31. *Printers & Scanners navigation pane*

Important Features and Improvements

Let's discuss some of the important features and improvements in macOS Ventura.

Weather: The Weather app is now available for Mac, with a design that is designed for a larger display. It has interactive forecast modules, immersive animations, and extensive maps. Use a color-coded scale to track the level and classification of the air quality. Easily determine whether the air quality is better or worse than the day before. View health advice, a breakdown of pollutants, and other information linked to air quality on a map. See a map of the weather that displays temperature, precipitation, and air quality. Explore the map. Take advantage of countless animated background variants that depict the sun's position, clouds, and precipitation.

Translate: Support for Turkish, Thai, Vietnamese, Polish, Indonesian, and Dutch has been added to the system.

Stocks: Check the date of the next earnings report for a corporation and mark it on your calendar. To view even more symbols, use the new two-column style in the medium-sized and big Stocks widgets. To organize the tickers you follow, make several unique watchlists. Add any criteria you specify, such as industry, asset type, ownership status, and more. You can also group symbols.

Siri: You get precisely the information you're seeking thanks to Siri's improved design, which produces results that are more focused.

Reminders: To easily access your favorite lists, pin them. View all your accomplished reminders together with information like the completion time in one location. To display a consolidated view of the lists and reminders contained in a group, click it. It is simpler to view and create reminders when grouping is done using time and date. The Morning, Afternoon, and Tonight categories on the Today List can help you organize your day. New Week and Month categories have been added to the Scheduled List to aid with longer-term organization.

With Reference Mode, Sidecar: Use Apple Silicon and the 12.9-inch iPad Pro as a supplementary reference display for your Mac.

Mail: Correcting typos and using synonyms for your search phrases are two ways that intelligent search improves your results. Receive alerts whenever you neglect to add a crucial component of your message, such as an attachment or a recipient. Emails can be scheduled to go out at the ideal time. A message you opened but didn't respond to should never be forgotten. Determine a reminder date and time for when messages should reappear in your inbox.

Spotlight: To see files in Quick Look on a result, press the Space bar. This combines all the data you're looking for into a single, rich result. It's contactable for businesses, sports, movies, TV shows, actors, musicians, and contacts. You can use Spotlight to look for photographs of people, animals, buildings, and more online. Spotlight can help you act rapidly. Set a countdown, activate a Focus, use Shazam to identify a song, use any shortcut, and more. In order to enable searching by places, sceneries, or even objects in the photographs, like text, a puppy, or a car, Spotlight uses information from images in Photos, Messages, Notes, and Finder. See Figure 4-32.

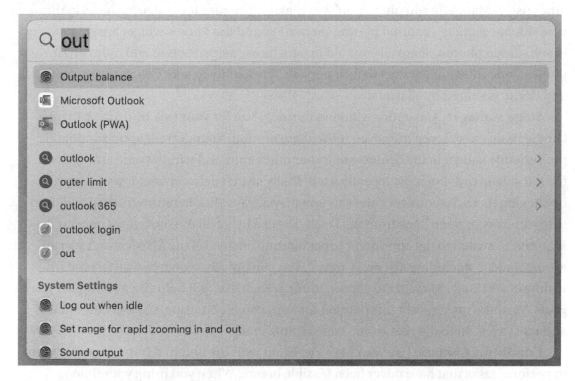

Figure 4-32. *Usage of Spotlight*

Safari: A group of tabs can be shared with friends. Everyone can add their own tabs, and as you collaborate, the Tab Group will automatically update to reflect your changes. Pin tabs to each group to personalize your Tab Groups. In macOS, add support for opt-in notifications from Safari sites. Check out the list of accessible extensions from your other devices in Safari's options. An extension that has been installed will sync so that you only need to turn it on once. The Safari web page translation now includes support for Arabic, Korean, Turkish, Thai, Vietnamese, Polish, Indonesian, and Dutch. Your Wi-Fi passwords can be found and managed in Network Preferences. Passwords can be referred to, shared, or deleted.

Passkeys: Passkeys are a quicker and safer sign-in alternative to passwords. You don't need to be concerned that website leaks could compromise your accounts because nothing confidential is saved on a web server. Passkeys can hardly ever be phished because they never leave your device and are unique to the website you made them for.

Passkeys are synced between all your Apple devices using iCloud Keychain and are end-to-end encrypted.

iCloud Shared Photo Library: iCloud photo libraries can be shared with up to five other users. Manually add photographs or make use of the clever sharing ideas in the new sidebar section. Featured photos, memories, and the Photos widget are great places to see shared photos. Share all your old images or use setup tools to add only certain photos depending on the start date or persons. The ability to add, edit, favorite, caption, and delete is shared by all users.

Stage Manager: Make your windows the ideal size for your task by resizing them. On the main canvas, you may even move them around. Your current app's window is prominently shown in the center, while your other apps and windows are arranged on the left side in order of most recently used. Easily switch between windows and apps by clicking them. To construct app sets you may always click to return to, drag and drop side windows or open apps from the Dock. To get a list of all the open apps on your Mac and to switch to the app you're concentrating on, use all the Mac features you are accustomed to, including Mission Control. You can quickly switch between standard windows and Stage Manager to choose the approach that will help you accomplish your goals. View the most recent information for apps you aren't using, such as new emails and messages, off to the side so you can stay informed.

Continuity Camera: Use your Mac's webcam with the potent iPhone camera system to perform tasks that have never been feasible before. When you bring your iPhone close to your Mac, your Mac will immediately switch to using the iPhone as a camera input. It works both wired and wirelessly. Any Mac may now use portrait mode thanks to Continuity Camera. In portrait mode, the background is blurred to keep the attention on you. You won't need to clutter your workstation with external illumination since a beautiful video effect skillfully darkens the background and illuminates your face. For complex lighting circumstances, such as scenarios in front of a window that are backlit, Studio Light is fantastic. Desk View on the iPhone lets you use the ultra-wide camera to show what's on your desk during a video chat. Without complicated setup, it allows you to simultaneously share your workstation and your face in a manner like an overhead camera.

Alongside an addition of new features and applications, in macOS Ventura, certain features have been removed to streamline the user experience.

The Preview app no longer supports PostScript (.ps) and Encapsulated PostScript (.eps) files. However, users can still print these files by accessing the Printer Queue from System Settings and dragging the file into the queue window.

Network Utility is no longer available as a standalone app.

The Network Locations feature has been removed from the graphical user interface. However, users can still access it via the command line.

Additionally, help files related to dial-up modems have been removed from the operating system.

These changes aim to simplify the macOS interface and enhance overall performance, while some functionalities are still accessible through alternative methods.

Summary

You now have better understanding of how to approach unique issues on a Mac. You can now troubleshoot different issues on a Mac. You also have fair understanding about macOS Ventura System Settings along with the important features and improvements.

In the next chapter, you will explore Apple Enterprise Management and a scalable and leading Enterprise Mobility Management solution which is oriented only to Apple devices, called Jamf to manage macOS, iOS and other Apple Family.

## CHAPTER 5

Introduction to Jamf and Apple Enterprise Management

This chapter will discuss about Apple Enterprise Management and why we need it. Additionally, you will find out why Jamf is one of the leading and scalable Apple Enterprise Management products along with its product portfolio, licensing, architecture, and other important components. Jamf Pro is used to manage macOS, iOS, and Apple TV devices. However, since our focus is on macOS devices, we will only touch on a few concepts of mobile devices wherever required. To understand more about Apple Enterprise Management and Jamf, let's focus on the following topics:

- Apple Enterprise Management

- Overview of Jamf and its capabilities

- Jamf Pro benefits

- Data gathering by Jamf Pro

- Jamf product portfolio with its features

- Enterprise and Education License pricing

- Overview of Jamf Cloud and on-premises

- Architectural diagram of Jamf Cloud and on-premises

- Jamf Cloud benefits and features

- Computer enrollment methods offered by Jamf Pro

- Jamf Pro's important components

© Sagar Rastogi and Jasdeep Singh 2023
S. Rastogi and J. Singh, *Exploring macOS*, https://doi.org/10.1007/978-1-4842-9882-4_5

- Security compliance and its frameworks

- Jamf Integration and Jamf Marketplace

- Overview of Jamf Pro Dashboard

- Useful resource URLs

Apple Enterprise Management

Before we discuss Apple Enterprise Management, let's understand why we need Apple Enterprise Management. Essentially MDM (Mobile Device Management) is not sufficient for enterprises to augment the Apple Leads, just the supervision of Apple Fleet devices doesn't help in the safeguarding of devices' data and user confidentiality. In order to access materials on devices, security should be in place plus automation of recurring tasks on devices and app management customization. Apple Enterprise Management can be reffered as a scalable and programmed solution, which is aimed to design explicitly for Apple devices. It is one of the finest techniques to achieve, associate, and safeguard the Apple ecosystem.

Basically, AEM is required to bring the finest capability to Apple devices. With the increasing demand of Apple Fleet in organizations, AEM fills the need of the hour. There are few AEM solutions like Jamf, Microsoft Intune, Kandji, Addigy, VMWare Workspace One and more. We decided to discuss Jamf in this chapter for the following reasons:

- It's the leading and scalable AEM solution in the market.

- It provides security, device protection, user confidentiality, app management customization and deployment.

- It comes with one of the best end user experience plus an excellent service by the Jamf Support team.

- Jamf offers integration with a wide range of third-party tools.

Overview of Jamf and Its Capabilities

Jamf Pro is a complete management solution for Apple devices like Macs, iPhones, iPads, and Apple TV. It makes life easier for IT teams because they can deliver the best services in less time and this is only possible with a programmed management solution and authoritative customization opportunities. Additionally, it ensures that users have an access to the best of capability which Apple has to offer via Jamf Enterprise Management Solution. JAMF provides the following capabilities:

- Zero-touch deployment

- On-demand collections of resources

- Access based on identity

- Device administration

- Inventory control

- Management of apps

- Threat reduction and averting damage

- Management of security and complete visibility

What Advantages Does Jamf Pro Offer to Its Customers?

Your computer's security will be managed by IT professionals, so you don't have to worry about that part. Additionally, endpoint protection, OS updates, application updates, and all compliance benchmarks are current without your intervention.

Using the Self Service part, you may choose when and where to install a specific application as per your need. Deployment and upgrade processes operate in the background, so it will not impact your productivity. Most device and app issues can be fixed by going into Self Service just with one click and without IT assistance.

Data Gathering by Jamf Pro

Jamf Pro has been adapted to only gather the information needed for asset tracking. Additionally, it supports Apple devices with hardware requirements, installed apps, available services, software updates, and usage of disk space. No personal information like, text messages, contacts, and browser history, is captured.

Product Portfolio and Features Offered by Jamf

It doesn't matter how many Apple devices you want to manage. Jamf provides a management solution designed for your needs, regardless of whether your company is a large organization, small business, or educational institution.

The Jamf product portfolio is split into three major categories.

Jamf Pro: The Enterprise Mobility Management (EMM) product provides unified endpoint management for Apple devices to IT experts and users.

Jamf Now: It's the simplest method for your organization to execute small business MDM activities on Apple devices, which helps to grow your business.

Jamf School: It is an MDM system designed specifically for education. Via its easy web-based interface, deploying, inventorying, and securing Macs, iPads, iPhones, and Apple TVs has never been easier. It allows you to easily administer Apple devices that focus on kids. You can integrate Apple devices into your learning syllabus along with interactive ways for learning for students and teachers.

Jamf Pro comes with the following features:

Deployment: It offers a fully personalized onboarding experience for your customers. Set up the ideal Mac, iPad, iPhone, or Apple TV, and have them all deployed in accordance with your preferred workflow.

Device administration: It is used to configure your Apple devices to operate exactly as required, for which you can use configuration profiles, policies, and scripts. It uses a unique Smart Groups technique, which is an effective way to extract real-time warnings and actions from inventory data, along with the automation of management.

App administration: By acquiring and installing apps in mass, you can streamline app management. It's simple to assign apps to users or devices using Jamf Pro's integration with Apple Business Manager and Apple School Manager. Deploy apps created in-house, from the App Store, the Business-to-Business App Store, or both. App licenses can be reclaimed to use them if required.

Inventory: User, hardware, software, and security device data can all be collected automatically. Software versions and warranty expirations are tracked by dynamic Smart Groups.

Self Service: This provides a single location for your users to access reliable apps and corporate resources and even short cuts for fixing issues like password resets, device slowness, and more. The ideal option to give end users more control while reducing the need for IT help is Jamf Self Service, a completely customized, on-demand app store that you manage.

Security: Use inbuilt security capabilities to secure Apple devices. Manage device settings and configurations, block harmful applications, and fix all your Apple devices without requiring any user contact. Jamf Pro with Jamf Protect is a Mac-specific endpoint protection solution.

Jamf Now comes with the following features:

Self-Service: The on-demand Mac App Catalogue offers third-party and Mac App Store apps that have been endorsed by organizations.

Prevention of malware: Use a "check box and deploy" procedure to prevent unwanted software, malware, and other dangers from executing on the Mac devices.

Device inventory: Monitor device settings with up-to-date information and status updates.

Distribution of apps: Distribute apps that are either free or were acquired through volume purchasing.

Single app mode: To concentrate the device for a particular use, limit your supervised iOS or iPadOS device to a single app.

Password sync: Enforce password policies from identity providers (IDP) like Microsoft Azure AD and Okta, and keep Mac passwords up to date using cloud credentials.

Custom apps and profiles: Jamf Now gives you even more versatility by allowing you to deploy custom applications and profiles.

Automatic configuration: Enroll devices automatically to avoid time-consuming manual setups and configure Wi-Fi and business email accounts.

Device security: If a device is misplaced or stolen, it can be remotely locked or wiped clean.

OS updates: Manage OS updates in order to keep the device compliant.

Jamf School comes with the following features:

Insights dashboard: You can observe managed apps, users, and devices. You can quickly and easily check the status of devices and isolate problems that need remediation.

Classroom administration: Drag and drop the necessary apps and material, and then set limits, make managing classes simple. It allows teachers to request apps, which are then distributed with IT administrators.

Incident management: Keep track of whether and when devices have been damaged or other potential issues using the incident system.

Locations: Easily handle many locations or schools. Manage each place, its devices, users, and groups independently with location support, pushing down profiles, apps, and more from a single location.

Management of student, teacher, and parent apps: Jamf School enables rapid, simple control and management of Apple devices. With Jamf Student, students set up their own device and maintain focus. With Jamf Teacher, teachers create lesson plans and interact with students. With Jamf Parent, parents assist in ensuring that homework sessions are focused and free of interruptions.

Endpoint security for Apple devices: The following are the ways to secure Apple devices:

Jamf Protect: Jamf Protect is an endpoint security solution designed to detect threats, fight against Mac and mobile attacks, and provide clear visibility on device compliance.

Jamf Connect: Jamf Connect allows users to access their Mac and applications with a single identity, eliminating the need for numerous accounts or a bind to Active Directory. It also improves the user experience during setup and day-to-day logins by supporting cloud identity providers (ID) such as Okta, Microsoft Azure Active Directory, Google Cloud, and Apple's enrollment customization tool.

Jamf Safe Internet: It protects student and organization devices from malware and phishing attacks by using content filtering and network security. Integrating Jamf Safe Internet with Jamf School allows you to automate the provision of Jamf Safe Internet services to preconfigured Jamf School devices or device groups.

Jamf Protect comes with the following features:

Endpoint protection: Jamf Protect detects and protects Mac and mobile devices comprehensively to keep endpoints secure, identify dangerous applications, and automatically quarantine malware.

Compliance and transparency: Jamf Protect assists organizations in maintaining compliance across all devices. You can customize benchmark reporting, collect comprehensive telemetry data, and perform audits against industry leaders like the Center for Internet Security (CIS).

High-quality endpoint telemetry: Jamf connects with SIEM (Security Incident and Event Management) and SOAR (Security Orchestration, Automation, and Reaction) systems to send Apple-best insights that boost capabilities for investigation and reaction.

Threat reduction and removal: Jamf Protect leverages the machine learning engine of Jamf to block risks to people and devices such rogue URLs, cutting-edge phishing scams, and crypto jacking. To guard against unintentionally initiating risk on the part of the user, it automatically disables harmful web content.

User experience: Security technologies must do more than just stop threats; they must also have a low user effect. Jamf Protect protects the Apple user experience by utilizing minimal system resources. It runs without the use of a kernel extension and provides same-day support for Apple releases.

Jamf Connect comes with the following features:

Account setup and verification: With a single set of cloud identification credentials, you can create secure accounts that get users up and running right away. With the enhanced security of multi-factor authentication, users may safely access devices and resources from anywhere.

Logical split tunnelling: This enables non-business applications to route directly to the Internet while ensuring secure business connections. As a result, network infrastructure is optimized, and end user privacy is protected.

Efficient and quick connectivity: Users can access business apps without affecting battery life. Jamf runs in the background without affecting the user experience.

Policies for risk-aware access: Improve security by blocking unauthorized access from users and devices.

Model of identity-centric security: Only authorized users are permitted to connect. They benefit from policy enforcement that is uniform across data centers, clouds, and SaaS apps. SSO (single sign-on) eradicates the need for certificate management.

Jamf Safe Internet comes with the following features:

Jamf School has been merged to improve education: A brand-new console with procedures tailored exclusively for school users has been developed from the ground up with seamless Jamf School integration to enable deployment and ongoing syncing from the platform you're accustomed to. It's straightforward and intuitive. Jamf Pro and Jamf Safe Internet are already integrated by default.

Simple reporting: Security experts recognize that threat management does not end with defensive tooling; you must also report on and comprehend the implications of your efforts.

Activate YouTube Restricted Mode: Use YouTube's Restricted Mode features to block links to mature content in comments, embedded videos, and search results.

Make Google Safe Search mandatory: For a secure learning environment, Jamf Safe Internet enforces Google's Safe Search to help suppress explicit content from Google search results.

Searchable database for content: It's a comprehensive content filtering system coupled with MDM for easy, effective user and student safety. Jamf Safe Internet is made to assist schools in guarding against harmful internet content and enforcing acceptable-use guidelines without compromising the learning environment that Apple devices offer. Administrators can establish and alter the content filter results to meet their school's needs using Jamf Safe Internet's lightweight, effective domain name system (DNS) technology without violating anyone's privacy.

License Pricing for Enterprise and Education

To know more about Jamf License Pricing for Enterprise and Education, please refer www.jamf.com/pricing/.

Overview of Jamf Cloud and Jamf On-Premises

Every organization's definition of success is different, so it's a good idea to periodically review how well your tools are serving your business as it develops and changes. Even if you've been happy with Jamf Pro on-premises up to this point, your organization may have more success hosting Jamf Pro in Jamf Cloud depending on scalability, business goals, and long-term planning. Let's talk about which one is more suited as per your requirements.

Availability: A quick, agile response is better suited to the cloud, and Jamf Cloud provides high availability by design. Every instance of the production infrastructure of Jamf has N+1 configuration parallel redundancy. This is a precaution to maintain continuous access to all infrastructure. When comparing on-premises hosting to Jamf Cloud, you should consider the cloud's many data centers and parallel architecture for these layers: firewalls, load balancers, DNS servers, Apache servers, application servers, database servers (MySQL), caching servers, storage servers (i.e., distribution points and backup server infrastructure), content delivery networks, network and data transfers, and Infrastructure as Code, rather than physical gear or setup tools. This provides significantly greater flexibility.

Backup and restore: It offers a data retention period of 30 days, separation of responsibilities automated backups before any modifications, like upgrades, and an infrastructure reserve.

Facilities: It consists of choosing a location, datacenters, physical security, media eradication, capacity estimating, and provisioning of instances.

Service and support: Jamf comes with excellent customer satisfaction while supporting customers. Jamf Cloud users statistically refer more peers to Jamf than the already strong on-premises referral rate. Because of the global coverage and rapid feedback loops between Jamf engineers, the global teams can work across time zones and between Jamf teams to ensure that the customer receives faster troubleshooting.

The global cloud operations team is available around the clock: The team is available in Minneapolis (MN), Eau Claire (WI), Amsterdam (The Netherlands), Katowice (Poland), and Sydney (Australia).

If you self-host with the same provider, enterprise support costs at least $15,000 per month: It comes with these benefits: immediate access to a senior cloud engineer around the clock, a specialized Solutions Architect, a Technical Account Manager, and account management staff dedicated to the billion-dollar portfolio (only Vista companies).

Jamf Account regional teams: You are represented by a global account team at Jamf. To make sure your needs are being met, they communicate with Jamf Cloud developers directly. Jamf Account regional teams are located in Minneapolis (MN), Eau Claire (WI), Austin (TX), Cupertino (CA), New York (NY), Amsterdam (The Netherlands), Katowice (Poland), Sydney (Australia), Emmen (The Netherlands), Causeway Bay (Hong Kong), London (United Kingdom), Munich (Germany), Stockholm (Sweden), and Tokyo (Japan).

Platform: The software versions that Jamf Pro supports are decided by direct collaboration between Jamf Cloud and the software engineering teams. This includes the technologies that Jamf Pro currently supports, such as cloud-optimized settings for Jamf Cloud. Beyond the usual fundamental prerequisites like Java, MySQL, and Tomcat, this goes farther. It includes promoting and standardizing technologies like Amazon Linux, Amazon Aurora, elastic load balancers, and application load balancers. Because of this close association, Jamf Cloud clients' Jamf Pro setups are optimized for both the platform and the configuration level. Jamf Cloud adoption promotes best practices within an organization. Jamf Pro is becoming increasingly connected with the marketplace. Partners are developing for Jamf Cloud workloads, and they anticipate that Jamf Cloud integrations will be easier to analyze and deploy. Customers who self-host on Amazon Web Services can use of some of Jamf Cloud's advantages.

Compliance: When hosting Jamf Pro for customers, they hold to high standards. This includes a method to maintain the environment, the third parties Jamf pays to audit operations, and the assurance of the security of customer Jamf Pro instances. Self-hosting Jamf Pro and achieving the same degree of compliance would be a significant and costly task.

Security: Jamf's primary responsibility is information security, and the company has vast experience in this field. Jamf can alleviate the customer workload by ensuring that the environments have controls in place for areas as of vulnerability administration, event security management, monitoring of security configuration, reviewing and auditing of security, identity and access management, incident management for security, security evaluation, and patch management.

Alerting and monitoring: Customers are contractually guaranteed 99.9% system availability under the Jamf Hosting Terms and Conditions. If Jamf ever fails to uphold this guarantee, it will offer credits in accordance with the conditions of that agreement. Every year, Jamf invests hundreds of thousands of dollars in monitoring to make sure it is giving its clients the best service possible. The following areas are covered by this: monitoring of application performance, server monitoring, service monitoring, end-user monitoring, tools for incident communication, logging for businesses, and custom monitoring.

Architecture of Jamf Cloud and Jamf On-Premises

Figures 5-1 through 5-3 are architecture diagrams. The source of images can be found in https://docs.jamf.com/technical-papers/jamf-pro/integrating-ad-cs/10.40.0/ Overview_ADCS.html.

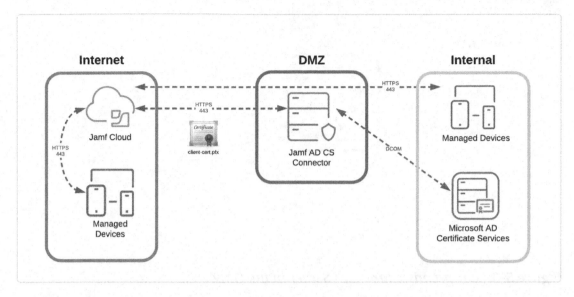

Figure 5-1. *Jamf Cloud with Jamf AD CS Connector in the DMZ*

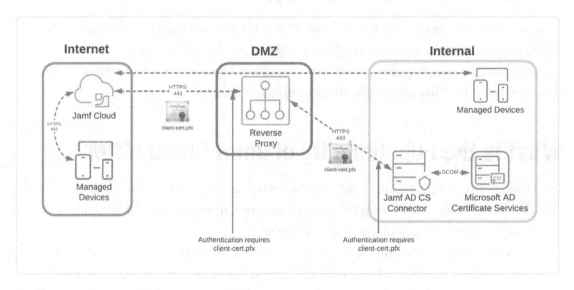

Figure 5-2. *Jamf Cloud with a DMZ Reverse Proxy Layer*

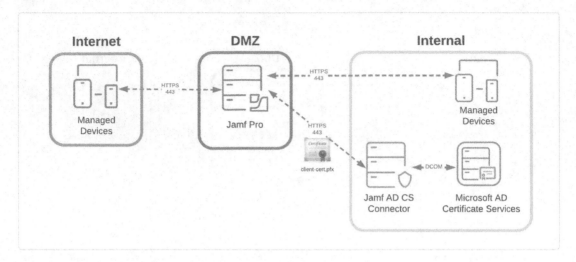

Figure 5-3. *On-premises Jamf Pro Server in the DMZ*

Benefits of Using Jamf Cloud

Here are the benefits of using Jamf Cloud: 99.9% uptime, 365 days a year with multi-tiered backup. Your business software stays up to date, minimizing the time needed for software updates. You also get identity provider integration (SSO using SAML 2.0), lowering infrastructure and application administration and support.

What is the Functionality of Jamf Cloud MDM?

Jamf Cloud, which operates on a subscription basis, includes a built-in cloud distribution solution for global package distribution and ensures 99.9% server availability. Here are some of the functionalities.

Data security: Jamf servers receive an automated upgrade with each release, and their data centers are situated in the United States, Germany, the United Kingdom, Australia, and Japan. If disaster recovery is required, automated daily backups are saved for 30 days.

Visibility: A Jamf status dashboard monitors cloud services and provides industry-standard security measures for hosting services.

Jamf collaborates effectively with others: The majority of enterprise authentication and identity services are fully integrated with Jamf Cloud. Additionally, Jamf Cloud offers expert migration assistance.

Computer Enrollment Methods by Jamf Pro

The process of enrolling Mac computers into Jamf Pro is called enrollment. Computer inventory data is sent to Jamf Pro when the computers are enrolled. Enrolling computers enables Jamf Pro to manage them. This enables you to execute inventory, remote management, and configuration operations on the PCs. When you enroll computers, you can provide a local administrator account called the "management account" that will be used to manage them. The management account can be used to accomplish the following computer tasks: screen sharing; using a Jamf policy to activate File Vault (when a secure token is enabled on the management account); using a policy to add or remove users from File Vault (when a secure token is enabled on the administration account); use a policy to generate a personal recovery key (when a secure token is enabled on the management account); and using a policy to perform authenticated restarts (when a secure token is enabled on the administration account).

There are two forms of computer enrollment, each with its own set of methods for enrolling a computer in that type.

Automated Device Enrollment (ADE) method: Organizations can configure and manage devices via automated device enrollment (often referred to as zero-touch deployment) as soon as the devices are taken out of the box. These devices now fall under supervision, and it is possible to set the MDM profile so that it cannot be removed by the user. Devices owned by the company are intended for Automated Device Enrollment.

Pre-stage registration is the only way to enroll devices with Automated Device registration and Jamf Pro. To cut down on the time and effort required to enroll computers with Jamf Pro, you can utilize a pre-stage enrollment to customize the computer enrollment process, distribute configuration profiles and packages during enrolment, and store setup settings. Computers running macOS 10.10 or later can also be handled automatically via a pre-stage enrollment. User-initiated enrollment for macOS must be enabled in Jamf Pro before using a pre-stage enrolment. Using this technique, you can become a User Approved MDM. Please take note that this method of enrollment needs an **Apple School Manager or Apple Business Manager** account.

Apple Business Manager: With Apple Business Manager, you can deploy Mac, iPad, iPhone, and Apple TV devices automatically to users, complete with settings, security controls, apps, and books. Automated Device Enrollment, formerly known as Apple Device Enrollment Program (Apple DEP), and Volume Purchasing, formerly known as Apple Volume Purchase Program (Apple VPP), are combined into one powerful service. Jamf Pro and Jamf now completely integrate with Apple Business Manager and offer same-day support for new features, allowing you to take advantage of device enrollment, security, volume purchasing, and roles.

Apple School Manager: Jamf Pro and Jamf School both interface with Apple School Manager to help schools automate and streamline device deployments. This integration significantly improves education workflows by providing IT with a single point of contact for all deployment and ongoing management requirements. This improves Apple deployment and continuing administration operations for you like creating the ideal learning environment for kids and teachers to thrive in with Apple School Manager, volume purchasing, managed Apple IDs, device setup, shared iPads, classroom management, and Student Information System (SIS) Integration.

The Device Enrollment method for computers: Device Enrollment enables organizations to manually enroll devices and regulate various elements of device use, including the option to wipe the device. When a user deletes an MDM profile, all settings and apps managed by the MDM solution are also deleted. There are several methods you can use to enroll computers with Device Enrollment and Jamf Pro which are user-initiated enrollment for computers, making use of a Recon Quick Add package, using the Recon Network Scanner to enroll multiple computers, remotely enrolling a computer with Recon, and running Recon locally to enroll a computer. However, the following is the recommended one: the **User-Initiated Enrollment** settings allow you to personalize the enrollment process for users down to the messaging that appears at each stage. By logging onto a web-based enrollment portal and following the onscreen instructions, users can enroll their own machines. Depending on the macOS version of the computer, customers are prompted to download either an MDM profile or a Quick Add package during registration. One approach for obtaining a User Approved MDM status is using the MDM profile mechanism.

Important Components of Jamf Pro

Jamf Policies: You can remotely automate routine administration tasks on managed computers using policies. You may distribute software, run scripts, and manage accounts using a policy. When you develop a policy, you describe the actions you want to automate, the frequency at which they should be performed (execution frequency), the occasion at which they should be carried out (trigger), and the users and computers for which they should be applied (scope). Users can access policies in Self Service and run them on their computers as necessary.

Frequency of policy execution: It consists of once per computer, once per user per computer, once per user, once every day, once every week, once every month, and ongoing.

Policy triggers: It consists of startup, login, logout, network state change, enrollment complete, recurring check-in, and custom. Computer Configuration Profiles are XML files called configuration profiles (.mobileconfig) and they offer a simple way to specify settings and limitations for users, computers, and devices.

Payload options for profile configurations: Payload variables can be used to add attribute values from Jamf Pro to configuration profile settings. As a result, you may produce payloads that include details on each device and user to whom you are disseminating the profile. When establishing a configuration profile in Jamf Pro, enter the $VARIABLE into any text field to use a payload variable. The value of the appropriate attribute in Jamf Pro is substituted for the $VARIABLE during profile installation.

Self Service: Self Service from Jamf offers a well-managed app catalogue, a potent tool for controlling and securing external applications. Additionally, it is a means to provide employees the authority and tools they require to be productive immediately. Self Service is an excellent tool for reducing end user wait times and for freeing up IT staff members from installing apps so they can work on other projects.

macOS application packaging: A self-contained collection of files known as a package can be distributed to distant computers. To create packages of software, applications, preference files, or documents, use Composer or a third-party packaging tool. To manage the packages you want to distribute to the computers in your environment, you can utilize Jamf Pro and Jamf Admin. Adding a package to your distribution point and Jamf Pro as well as modifying the package's settings are all part of managing packages. You can use a policy in Jamf Pro to distribute a package to computers after it has been added to the distribution point and Jamf Pro.

Security Compliance and its Frameworks

It's crucial to create a strong plan as more businesses introduce Apple devices into the office to make sure you can retain compliance with IT policies and adhere to industry security standards and regulations. Compliance with security legislation, industry standards, and data and security obligations is important. The device and data use cases, legal requirements, and industry in which an organization operates all have a significant impact on its compliance management strategy.

In the context of data security, it's crucial for organizations to comprehend that if compliance requirements aren't completed, you run the danger of decline in reputation; loss of clients, accounts, or employment; financial loss in the forms of fines or sanctions; and data leaks and breaches.

Advantages of compliance: Following security compliance in an organization has various advantages in addition to financial penalties and sanctions, such as keeping a competitive edge, increased operational effectiveness, increasing consumer trust, reducing security threats, and preserving the reputation of your business.

Compliance frameworks: Organizations frequently employ one of three compliance frameworks to make sure they adhere to security and legal requirements. The comprehensive guide on managing cybersecurity risk from the **National Institute of Standards and Technology (NIST)** focuses on five basic operations: identify, protect, detect, respond, and recover. It highlights the significance of risk management and assessment, as well as ongoing evaluation and improvement. Benchmarks from the **CIS (Center for Internet Security)** are recommendations for securing networks and systems in organizations. They concentrate on doable, realistic actions that businesses can take to reduce prevalent online dangers. A standard for information security management systems (ISMS) is ISO 27001, according to the **ISO (International Organization for Standardization).** It includes a broad variety of security controls, such as access control, physical security, and incident management.

The implementation of a security benchmark is also needed for many regulated businesses, including systems covered by **PCI DSS (Payment Card Industry Data Security Standard)**, which may be used by retail or online businesses that process credit card transactions. **Health Insurance Portability and Accountability Act (HIPAA)** regulations must be followed by healthcare organizations. Under the **Family Educational Rights and Privacy Act (FERPA),** schools and colleges are required to implement safeguards to ensure the confidentiality of student education records.

Jamf Integrations and its Marketplace

Jamf customers, who range from small businesses to bigger enterprise organizations, use several enterprise products to provide employees with a great work and support environment. The Jamf platform seamlessly integrates into your IT stack and offers hundreds of tool connectors to optimize IT procedures.

Jamf Marketplace: The Marketplace is a one-stop shop for finding, learning about, and using essential tools that integrate with and enhance the Jamf platform. Some of the third-party approved applications available in Jamf Marketplace are Splunk, Rapid Deployment Tool, Blink, Trellix Endpoint Security, Zero Networks, Jamf Protect or Microsoft Sentinel, App Catalog, Setup Your Mac, CloudworkSSO, PatchBot, Beyond Identity, EasyLAPS, Installomator, Okta, Prune, JamfLog for Sublime Text, Jamf for Jira, Power BI, JSSImporter, Google Secure LDAP, Azure Active Directory, Jamf Tableau Integration, Microsoft Intune, TeamViewer, AutoPkg and more. Entire details which Jamf Marketplace can offer, can be found on their website `https://marketplace.jamf.com/`.

Overview of Jamf Pro Dashboard

Note   We explain all of the available components in Jamf Pro 10.46.0 version. Components may be added or removed as per Jamf.

You can keep track of the status of frequently accessed Jamf Pro items, such as smart groups, policies, configuration profiles, patch reports, and licensed software, in one place using the Jamf Pro Dashboard. By selecting the Jamf Pro icon in the top-left corner of the page, you may enter the Dashboard. See Figure 5-4.

Figure 5-4. *Jamf Pro Dashboard navigation*

For the Jamf Pro Dashboard to show updated data, you must manually refresh it. Data on the Jamf Pro Dashboard is not updated automatically. By checking the box that appears after creating any of the following things, you can add widgets to the Jamf Pro

Dashboard: Policies, Licensed Software, Configuration Profiles, Patch Management, Smart Groups, and Third-Party PKI Certificate. You can click the statistics shown in each widget after adding items to the Jamf Pro Dashboard to get directly to the section of Jamf Pro you want to view.

Jamf Pro Dashboard comes with the settings shown in Figure 5-5.

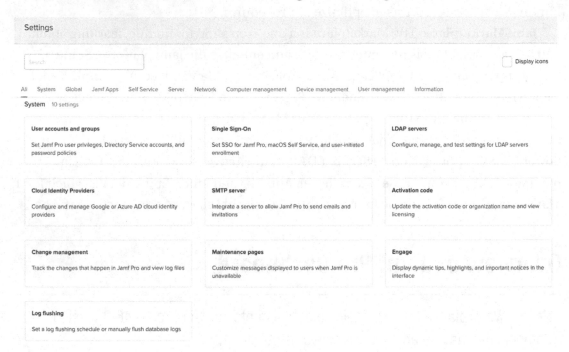

Figure 5-5. Jamf Pro System Settings overview

User accounts and groups: Jamf Pro is an app with many users. You may give each user a separate set of rights and levels of access with Jamf Pro user accounts and groups. You have the option of granting access to the entire Jamf Pro or only one site when configuring a Jamf Pro user account or group. By selecting one of the following privilege sets, you can grant privileges: Administrator, Auditor, Enrollment Only, and Custom.

LDAP servers: Incorporating with an LDAP directory service enables you to for the purpose of inventory, look up and populate user data from an LDAP directory service; add LDAP directory service user accounts or groups to Jamf Pro; and require users to utilize their LDAP directory accounts to access Self Service or the enrollment portal. The scope of remote administration tasks should be based on users or groups from the directory service.

Cloud identity providers: You may easily and securely access user information kept in the provider's configuration by integrating Jamf Pro with a cloud identity provider.

You may carry out the following: search for and fill up user data for inventory needs and add users or groups from the cloud identity provider to Jamf Pro. Users must use their directory accounts to access Self Service or the enrollment portal. Users or groups from the cloud identity provider inform the scope of remote management tasks.

Single sign-on: For some features of Jamf Pro, single sign-on can be enabled by integrating with a third-party identity provider (IdP). Users are automatically forwarded to your company's IdP login page after SSO has been configured and enabled. User access to the resource they were attempting to access is granted upon authentication

SMTP server: As a result of integrating with an SMTP server, you can inform Jamf Pro users by email when specific events take place. Email invites for user-initiated enrollment are sent.

Activation code: You can update the activation code for your license using Jamf Pro's Activation Code settings. Additionally, you can check licensing details and alter the name of the organization that holds the license.

Change management: You can keep track of Jamf Pro changes, including the establishment of a user account, with the help of change management. You can log those modifications to a syslog server and a log file (`JAMFChangeManagement.log`) on the Jamf Pro host server using the Change Management options in Jamf Pro.

Maintenance pages: For each language used in your environment, you can design a unique maintenance page using the Maintenance Pages setting. Users see the maintenance page while Jamf Pro is starting up or when getting an upgrade during enrollment.

Engage: As part of an ongoing effort to enhance your Jamf Pro experience, Engage gathers anonymous usage information. Additionally, it enables Jamf Pro to show pertinent data from within the Jamf Pro interface.

Log flushing: Flushing logs can speed up searches and reduce database size.

Global Management Settings

Categories: In Jamf Admin and Jamf Pro, categories are organizational elements that let you organize policies, packages, scripts, and printers. In Jamf Self Service, categories can be used to classify apps, configuration profiles, rules, and books. This makes it simpler to find certain goods. See Figure 5-6.

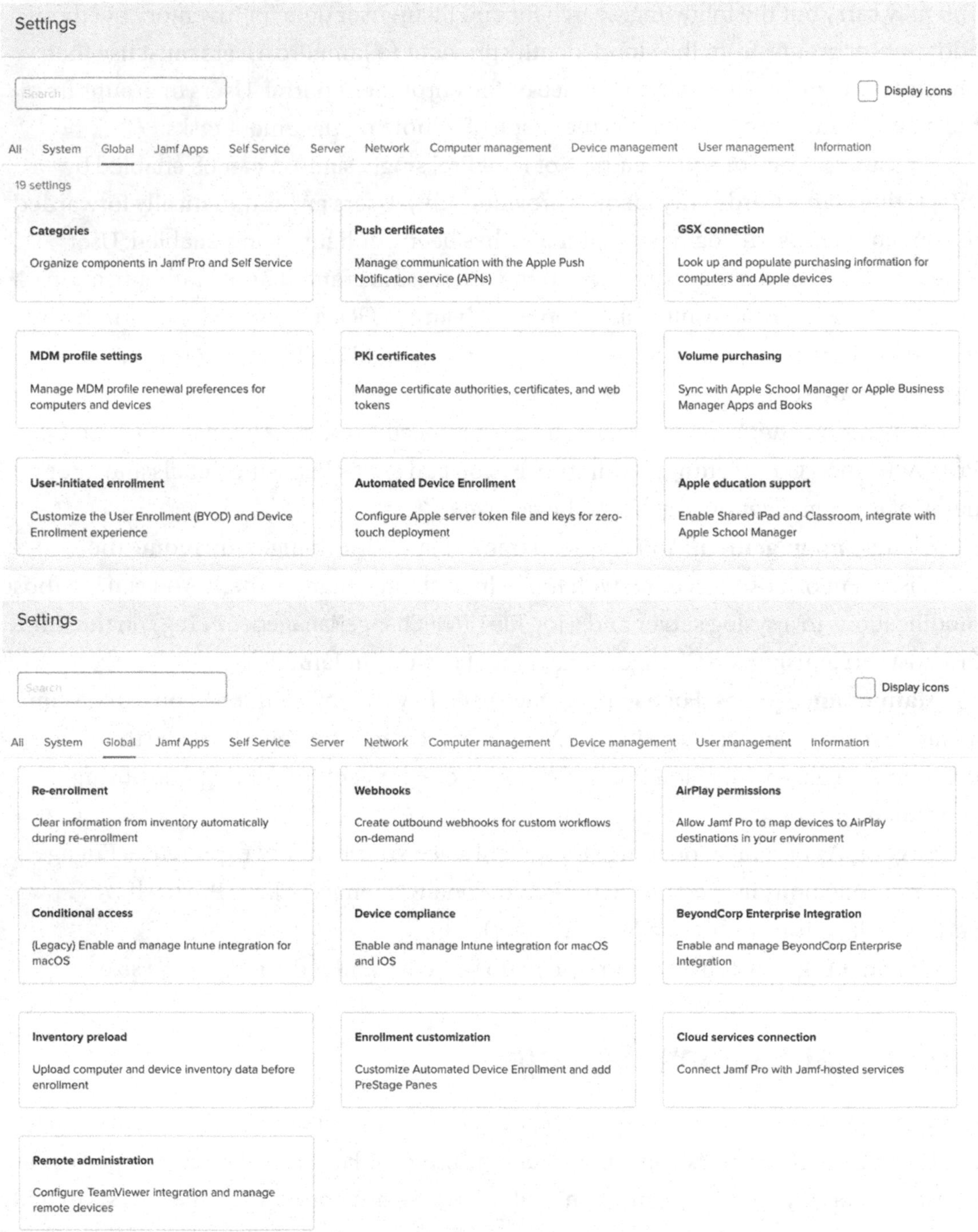

Settings

Search   ☐ Display icons

All   System   Global   Jamf Apps   Self Service   Server   Network   Computer management   Device management   User management   Information

19 settings

Categories

Organize components in Jamf Pro and Self Service

Push certificates

Manage communication with the Apple Push Notification service (APNs)

GSX connection

Look up and populate purchasing information for computers and Apple devices

MDM profile settings

Manage MDM profile renewal preferences for computers and devices

PKI certificates

Manage certificate authorities, certificates, and web tokens

Volume purchasing

Sync with Apple School Manager or Apple Business Manager Apps and Books

User-initiated enrollment

Customize the User Enrollment (BYOD) and Device Enrollment experience

Automated Device Enrollment

Configure Apple server token file and keys for zero-touch deployment

Apple education support

Enable Shared iPad and Classroom, integrate with Apple School Manager

Settings

Search   ☐ Display icons

All   System   Global   Jamf Apps   Self Service   Server   Network   Computer management   Device management   User management   Information

Re-enrollment

Clear information from inventory automatically during re-enrollment

Webhooks

Create outbound webhooks for custom workflows on-demand

AirPlay permissions

Allow Jamf Pro to map devices to AirPlay destinations in your environment

Conditional access

(Legacy) Enable and manage Intune integration for macOS

Device compliance

Enable and manage Intune integration for macOS and iOS

BeyondCorp Enterprise Integration

Enable and manage BeyondCorp Enterprise Integration

Inventory preload

Upload computer and device inventory data before enrollment

Enrollment customization

Customize Automated Device Enrollment and add PreStage Panes

Cloud services connection

Connect Jamf Pro with Jamf-hosted services

Remote administration

Configure TeamViewer integration and manage remote devices

Figure 5-6. *Jamf Pro Global settings overview*

258

Push certificates: An encrypted file called a push certificate, created by Apple, creates a trust relationship between a third-party service like Jamf Pro and the Apple Push Notification service (APNs). Jamf Pro commands and data are transmitted to and from devices using APNs as the communication channel. After receiving commands, devices continuously monitor APNs for messages to send back to Jamf Pro over APNs.

GSX connection: You may combine Jamf Pro with Apple's Global Service Exchange (GSX) using the GSX Connection settings to look up and populate the following purchase data for computers and mobile devices: purchase date and warranty expiration date.

MDM profile settings: You can set the MDM profile settings to control when computers and mobile devices will automatically renew their MDM profiles. The device identity certificate, which is contained in the MDM profile, is likewise renewed for a period of two years when the MDM profile is renewed.

PKI certificates: The PKI Certificates settings give you the ability to control the public key infrastructure required to create communication between computers, mobile devices, and certificate authority (CA). A PKI with certificate-based authentication functionality is necessary for Jamf Pro.

Volume purchasing: In order to control the distribution of your apps and books to devices or users, Jamf Pro's volume purchase connection syncs with Apple School Manager or Apple Business Manager.

User-initiated enrollment: Jamf Pro enrolls computers and mobile devices through the enrollment procedure. By doing this, a link is made between the Jamf Pro server and the computers and mobile devices. By going to an enrollment URL on their own, people can start the enrolling process via user-initiated enrollment. Go to `https://JAMF_PRO_URL.jamfcloud.com/enroll` (hosted by Jamf Cloud) and `https://JAMF_PRO_URL.com:8443/enrol` (on-premises hosting). These are customised URLs wherein "JAMF_PRO_URL" refers to the hostname or company name. These URLs are setup by the Jamf team and is unique to every organisation.

Automated device enrollment: When a user turns on a device, Apple's Automated Device Enrollment, commonly referred to as zero-touch deployment, immediately enrolls and configures it. IT does not communicate with users. The following device statuses are established using this enrollment technique, which is the one that is most frequently used for devices owned by your company: Supervised and User-Approved MDM.

Apple Education Support: You can perform the following with Jamf Pro's Apple Education Support settings: enable the usage of the Apple Classroom app with the Shared iPad by allowing computers and iPads to be added to Classes in Jamf Pro.

Reenrollment: When a computer or mobile device is reenrolled with Jamf Pro, you can clear specific inventory data from it using the Reenrollment options in Jamf Pro.

Webhooks: For any event in the Events API, you can create outbound webhooks using Jamf Pro's Webhooks option. Webhooks operate in conjunction with the Events API to let you create custom processes whenever you want in the programming language of your choice utilizing real-time events from Jamf Pro. For instance, you can set up a webhook to alert a chatroom whenever a third-party macOS app in Jamf Pro has been updated. The event is sent to the chatroom's instant message plug-in that you wrote.

AirPlay permissions: You can map one or more mobile devices to an AirPlay destination, like an Apple TV, using AirPlay Permissions, enabling those mapped mobile devices to automatically pair with the AirPlay destination. You can decide whether to automatically provide the mobile device the password for the AirPlay destination when it is mapped to one using AirPlay Permissions, or to restrict that device's access to only the authorized AirPlay destinations.

Conditional Access: Due to the transition away from Microsoft's Partner Device Management legacy API, Jamf will stop providing Conditional Access support in a later version of Jamf Pro (expected removal date: mid-2024). As an alternative, Jamf now provides macOS Device Compliance, which makes use of Microsoft's brand-new Partner Compliance Management API. The transition from the old Partner Device Management API to the new Partner Compliance Management API is being developed jointly by Jamf and Microsoft. The legacy Partner Device Management API will continue to function for a year after the migration path is made available to give organizations using the historical API time to switch to the new API. To ensure the easiest transition to the new macOS Device Compliance (Partner Compliance Management API), Jamf advises environments using the macOS Conditional Access (Partner Device Management API) to wait until the migration path is made available. Before the Microsoft Partner Device Management API is deprecated in the future, Jamf users will need to migrate their workflows to macOS Device Compliance in Jamf Cloud. Customers who presently use macOS Conditional Access will need to switch their workflows over to Jamf cloud's macOS device compliance. Contact Customer Success for more information about Jamf Cloud support. Only AWS GovCloud is supported for the creation of new Conditional Access integrations

Device compliance: You may enforce compliance on Jamf Pro-managed institutionally owned macOS, iOS, and iPadOS devices by integrating with Microsoft Intune. This enables businesses to guarantee that only authorized users using authorized devices have access to company resources. The Partner Compliance Management API is used for the Jamf Pro device compliance interface with Microsoft Intune.

BeyondCorp Enterprise Integration: Organizations may make sure that only dependable individuals with authorized computers and mobile devices can access organizational resources with Google BeyondCorp Enterprise. Administrators can create a compliance and security framework around end user devices without needing a network perimeter thanks to the BeyondCorp Enterprise interface between Jamf Pro and BeyondCorp.

Inventory preload: Before devices are enrolled, you can upload computers and mobile device inventory data using the Inventory Preload configuration. When inventory is gathered based on a matching serial number, the preloaded information will be applied to computers and mobile devices. When a comma-separated value (CSV) file is submitted, user data is immediately used.

Enrollment customization: The Automated Device Enrollment user experience can be tailored using the Enrollment Customization options in Jamf Pro.

Cloud services connection: By turning on the Cloud Services Connection, you may immediately link your Jamf Pro instance to any Jamf-hosted services that are accessible. The following services are offered: icon service, app installers, Jamf platform integration service, and Title Editor.

Remote administration: It contains TeamViewer Integration. You can create a remote screen-sharing connection between a Jamf Pro administrator and an end user's computer by integrating Jamf Pro with TeamViewer, an all-in-one remote access tool that is quick and safe.

Jamf Apps

Here is an overview of Jamf apps. See Figure 5-7.

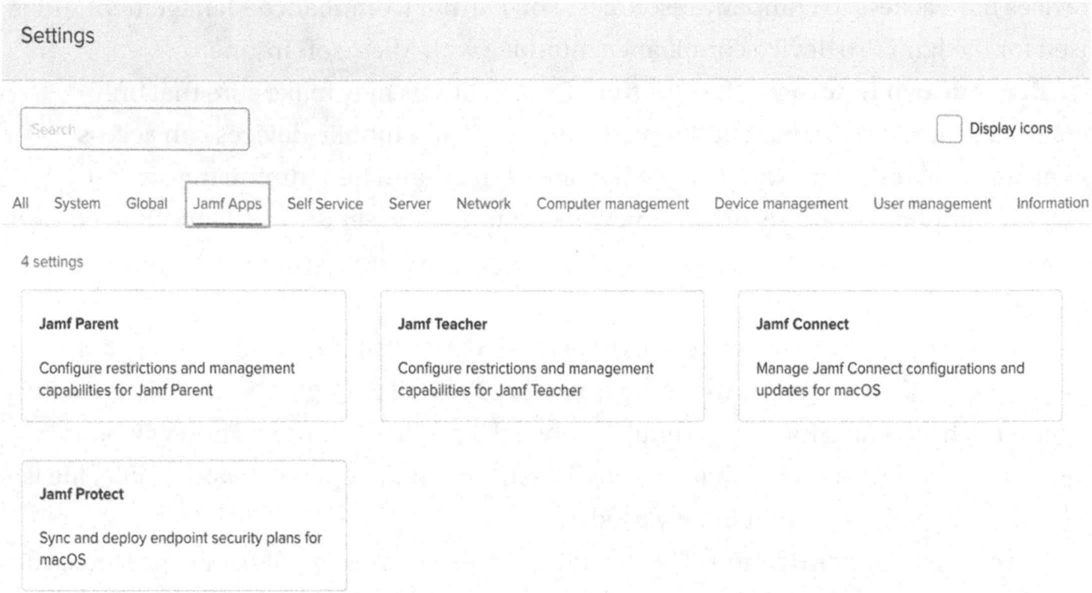

Figure 5-7. *Jamf Apps overview*

Jamf Parent: With the help of the free Jamf Parent app, parents can control the apps and device features that their kids have access to on their school-issued smartphones.

Jamf Teacher: Teachers may control student devices in the classroom with the help of Jamf Teacher, a free mobile, desktop, and online application.

Jamf Connect: With the help of the Jamf Connect app, administrators can control authentication by tying a user's local macOS account to the cloud identity (network account) of their company.

Jamf Protect: A cross-platform enterprise endpoint security solution called Jamf Protect gives administrators and security experts the power to safeguard devices utilizing a wide range of security features. With Jamf Protect's macOS endpoint security feature, you can make unique detections that safeguard computers by continuously watching out for suspicious and undesired activity while comparing machines to security standards set by the Center for Internet Security (CIS). In order to support ongoing macOS updates and maintain the Apple user experience, Jamf Protect runs without the usage of kernel extensions.

Self Service

Figure 5-8 shows the Self Service options.

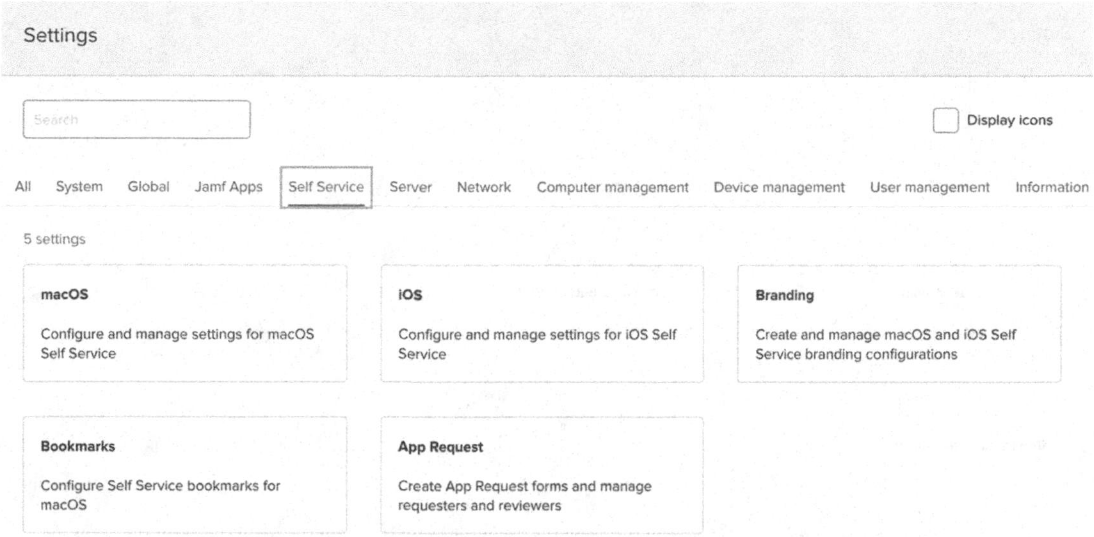

Figure 5-8. *Self Service overview*

macOS: Users can browse and download configuration profiles, Mac App apps, and books using Jamf Self Service for macOS. Users can also visit websites using bookmarks and run policies and updates to third-party applications via patch policies.

iOS: On controlled mobile devices, Jamf Self Service enables users to browse and download apps, books, and setup profiles for mobile devices. An easy-to-use interface allows users to navigate Self Service with their fingers.

Branding: To give your end customers a recognizable appearance and feel, you may customize several features in the Jamf Self Service for macOS and iOS apps using the branding settings.

Bookmarks: With the use of bookmarks, you can provide your users with quick access to web pages from within Jamf Self Service for macOS.

App Request: You can enable a chosen group of users to request iPad apps directly from Jamf Self Service for iOS by using the App Request feature. This is helpful in settings like schools where you want to give teachers the authority to request instructional apps on behalf of the students in their care.

Server

Figure 5-9 shows the Server options.

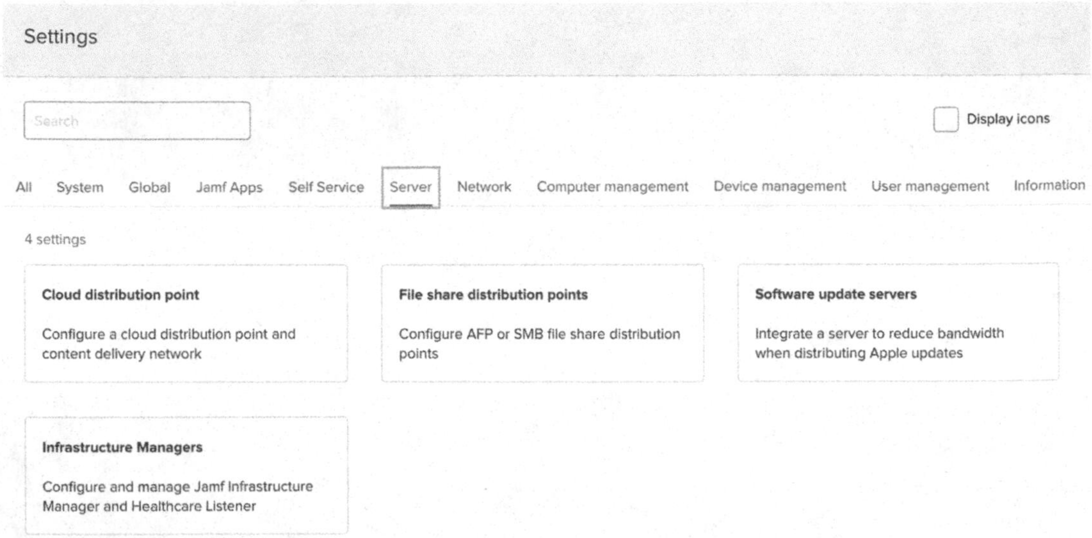

Figure 5-9. *Server settings overview*

Cloud distribution point: Packages, internal apps, and internal books are hosted by the cloud distribution point via a content delivery network (CDN).

File share distribution points: A file share distribution point can be a server having an AFP or SMB share. A file share distribution point must be configured and added to Jamf Pro before it can be used with Jamf Pro.

Software update servers: The first step in using a policy to run Software Update from an internal software update server is to add an internal software update server to Jamf Pro.

Infrastructure Managers: A service that is managed by Jamf Pro is an instance of Jamf Infrastructure Manager.

Network

Figure 5-10 shows the Network options.

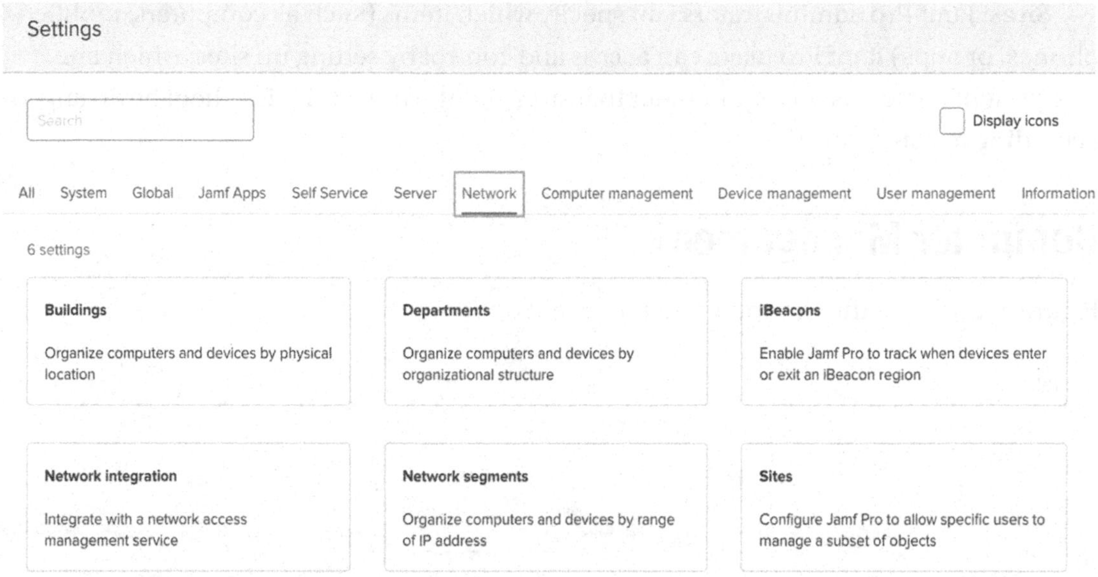

Settings

Search ☐ Display icons

All   System   Global   Jamf Apps   Self Service   Server   Network   Computer management   Device management   User management   Information

6 settings

Buildings

Organize computers and devices by physical location

Departments

Organize computers and devices by organizational structure

iBeacons

Enable Jamf Pro to track when devices enter or exit an iBeacon region

Network integration

Integrate with a network access management service

Network segments

Organize computers and devices by range of IP address

Sites

Configure Jamf Pro to allow specific users to manage a subset of objects

Figure 5-10. *Network Settings overview*

Buildings and Departments: You can organize computers and mobile devices based on their physical locations and organizational structure using departments and buildings. They may be used to configure the range of tasks for remote administration, conduct inventory searches, and make smart groupings.

iBeacons: Utilizing Apple's iBeacon technology, Jamf Pro enables you to keep track of when computers and mobile devices enter and leave an iBeacon area. By doing this, you can make sure that configuration profiles and policies are only applied to a device while it is in the designated region.

Network integration: A network access management service, such as Cisco Identity Services Engine (ISE), can be linked with Jamf Pro. In order to confirm that the computers and mobile devices on your network are consistent with your organization's standards, the service can communicate with Jamf Pro through network integration. The service can remind users to enroll their computers and mobile devices in Jamf Pro in order to become compliant, choose the amount of network access to allow to a computer or mobile device based on information from Jamf Pro, and send messages to end users.

Network segments: Depending on where on the network they are located, computers and mobile devices can be grouped using a network segment, which is a set of IP addresses. Class B or class C subnets, or any IP range inside them, may be considered network segments.

Sites: Jamf Pro administrators can specify which items (such as computers, mobile phones, or apps) Jamf Pro users can access and control by setting up sites, which are components. There is no requirement that sites and the objects inside them be arranged according to actual location.

Computer Management

Figure 5-11 shows the Computer management options.

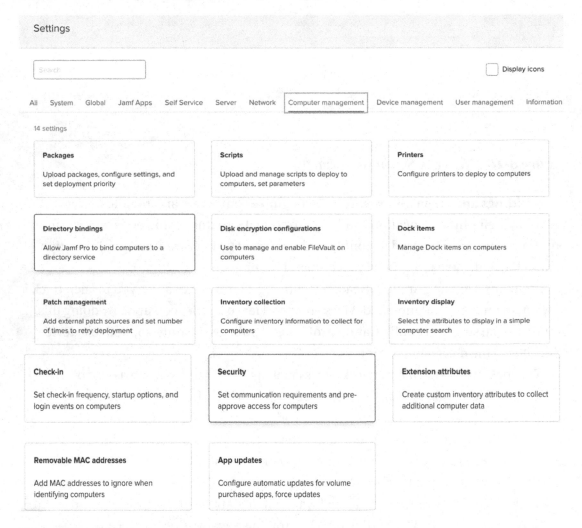

Figure 5-11. *Computer management overview*

Packages: A self-contained collection of files known as a package can be distributed to distant computers. When referring to Apple Installer packages (PKGs) and disc images (DMGs), which are used to distribute software and files to computers, Jamf uses the term "package."

Scripts: Scripts that have been added to Jamf Pro or Jamf Admin are automatically added to the database. As files on your distribution points, before you may execute a script in this kind of scenario, it must already be present in Jamf Pro and on the distribution point from which you intend to distribute it.

Printers: By adding printers to Jamf Pro or Jamf Admin, you may control printers in your environment.

Directory bindings: To connect computers to a directory service, add a directory binding to Jamf Pro. You may add and manage the following categories of directory bindings: Microsoft Active Directory, Apple Open Directory, ADmitMac, Centrify, and Power Broker Identity Services.

Disk encryption configurations: To manage and configure File Vault on machines, use Jamf Pro's disc encryption setup.

Dock items: Adding dock items to Jamf Pro or Jamf Admin allows you to manage dock objects on computers.

Patch management: Using Jamf Pro's built-in capabilities, you can manage software updates in your environment. By controlling software updates, you can make sure that the software on target machines is current in your environment and update it if necessary.

Inventory collection: The Update Inventory policy is automatically created when Jamf Pro is installed, and it is used by default to collect inventory from machines. This policy does a once-weekly inventory of all computers.

Inventory display: Each Jamf Pro user can customize the Computer Inventory Display settings to specify which attribute fields to show in the outcomes of a straightforward computer search.

Check-in: The period at which computers check in with Jamf Pro to see what policies are accessible is known as the recurrent check-in frequency.

Security: You can accomplish the following using Jamf Pro's security settings: enable authentication using certificates; enable push notifications; and install the Privacy Preferences Policy Control profile automatically.

Extension attributes: The use of extension characteristics enables the collection of additional inventory data.

Removable MAC addresses: The JAMF Software Server (JSS) can be made to ignore MAC addresses by adding detachable MAC addresses. In order to prevent the JSS from using certain MAC addresses as computer IDs, for instance, USB Ethernet dongle MAC addresses are frequently inserted as detachable MAC addresses.

App updates: This causes Jamf Pro to automatically update app descriptions, icons, and versions. During the specified time, this update occurs once each day. App Store software and apps purchased in bulk should be made to automatically update on devices. Every time a device checks in with Jamf Pro, this update is executed automatically.

Device Management

Figure 5-12 shows the Device management options.

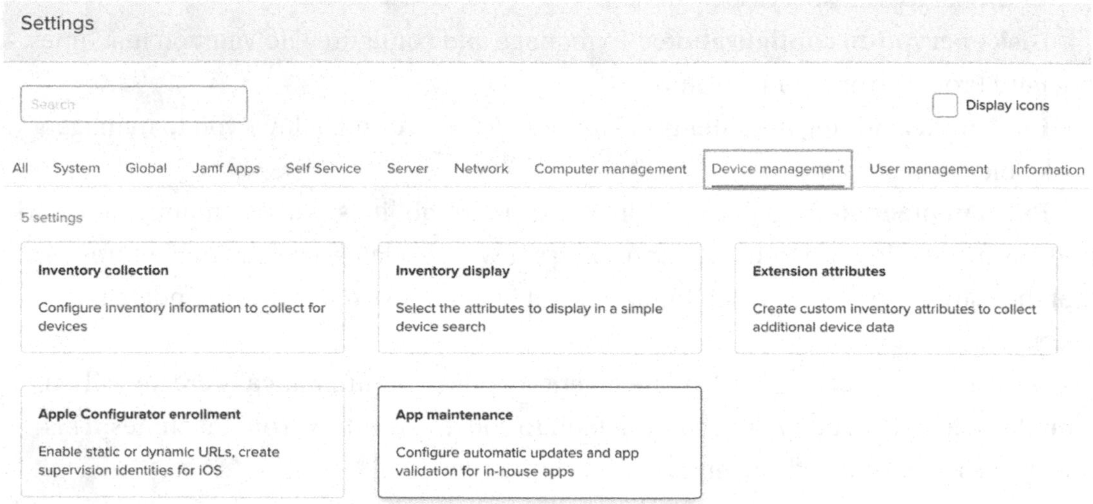

Figure 5-12. *Device management settings overview*

Inventory collection: Each controlled device is given a full inventory record in Jamf Pro. This data is viewable and editable in Jamf Pro. The availability of extra inventory information varies depending on the ownership type, device type, and OS version, whereas basic inventory information, such as hardware, OS version, storage, and apps, is often available for all devices.

Inventory display: Each Jamf Pro user can customize the Mobile Device Inventory Display settings to specify which attribute fields to show in the outcomes of a straightforward mobile device search.

Extension attributes: The use of extension characteristics enables the collection of additional inventory data. When populating extension attribute values, an input type is used, which can be any of the following: text field, pop-up menu, and LDAP attribute mapping.

Apple Configurator enrollment: You can enroll mobile devices with Jamf Pro utilizing Apple Configurator 2 and an enrollment URL by using the Apple Configurator enrollment settings. This entails enabling Apple Configurator enrollment in Jamf Pro and enrolling devices using Apple Configurator 2 and an enrollment URL by connecting the devices to a computer via USB.

App maintenance: For internal apps, you may do the automatic updates using Jamf Pro's App Maintenance settings. Jamf Pro can be set to automatically update all corporate apps that are downloaded and installed on mobile devices, including those that are included in Jamf Self Service for iOS.

User Management

Figure 5-13 shows the User Management options.

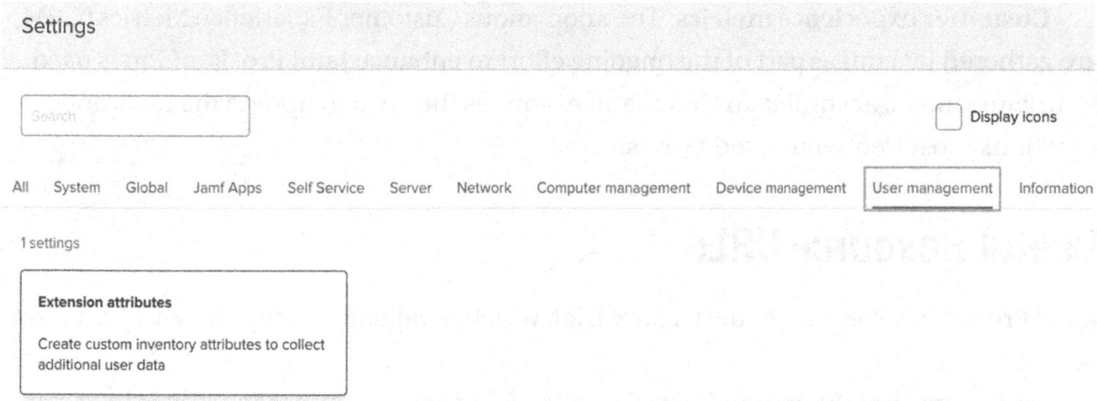

Figure 5-13. *User Management settings*

Extension attributes: The use of extension characteristics enables the collection of additional inventory data. When populating extension attribute values, an input type is used, which can be any of the following: script, text field, pop-up menu, and LDAP attribute mapping.

Information

Figure 5-14 shows the Information options.

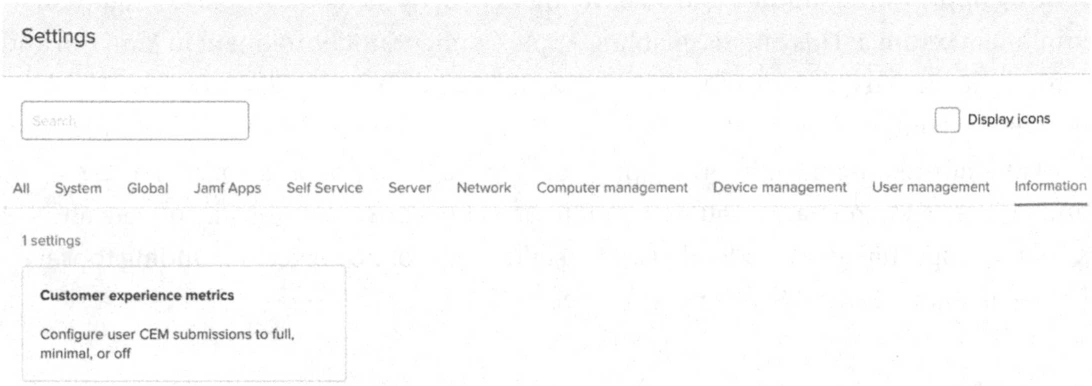

Settings

Search   ☐ Display icons

All   System   Global   Jamf Apps   Self Service   Server   Network   Computer management   Device management   User management   Information

1 settings

Customer experience metrics

Configure user CEM submissions to full, minimal, or off

Figure 5-14. *Information settings overview*

Customer experience metrics: The anonymous Customer Experience Metrics (CEM) are gathered by Jamf as part of the ongoing effort to enhance Jamf Pro. Jamf Pro is used by organizations, according to CEM. Jamf examines this data to update the tools and functions most frequently used by businesses.

Useful Resource URLs

Jamf Free Trial: You can request a Jamf trial, which is valid for 14 days, at `www.jamf.com/request-trial/`

    Jamf Instance URL format hosted on Cloud: `https://yourcompany.jamfcloud.com/`

    Jamf Instance URL format hosted on-premises :`https://JAMF_PRO_URL.com:8443/enrol`

    Jamf Marketplace URL: `https://marketplace.jamf.com/`

Summary

You should understand the significance of Apple Enterprise Management and why it's required to manage and secure Apple Fleet devices. Additionally, you should have A good understanding of why Jamf is one of the leading and scalable Apple Enterprise Management solutions on the market. You explored the Jamf product portfolio, which helped you to know about available Jamf offerings. At the same time, you explored the features for every Jamf product, which helps you to choose for your environment as per your requirements. Now you are in position to explain to your end users why Jamf is good and how it can make their life easy.

Your company management can get a holistic overview what data it can gather from Jamf Pro and this data can be presented in a visual report.

At the same time, you also learned about Jamf Cloud and the on-premises overview along with the architecture diagram, which helps you to select which one is better for your company. Additionally, you learned about Jamf Cloud features and its benefits.

You also have fair understanding about security compliance and its frameworks available as per your company requirement.

At this stage, you are familiar with Jamf integration and possible integration with approved third-party apps available in Jamf Marketplace.

You also have good understanding how enrollment works on a macOS computer managed by Jamf Pro and all the available enrollment options available. Now you are in a position to learn and manage macOS managed computers since you have explored all the settings available in Jamf Pro Dashboard.

Finally, you know useful Jamf URLs, which helps you to manage and secure macOS computers offered by Jamf Pro.

In the next chapter, you will investigate the command-line interface called Terminal, third-party text editors, Bash scripts, how to apply a shell script in real time, and more.

Glossary

Abbreviation	Description
MDM	Mobile Device Management
app	Application
AEM	Apple Enterprise Management
OS	Operating System
EMM	Enterprise Mobility Management
IDP	Identity Providers
CIS	Center for Internet Security
SIEM	Security Incident and Event Management
SOAR	Security Orchestration, Automation, and Response
SSO	Single Sign-On
DNS	Domain Name System
ADE	Automated Device Enrollment
DEP	Device Enrollment Program
VPP	Volume Purchase Program
NIST	National Institute of Standards and Technology
CIS	Center for Internet Security
ISO	International Organization for Standardization
PCI DSS	Payment Card Industry Data Security Standard
HIPAA	Health Insurance Portability and Accountability Act
FERPA	Family Educational Rights and Privacy Act

## CHAPTER 6

Automation

This chapter covers automation in macOS and how it can be useful for Mac system administrators, system engineers, DevOps engineers, and others. Automation makes the life of a system admin much easier and provides the best experience for the end user. To understand and apply automation on a macOS computer in real time, you need a clear understanding of the following topics in detail:

- The command-line interface (Terminal) and its usage
- Mac Terminal vs. the Windows command-line interface (CLI)
- Day-to-day/useful commands from the CLI (i.e., Terminal)
- Supported programming languages on macOS
- AppleScript and a slight introduction
- Basics of shell scripting and important components
- How to create and execute a shell script using Terminal or a third-party text editor
- Known third-party text editors for Macs
- Advanced shell scripting
- Use of the command line on macOS

Using the Command Line on macOS

In an earlier chapter, you explored the command-line interface (i.e., Terminal) basics, so now you'll learn how Terminal can be useful with macOS. The command line is a great way to relate to macOS without the use of a graphical user interface (GUI). Although most basic administrative tasks can be achieved using the GUI on macOS, in some cases

© Sagar Rastogi and Jasdeep Singh 2023
S. Rastogi and J. Singh, *Exploring macOS*, https://doi.org/10.1007/978-1-4842-9882-4_6

it is more sensible to perform them via Terminal. Terminal is built on the Unix operating system. Let's understand why and when it's required to use custom command-line commands in macOS along with useful commands.

Prerequisites to Using the CLI on macOS

You must know the fundamentals of the macOS ecosystem and be using a Mac device with administrator privileges.

Reasons to Use the Command-Line Interface

You can use the command line for administrative tasks instead of relying on the normal user interface, such as when you want to execute change permissions system-wide, batch commands, automate operational tasks, or diagnose issues. It comes with these benefits: you can access filesystem, remotely manage a Mac device over Apple Remote Desktop, remotely manage devices using MDM, automate recurring tasks using scripting, execute remote login using SSH, and execute commands as a root user.

Construction of a Command-Line Sequence

The command prompt is the beginning line where every macOS Unix command is input and executed. It delivers vital details to the user. It includes the current user, current directory, and machine name in the command prompt.

In Figure 6-1, % is the default zsh prompt symbol. Different shells use other symbols. For instance, the bash custom is $. Here the machine name is **Big-Sur**, the username is sagarmac, and the current directory is the home folder, signified by ~, which is a concise approach to point to the user's home folder.

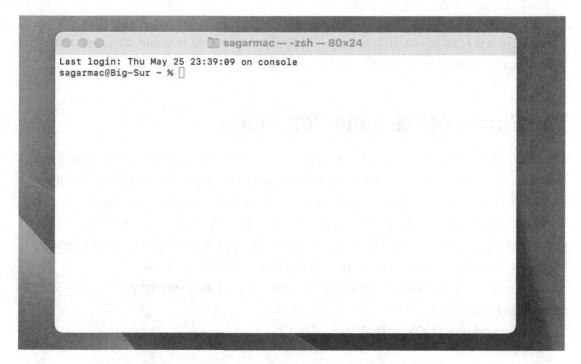

Figure 6-1. *Overview of a Mac Terminal command-line sequence*

Differences Between Mac Terminal and Windows Command Line

There are three major operating systems available: macOS, Linux, and Windows. macOS Terminal uses Unix commands and the Windows CLI is built on the MS DOS structure of commands.

Every OS comes with a selection for the shell. The macOS CLI is called Terminal and it customs the results of sh. Until 10.15 (i.e., Catalina OS) macOS came with the default of bash, but from 10.15 and onwards, macOS comes with the default of zsh. The syntax of sh programs are same. Overall, the purpose is to resolve the same issues.

Basically, bash is just sh but with additional types and better syntax. macOS uses bash. Windows uses PowerShell and cmd. Both come with a unique syntax. By default, PowerShell is installed on Windows 7 and further Windows versions.

To use the Unix command prompt on macOS, open the Terminal app, which is located by default in the Utilities folder. The Utilities folder exists inside the Applications folder (/Applications/Utilities). To use the cmd prompt in Windows 7, click the Start button and type cmd in search box. In later Windows versions, you can navigate to the Start menu, find Run, and input a cmd command.

The Power of the sudo Command

This is one of the most powerful and vital commands. The sudo command (or superuser do) permits you to execute commands as a root user. It is a transient approach to allow a user an administrative right. You will customize it when you need to accomplish administration activities. This will imitate the system or different users, which only superuser can perform, for modifying configuration files, installing software libraries, and more. To use the sudo command, you must be an admin at least.

For instance, if you are not an administrator or a root user, entering the sleep 2 command gives you an error:

Command used in Terminal: sudo sleep 2

See Figure 6-2.

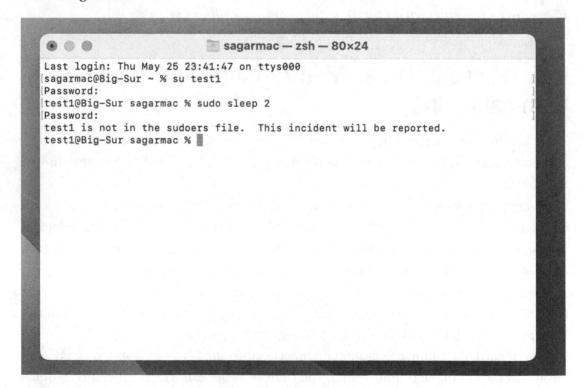

Figure 6-2. *Demonstration of the sudo command with a standard user*

The reason for this error is that the `sleep 2` command can only be executed by the root user or by an administrator with superuser do privileges.

Figure 6-3 shows the `sleep 2` command executed successfully because it was executed by the root user or by an administrator with superuser do privileges.

Command used in Terminal: sudo sleep 2

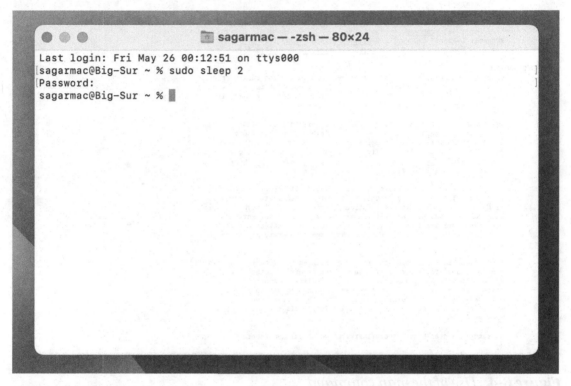

Figure 6-3. *Demonstration of the sudo command with the administrator user*

Useful Terminal Commands

man: The `man` command stands for **manual pages**. It is like a help structure for the command line and is mainly called to access help documents for specific Terminal commands. For example, if you want to know more about the `sudo` command, you must use the `man sudo` command in Terminal. Figure 6-4 shows how it looks in Terminal.

Command used in Terminal: man sudo

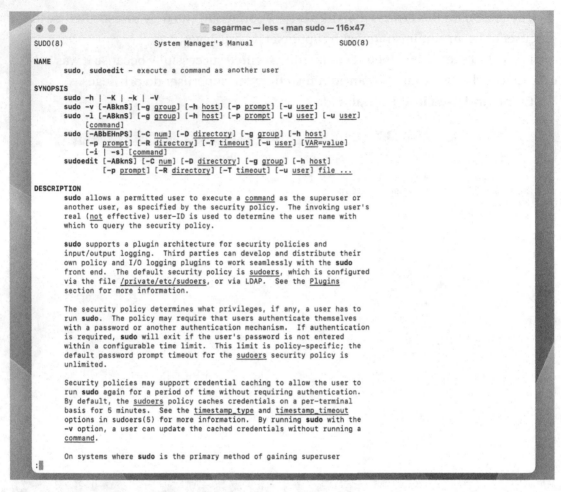

Figure 6-4. *Use of the man command*

pwd: The pwd command means **print working directory**, which provides the absolute path to the present working directory. See Figure 6-5.

Command used in Terminal: pwd

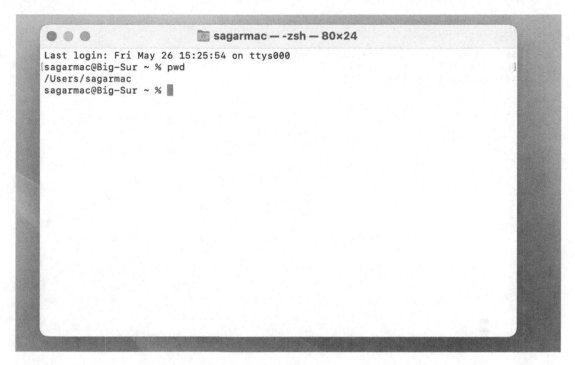

Figure 6-5. *Demonstration of the pwd command*

mkdir: The mkdir command means **make directory**. Let's create a directory on a macOS desktop named task. See Figure 6-6.

Command used in Terminal: mkdir task

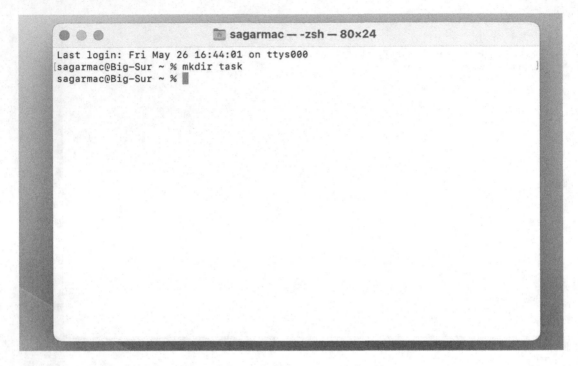

Figure 6-6. *Demonstration of the mkdir command*

Note that if you try to create same directory named task again, it will throw the error `mkdir: task: File exists`. See Figure 6-7.

Command used in Terminal: `mkdir task`

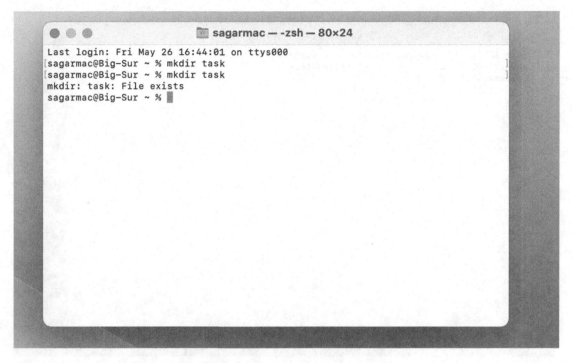

Figure 6-7. *Demonstration of the mkdir command*

You can create multiple directories using the -p option. For example, the mkdir -p actions/task command will make a folder known as actions and a nested folder or subfolder named task. See Figure 6-8.

Command used in Terminal: mkdir -p actions/task

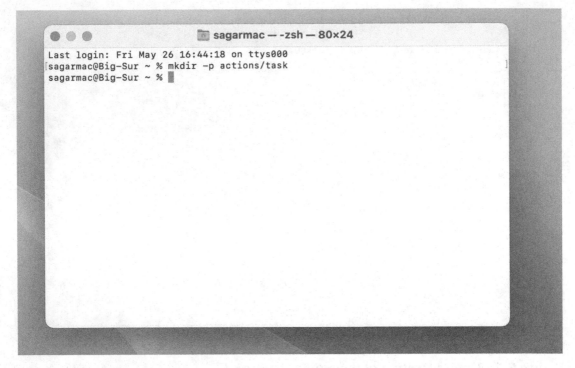

Figure 6-8. Demonstration of the mkdir command with the -p flag

cd: The cd command means to **change directory**. Let's leverage this command to access the task directory you created above. See Figure 6-9.

Command used in Terminal: cd task

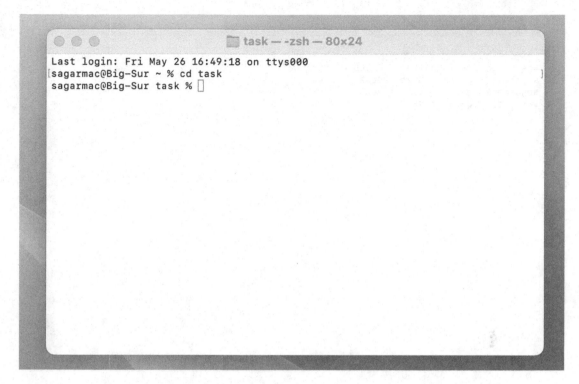

Figure 6-9. *Demonstration of the cd command*

touch: With the help of the touch command, you can create a file. First, navigate to the task folder on the desktop using cd ~/Desktop/task and then create file named test.txt using the touch test.txt command, which basically stores it in task folder on macOS Desktop. See Figure 6-10.

Command used in Terminal: cd ~/Desktop/task

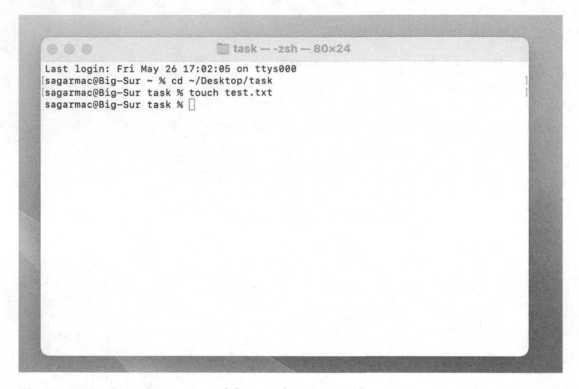

Figure 6-10. *Demonstration of the touch command*

Figure 6-11 shows the test.txt file created in the task folder on a macOS desktop.

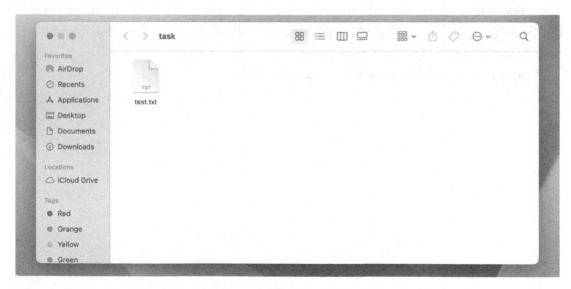

Figure 6-11. *Location of the test.txt file in the task folder*

ls: The ls command means **list**. It is used to show all the contents of the indicated directory. If no path is indicated, it will show all in the current directory. Figure 6-12 shows everything with ls because you haven't indicated the path.

Command used in Terminal: ls

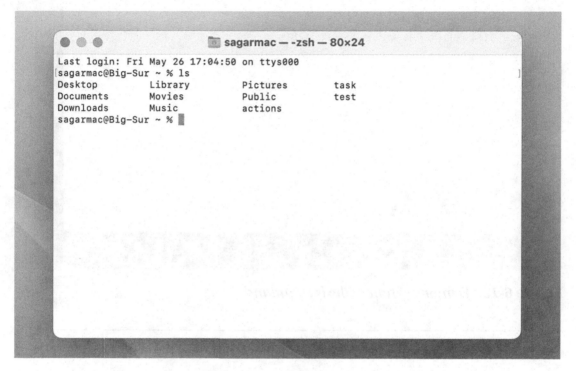

Figure 6-12. *Demonstration of the ls command*

Let's talk about ls with the absolute path indicated. Here is the workflow:

```
cd ~/Desktop/task
mkdir work
ls
```

Figure 6-13 shows how it looks in Terminal.

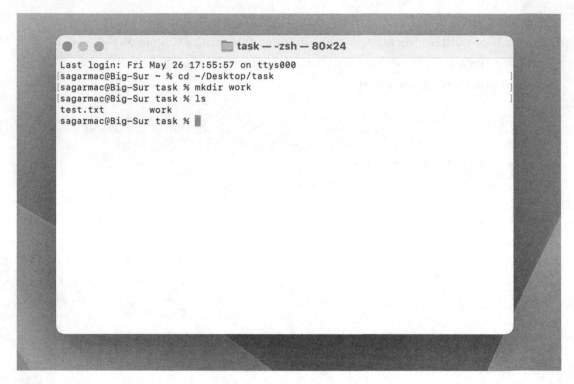

Figure 6-13. *Demonstration of the ls command*

Note   The -a flag shows hidden files and directories. See Figure 6-14.

Command Used in Terminal: `ls -a`

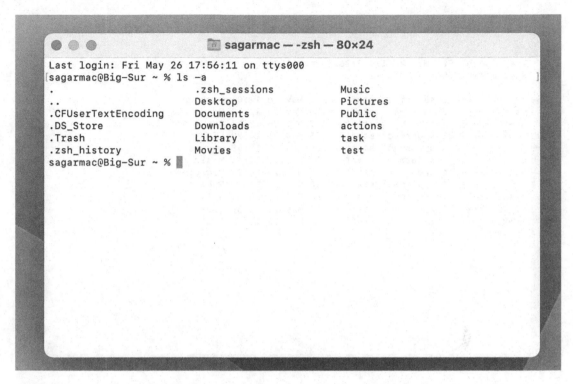

```
● ● ●                    sagarmac — -zsh — 80×24
Last login: Fri May 26 17:56:11 on ttys000
[sagarmac@Big-Sur ~ % ls -a                                                  ]
.                       .zsh_sessions           Music
..                      Desktop                 Pictures
.CFUserTextEncoding     Documents               Public
.DS_Store               Downloads               actions
.Trash                  Library                 task
.zsh_history            Movies                  test
sagarmac@Big-Sur ~ %
```

Figure 6-14. *Demonstration of ls command with -a flag*

Note   Use the -l flag to show detailed information. See Figure 6-15.

Command Used in Terminal: ls -l

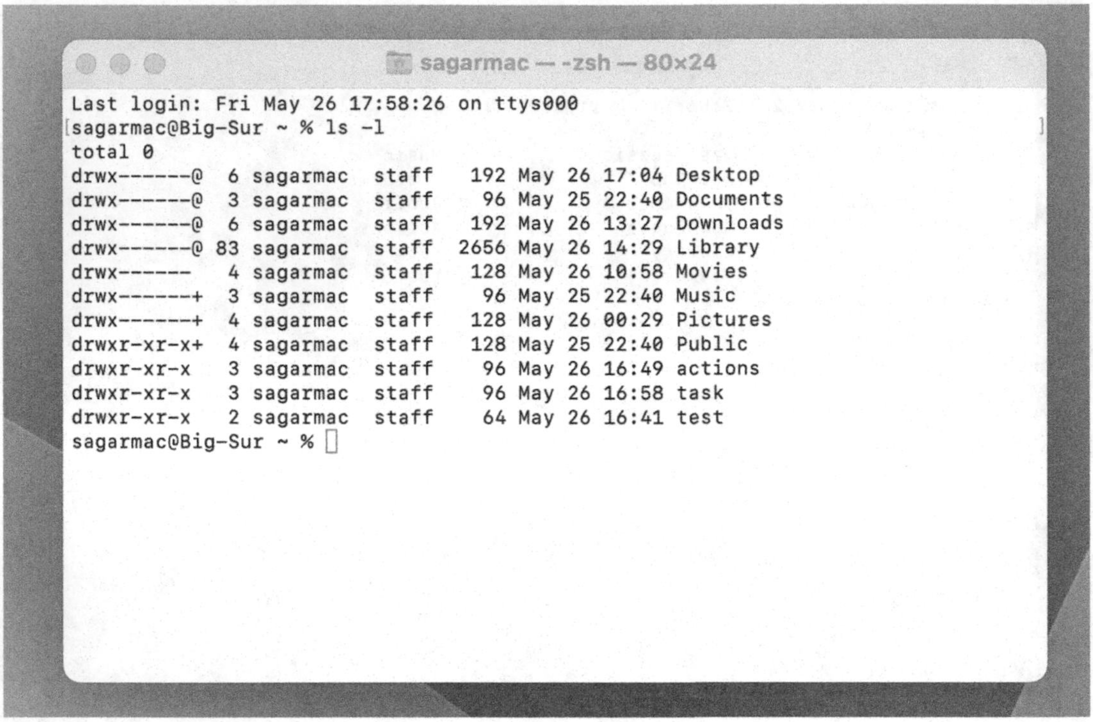

```
● ● ●                    📁 sagarmac — -zsh — 80×24
Last login: Fri May 26 17:58:26 on ttys000
[sagarmac@Big-Sur ~ % ls -l
total 0
drwx------@  6 sagarmac  staff   192 May 26 17:04 Desktop
drwx------@  3 sagarmac  staff    96 May 25 22:40 Documents
drwx------@  6 sagarmac  staff   192 May 26 13:27 Downloads
drwx------@ 83 sagarmac  staff  2656 May 26 14:29 Library
drwx------   4 sagarmac  staff   128 May 26 10:58 Movies
drwx------+  3 sagarmac  staff    96 May 25 22:40 Music
drwx------+  4 sagarmac  staff   128 May 26 00:29 Pictures
drwxr-xr-x+  4 sagarmac  staff   128 May 25 22:40 Public
drwxr-xr-x   3 sagarmac  staff    96 May 26 16:49 actions
drwxr-xr-x   3 sagarmac  staff    96 May 26 16:58 task
drwxr-xr-x   2 sagarmac  staff    64 May 26 16:41 test
sagarmac@Big-Sur ~ % ▯
```

Figure 6-15. *Demonstration of the ls command with the -l flag*

clear: It clears the Terminal screen. See Figure 6-16.

Command used in Terminal: clear

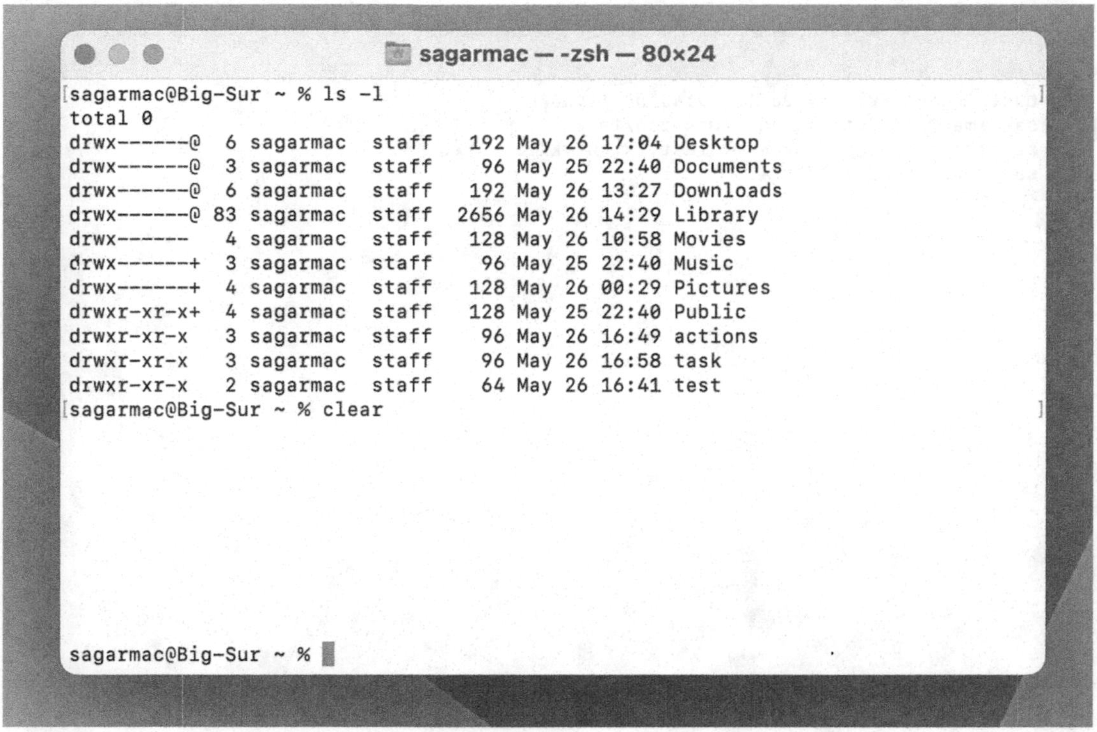

```
●  ●  ●                    🗀 sagarmac — -zsh — 80×24
[sagarmac@Big-Sur ~ % ls -l
 total 0
 drwx------@  6 sagarmac   staff    192 May 26 17:04 Desktop
 drwx------@  3 sagarmac   staff     96 May 25 22:40 Documents
 drwx------@  6 sagarmac   staff    192 May 26 13:27 Downloads
 drwx------@ 83 sagarmac   staff   2656 May 26 14:29 Library
 drwx------   4 sagarmac   staff    128 May 26 10:58 Movies
 drwx------+  3 sagarmac   staff     96 May 25 22:40 Music
 drwx------+  4 sagarmac   staff    128 May 26 00:29 Pictures
 drwxr-xr-x+  4 sagarmac   staff    128 May 25 22:40 Public
 drwxr-xr-x   3 sagarmac   staff     96 May 26 16:49 actions
 drwxr-xr-x   3 sagarmac   staff     96 May 26 16:58 task
 drwxr-xr-x   2 sagarmac   staff     64 May 26 16:41 test
[sagarmac@Big-Sur ~ % clear




 sagarmac@Big-Sur ~ % █
```

Figure 6-16. *Demonstration of the clear command*

mv: The mv command is for **move**. This command is used to move files and directories from one place to another. It can also be used to rename files and directories. The following command will move the test.txt file from its current directory to its child directory named work. Here is the workflow. See Figures 6-17 and 6-18 for the results.

```
cd ~/Desktop/task
mv test.txt work/test.txt
```

Figure 6-17. *Demonstration of the mv command*

Figure 6-18. *Snapshot of the test.txt file*

cp: The cp command is used to copy. Here is the syntax for copying files and folders:

```
cp source target
```

Let's understand more about the cp command with the example. To copy the file called test.txt from the macOS Desktop folder to the Documents folder, you input the following command in Terminal. See Figures 6-19 and 6-20.

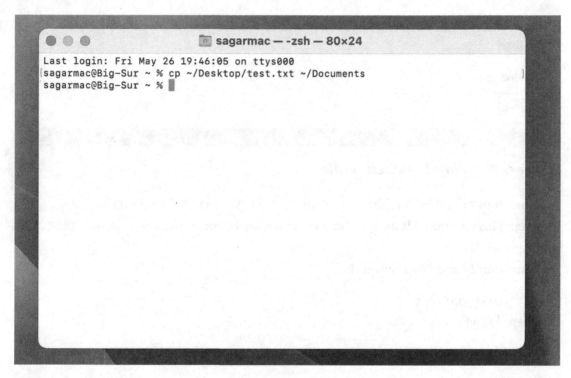

Figure 6-19. Demonstration of the cp command

Figure 6-20. *Snapshot of test.txt file*

Command used in Terminal: `cp ~/Desktop/test.txt ~/Documents`

grep: This command is used for pattern searching. For example: `grep 'find' test.txt`. See Figure 6-21.

Commands used in Terminal:

```
cd ~/Desktop/Test
grep 'find' test.txt
```

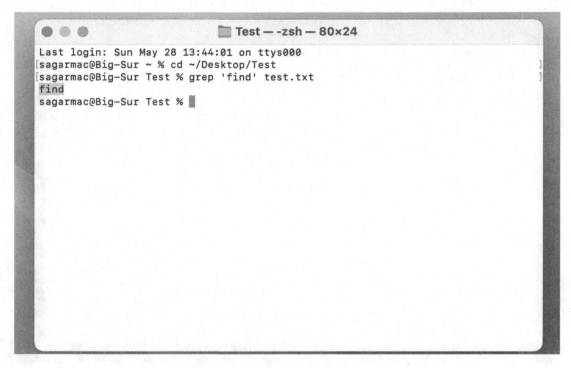

Figure 6-21. *Demonstration of the grep command*

awk: This command is used for pattern scanning and processing. For example: awk '{print $1}' test.txt. See Figure 6-22.

Commands used in Terminal:

cd ~/Desktop/Test
awk '{print $1}' test.txt

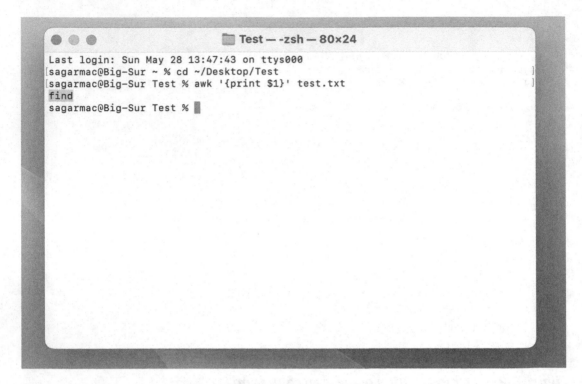

Figure 6-22. *Demonstration of the awk command*

chmod: This command is used for changing the file permissions. For example: chmod
751 /path/to/file (i.e., chmod 751 /Users/sagarmac/Desktop/Test/test.txt). This
indicates that the file permissions have been modified to the following:

rwx for owner

rx for group

x for others

r stands for read

w for write

x for execute

(x=1, r=4, w=2)

See Figure 6-23.

Command used in Terminal: chmod 751 /Users/sagarmac/Desktop/Test/
test.txt

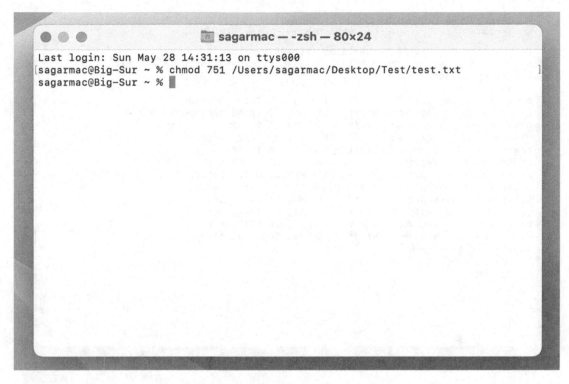

Figure 6-23. *Demonstration of the chmod command*

Figure 6-24 shows how you can validate the file permission for chmod 751 /Users/
sagarmac/Desktop/Test/test.txt.

Commands used in Terminal:

chmod 751 /Users/sagarmac/Desktop/Test/test.txt

ls -l

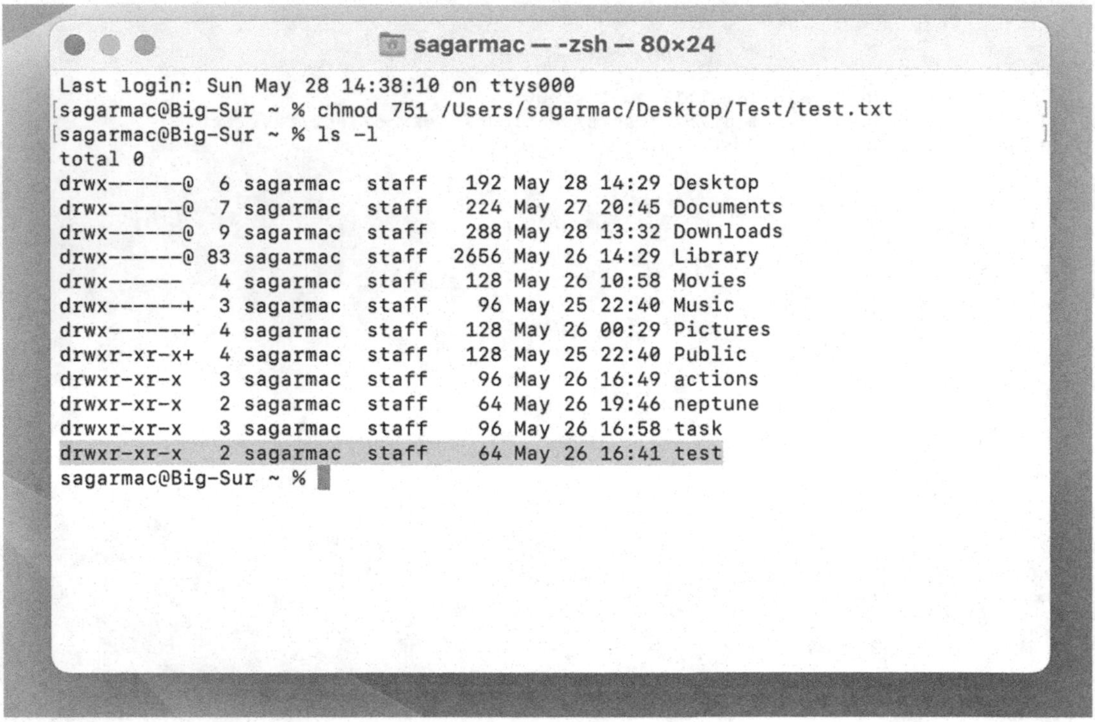

```
● ● ●                🖥 sagarmac — -zsh — 80×24

Last login: Sun May 28 14:38:10 on ttys000
[sagarmac@Big-Sur ~ % chmod 751 /Users/sagarmac/Desktop/Test/test.txt    ]
[sagarmac@Big-Sur ~ % ls -l                                              ]
total 0
drwx------@  6 sagarmac  staff   192 May 28 14:29 Desktop
drwx------@  7 sagarmac  staff   224 May 27 20:45 Documents
drwx------@  9 sagarmac  staff   288 May 28 13:32 Downloads
drwx------@ 83 sagarmac  staff  2656 May 26 14:29 Library
drwx------   4 sagarmac  staff   128 May 26 10:58 Movies
drwx------+  3 sagarmac  staff    96 May 25 22:40 Music
drwx------+  4 sagarmac  staff   128 May 26 00:29 Pictures
drwxr-xr-x+  4 sagarmac  staff   128 May 25 22:40 Public
drwxr-xr-x   3 sagarmac  staff    96 May 26 16:49 actions
drwxr-xr-x   2 sagarmac  staff    64 May 26 19:46 neptune
drwxr-xr-x   3 sagarmac  staff    96 May 26 16:58 task
drwxr-xr-x   2 sagarmac  staff    64 May 26 16:41 test
sagarmac@Big-Sur ~ % ▊
```

Figure 6-24. *Validating file permissions for chmod 751*

For instance, chmod go=+r /path/to/file (chmod go=+r /Users/sagarmac/
Desktop/Test/test.txt) indicates read permission have been added to the group and
others. The characters stand for the following:

u for user

g for group

o for other

+ to add permission

- to remove permission

r for read

w for write

x for execute

See Figure 6-25.

Commands used in Terminal:

chmod go=+r /Users/sagarmac/Desktop/Test/test.txt

ls -l

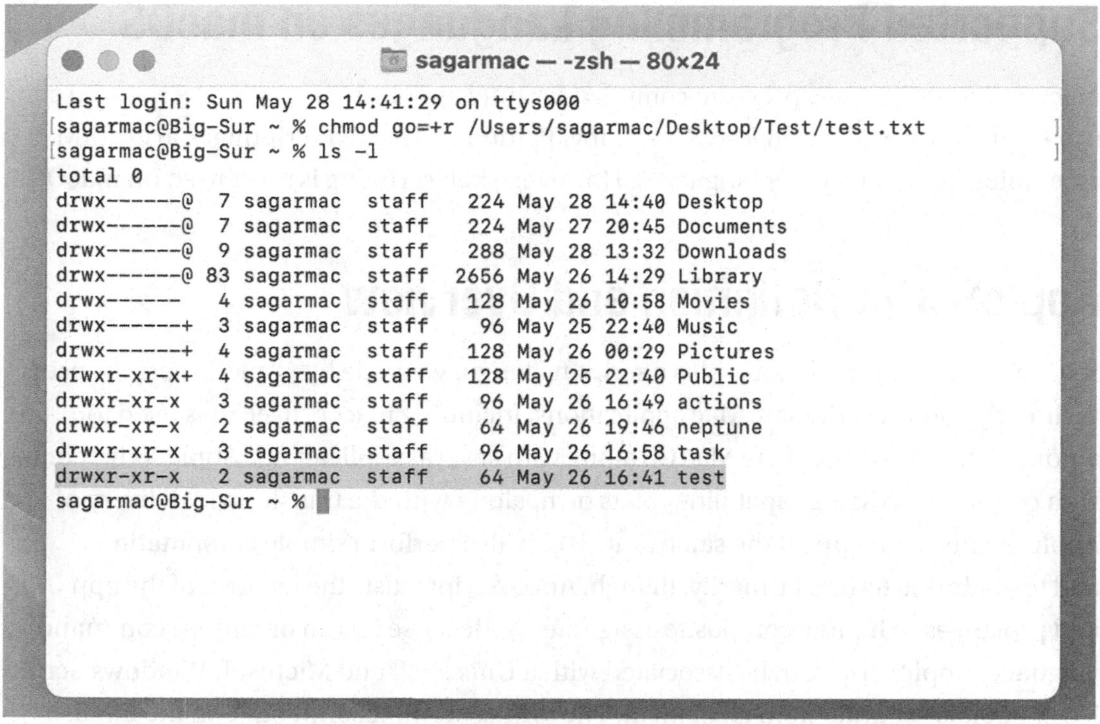

```
● ● ●                  ⬜ sagarmac — -zsh — 80×24
Last login: Sun May 28 14:41:29 on ttys000
[sagarmac@Big-Sur ~ % chmod go=+r /Users/sagarmac/Desktop/Test/test.txt  ]
[sagarmac@Big-Sur ~ % ls -l                                              ]
total 0
drwx------@  7 sagarmac  staff   224 May 28 14:40 Desktop
drwx------@  7 sagarmac  staff   224 May 27 20:45 Documents
drwx------@  9 sagarmac  staff   288 May 28 13:32 Downloads
drwx------@ 83 sagarmac  staff  2656 May 26 14:29 Library
drwx------   4 sagarmac  staff   128 May 26 10:58 Movies
drwx------+  3 sagarmac  staff    96 May 25 22:40 Music
drwx------+  4 sagarmac  staff   128 May 26 00:29 Pictures
drwxr-xr-x+  4 sagarmac  staff   128 May 25 22:40 Public
drwxr-xr-x   3 sagarmac  staff    96 May 26 16:49 actions
drwxr-xr-x   2 sagarmac  staff    64 May 26 19:46 neptune
drwxr-xr-x   3 sagarmac  staff    96 May 26 16:58 task
drwxr-xr-x   2 sagarmac  staff    64 May 26 16:41 test
sagarmac@Big-Sur ~ % ▮
```

Figure 6-25. *Demonstration of chmod go=+r /path/to/file*

chown: This command is used to change the owner.

cat: This command is used to read and display the contents of one or more files.

curl: This is a utility for sending the data to or from a web server.

defaults: This command is used to read, write, and delete software preferences.

echo: This command is used to return the result of a command to standard output.

killall: This command is used to stop a running process or application.

rm: This command is used to delete files.

rmdir: This command is used to delete a directory.

date: This command is used to display the current date.

open: This command is used to open either file you call.

find: This command is used to search for files.

which: This command find a program file in user's path

Supported Programming Languages on macOS

macOS can execute any program compiled for Intel or M1 Mac models. Overall, you can run AppleScript, C, Objective-C, C++, Ruby, Python, PHP, shell scripting, x86 or ARM assembler, and many other languages. However, shell scripting is most used on macOS.

AppleScript Definition and Overview

Similar to bash, AppleScript is also a scripting language made by Apple. It permits users to directly control scriptable Mac applications, including macOS itself. It is used to automate the activities of the Mac OS along with several applications. AppleScript comes with certain processing capabilities of its own, along with the transfer and delivery of Apple events to an app. At the same time, it can also perform simple computations and text administering. Primarily, though, AppleScript trusts the features of the app and processes to handle composite assignments. Because it is an organized command language, AppleScript can be associated with a Unix shell and Microsoft Windows Script Host, but it is separate from all of them. The syntax of AppleScript built on the English syntax, so if someone has no coding knowledge, they can still understand it just by reading it.

Syntax and how to write a simple script in AppleScript: To create and execute simple AppleScript, you must have the Script Editor application, which is an inbuilt app on macOS. It can be open from the Utilities\Application folder or from Spotlight to open Script Editor.

Example 1: To display a prompt on a user Mac computer with two buttons, here is the code:

```
display dialog "Know more about AppleScript." buttons {"Read", "Skip"}
```

In Figure 6-26, we have just typed the command. Since we haven't run the command, the colors are same throughout the command. In Figure 6-27, the Script Editor colors will be changed in the command.

Figure 6-26. *Demonstration of the display dialog in the Script Editor*

It will display the message along two buttons when you click Run in Script Editor. See
Figure 6-27.

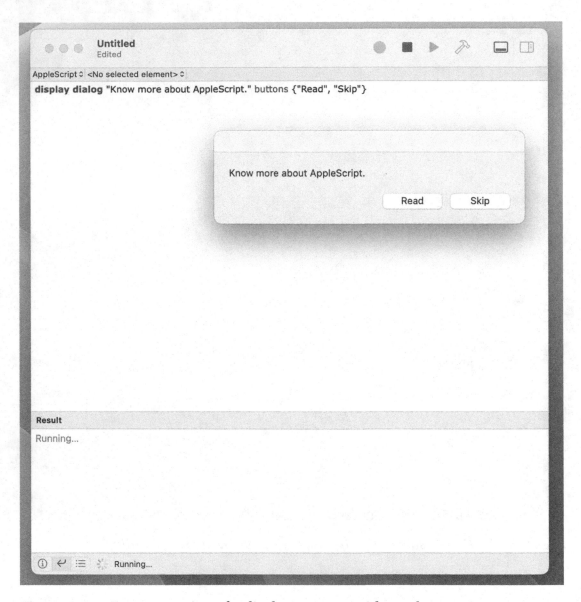

Figure 6-27. *Demonstration of a display message with two buttons in*
Script Editor

Once you click the Read button it will show the command execution in Result as {
{button returned:"Read"}. See Figure 6-28.

Figure 6-28. *Output of the Read button in Script Editor*

Once you click the Skip button it will show the command execution in Result as { {button returned:"Read"}. See Figure 6-29.

Figure 6-29. *Command execution result of the Skip button in Script Editor*

Exmaple2: To display an alert on a Mac computer, here is the code along with a Script Editor Screenshot:

display alert "Learn AppleScript"

In Figure 6-30, we have just typed the command. Since we haven't run the command, the colors are same throughout the command. In the next image, the colors will be changed.

Figure 6-30. *Demonstration of a display alert in Script Editor*

It will display alert message and OK button when you click Run in Script Editor. See Figure 6-31.

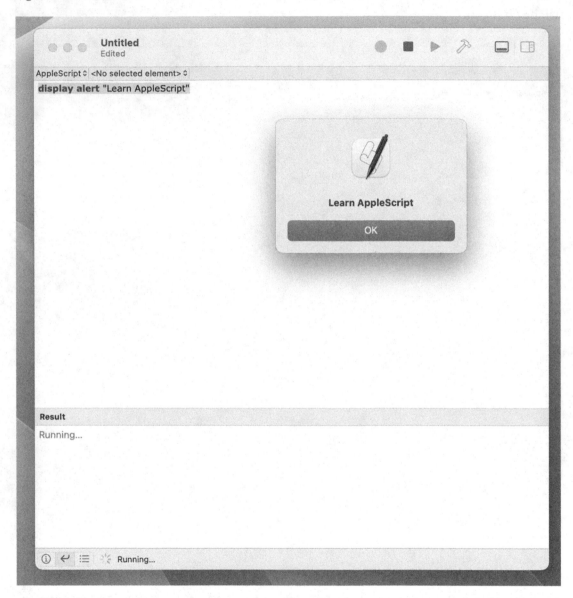

Figure 6-31. *Demonstration of a display message with button in Script Editor*

Once you click OK, it will show the command execution in Result as {button returned:"OK"}. See Figure 6-32.

Figure 6-32. *Command execution result of the OK button in Script Editor*

Note   AppleScript is hardly used on macOS. Rather, bash script is frequently used to automate tasks on macOS.

Shell Scripting and Its Usage

A shell script is a computer program intended to run in a shell. Scripts can be written in many scripting languages. Distinctive functions are file manipulation, program executing, and printing text. Shell scripts are robust in deploying data. Shell scripts provide a seamless solution to do so. They are also easy to develop and easy to run on macOS. They can be easily used to filter ranges and data alteration on an enormous scale. Because of that reason, shell scripts are frequently used in data science and other specialized environments. Each shell has a precise feature set, therefore bash features may not occur in different shells. To confirm a bash script is construed the correct way, it must begin with #!/bin/bash. In order for bash to operate, the bash shell needs be installed on the present operating system.

Differences Between bash vs. zsh

bash and zsh (i.e., part of Bourne shell family) share central features. Zsh stands for Z shell, which is the supplement of Bash along with numerous features. But there are differences. Auto completion is much quicker in zsh as compared to bash. zsh comes with inline wildcard expansion; bash doesn't support this feature. zsh comes with prefix and suffix command aliases; bash doesn't support these features. Zsh comes with numerous themes and plugins; bash offers less themes and plugins. By default, zsh doesn't handle # as a comment; # is a comment in bash by default. Zsh is more accurate and in case of an issue it throws an error; bash does items on its own. zsh holds the user configuration settings in .zshrc; bash holds the user configuration settings in .bashrc. zsh comes with numerous superior features compared to bash.

Modifying the Default Shell on macOS

Launch Terminal on Mac and type the following command:

```
cat /etc/shells
```

See Figure 6-33 for all the existing shells for Mac.

Command used in Terminal: `cat /etc/shells`

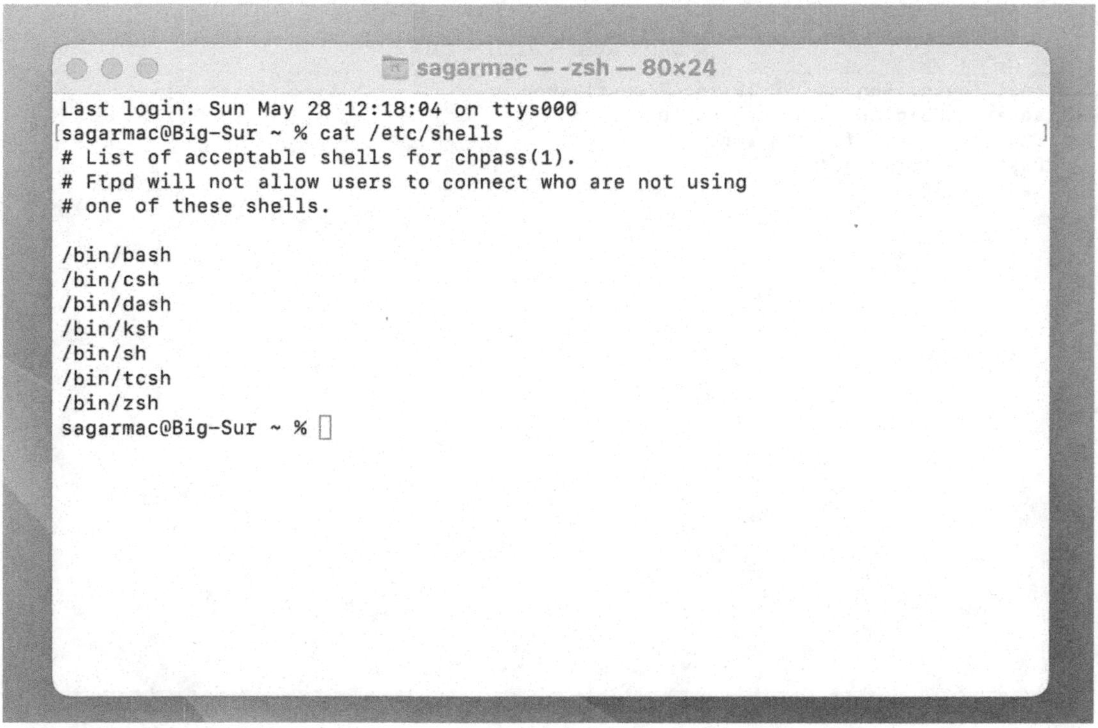

```
●●●                    sagarmac — -zsh — 80×24
Last login: Sun May 28 12:18:04 on ttys000
[sagarmac@Big-Sur ~ % cat /etc/shells                                          ]
# List of acceptable shells for chpass(1).
# Ftpd will not allow users to connect who are not using
# one of these shells.

/bin/bash
/bin/csh
/bin/dash
/bin/ksh
/bin/sh
/bin/tcsh
/bin/zsh
sagarmac@Big-Sur ~ % ▯
```

Figure 6-33. *Available shells in Terminal*

Let's explore how to convert the zsh shell model to the bash shell mode and vice versa.

This command will convert zsh to bash shell (chsh -s /bin/bash). See Figure 6-34.

zsh to bash conversion command used in Terminal: chsh -s /bin/bash

Figure 6-34. *zsh to bash conversion*

This command will help you validate the current shell mode (echo $0). **From Figure 6-35 its clearly understood that the current shell mode is bash (the highlighted one).**

chmod go=+r /Users/sagarmac/Desktop/Test/test.txt

Command used in Terminal: echo $0

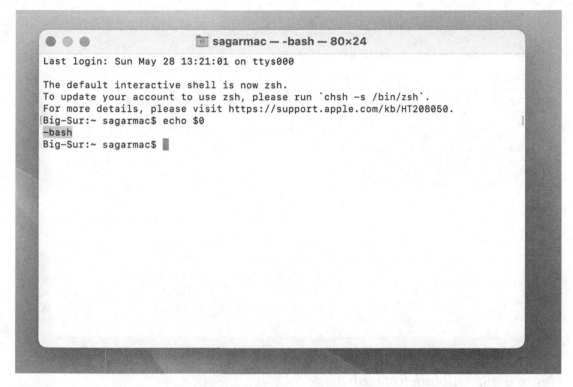

```
● ● ●                    📁 sagarmac — -bash — 80×24
Last login: Sun May 28 13:21:01 on ttys000

The default interactive shell is now zsh.
To update your account to use zsh, please run `chsh -s /bin/zsh`.
For more details, please visit https://support.apple.com/kb/HT208050.
[Big-Sur:~ sagarmac$ echo $0                                            ]
-bash
Big-Sur:~ sagarmac$ █
```

Figure 6-35. *How to check the shell mode*

If you again try to change the zsh mode to bash, it will throw an error that says chsh: no changes made. See Figure 6-36.

Command used in Terminal: chsh -s /bin/bash

Figure 6-36. *Validation of bash mode*

This command will convert bash to zsh shell (chsh -s /bin/zsh). See Figure 6-37.

bash to zsh conversion command used in Terminal: chsh -s /bin/zsh

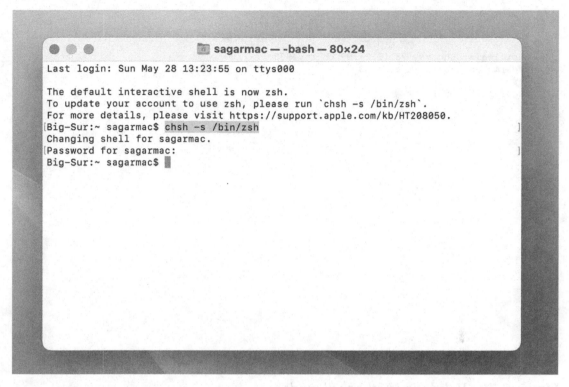

```
●  ●  ●              🔲 sagarmac — -bash — 80×24
Last login: Sun May 28 13:23:55 on ttys000

The default interactive shell is now zsh.
To update your account to use zsh, please run `chsh -s /bin/zsh`.
For more details, please visit https://support.apple.com/kb/HT208050.
[Big-Sur:~ sagarmac$ chsh -s /bin/zsh                                          ]
Changing shell for sagarmac.
[Password for sagarmac:                                                        ]
 Big-Sur:~ sagarmac$ ▮
```

Figure 6-37. *bash to zsh conversion*

This command will help you validate the current shell mode (echo $0). **From Figure 6-38, it is clearly understood that the current shell mode is zsh.**

Command used in Terminal: echo $0

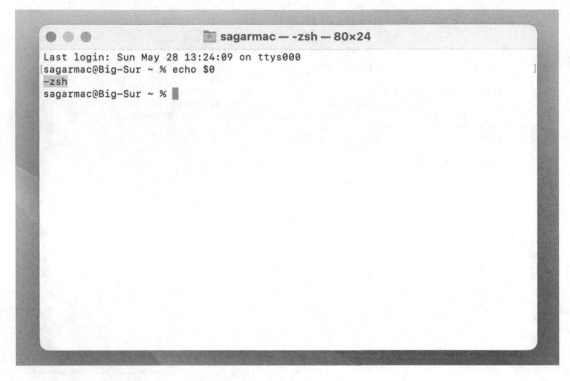

Figure 6-38. *Validation of the shell mode*

Basic Building Components for Writing a Simple Bash Script

What are variables? Variables are used to store data. You can customize variables to read, manipulate, and access data during the script. The macOS and Linux operating systems have variables by default. You can use env to display a list of environment variables. To write an effective shell script, it's always good to use variables.

In bash, a variable can store numeric values, characters, or strings of characters.

Syntax: Key=Value (This the way variable can be defined.)

To describe a variable for the present shell and all subshells, customize **export key=value**. To ensure a variable is automatically set, put it in one of the bash startup files. Refer to a variable using echo $key. To prevent opacity, customize echo ${key}; compare echo ${key}1 with echo $key1. See Figure 6-39.

Commands used in Terminal:

```
key=value
echo $key
echo ${key}
echo ${key}1
echo $key1
```

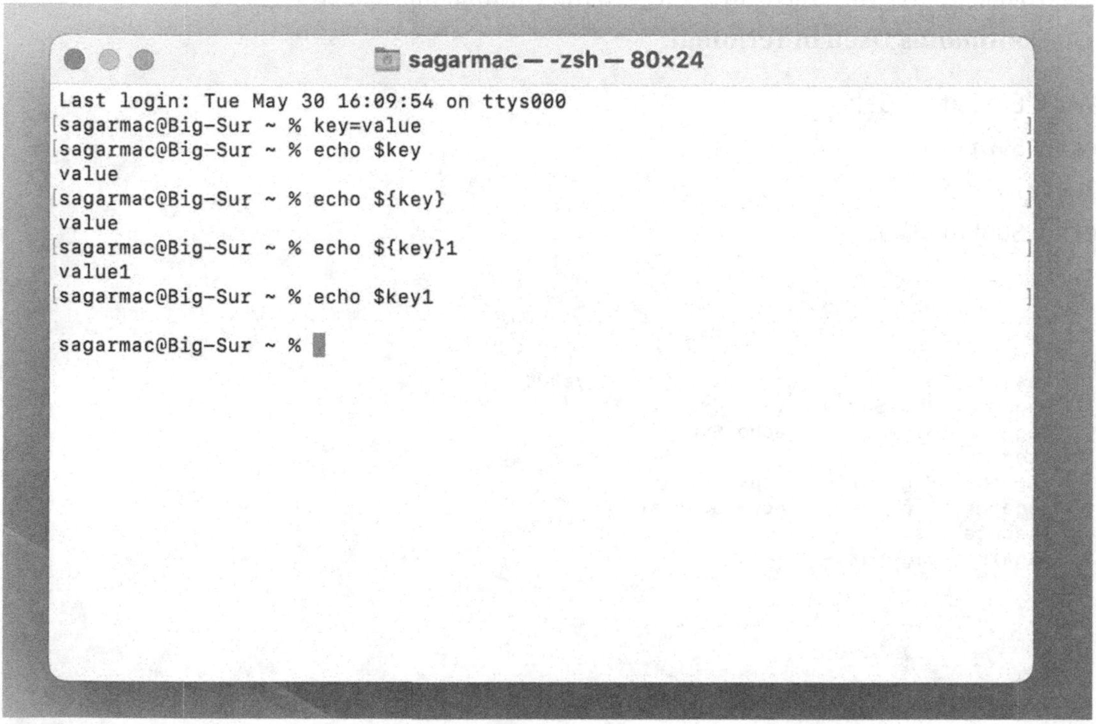

Figure 6-39. *Demonstration of a variable*

The organization of variables doesn't make any impact on the shell. In a similar way, variables hold strings, real numbers, and integers. It's important to understand that a variable can store one value at a time. Subsequently, string split using spaces are require to have quotes. For example, the following variable holds the string Execute, but because of the space after Execute, it will not store Task.

```
Var=Execute Task
```

Thus, the correct assignment for a variable is the following:

```
Var="Execute Task"
```

You can allocate the value centered on the output attained from the above command by means of command substitution. Note that $ is essential to access the current variable's value.

SubVar=$Var (This will allocate the value of Var the new variable SubVar)

To access the variable value, add $ to the variable name. See Figure 6-40.

Commands Used in Terminal:

```
Var="Execute Task"
echo $Var
SubVar=$Var
echo SubVar=$Var
```

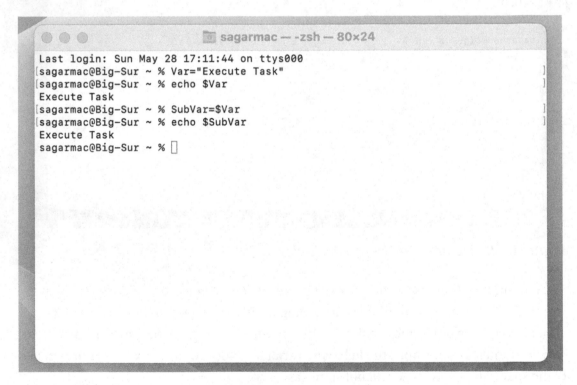

Figure 6-40. *Understanding variables with examples*

There are mainly three types of variables:

Global variables comes with a global scope and are easily available during the program. The main benefit of global variables are that they can be declared externally in the chunk of code or the function.

Local variables are only available within a particular function or chunk of code. Local variables can supersede an identical variable name in the bigger scope.

Special variables are built and retained through bash itself and at the same time are needed with the shell to function accurately. To outline in uppercase and to get every part of them, use the set / env / printenv command. See Figure 6-41.

Commands used in Terminal:

```
set / env / printenv
printenv
```

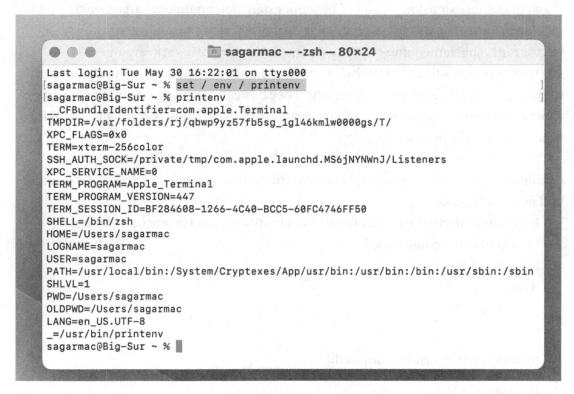

Figure 6-41. *Demonstration of the set/ env /printenv command*

Naming conventions for variables: The following are the variable naming conventions in bash scripting: letters, underscores (_), and numbers. A variable must begin with a letter or underscore (_). No spaces or special characters are allowed. They are case-sensitive and custom descriptive names that suggest the purpose of the variable. Reserved keywords are if, then, else, fi, and etc.

`Var`, `sum`, `Var`, `Do_Var`, and `DoVar` are some valid variable names in bash scripting. Here are some invalid names: `3rdVar` (a variable name can't begin with a number), `Do Var` (a variable name can't have a space), and `Do-Var` (a variable name can't include a hyphen).

What are arguments and their uses? A command-line argument is a value that can be passed to the shell script as it executes. Additionally, it permits the user to modify events the script executes. To authorize an argument with the shell script, it's required to input in the arguments just after the script name, during the execution of script.

Syntax shellextension ./NameoftheScript.extenstion argument1 argument2.

For instance, `sh ./testscript.sh do work` (wherein `sh`=shellextension, `testscript.sh`=NameoftheScript.extenstion, `do`=argument1, `work`=argument2)

What are conditionals and their use? Conditional statements are mostly used in scripting to achieve decision-making jobs. They basically allow you to modify the drift of control in a script. Conditional statements come with five unique statements that can be used in shell scripting when required.

Expressions generate a Boolean output, either true or false, and are known to be conditions. There are various ways to assess conditions, including if, if-else, if-elif-else, and nested conditionals.

Let's understand the syntax for all five conditional statements one by one:

Syntax of the if conditional:

if [`condition`]

then

    `statement`

fi

Syntax of the if-else conditional:

if [`condition`]

then

    `statement1`

else

    `statement2`

fi

Syntax of the else-if ladder conditional:

if [condition1]
then
    statement1
elif [condition2]
then
    statement2
else
    statement3
fi

Syntax of the nested if conditional:

if [condition1]
then
    statement1
else
    if [condition2]
    then
    statement2
    fi
fi

Syntax of the switch conditional:

case in
    case2) Statement 1;
    case 2) Statement 2;
esac

Logical operators such as AND -a and OR -o are powerful for comparisons that have more impact. If [$x -gt 50 -x $y -lt 90], this statement will validate if both conditions are true: x is greater than 50 AND y is less than 90, wherein gt stands for greater than and lt stands for less than.

Numeric comparison operators: Here are a few operations:

5 -eq 5 means 5=5

5 -ne 2 means 5 is not equal to 2

5 -gt 1 means 5 is greater than 1

5 -lt 6 means 5 is less than 6

5 -ge 5 means 5 is >=5

5 -le 5 means 5 <=5

What are wild cards? A wildcard is basically a concise written outline, frequently a specific character, that can match other character in a file path. Additionally, it is a form of shortcut that permits you to state a complete set of connected path names by means of a brief outline. Using the wildcard form, it is quite simple to copy, delete, or move a huge number of files by a specific command. In all, there are three types of wildcards which are described below.

Single wildcard (*): This is the most often used wildcard in shell scripting. For instance, file * shows all of the files that exist in the directory and their type. See Figure 6-42.

Command used in Terminal: file *

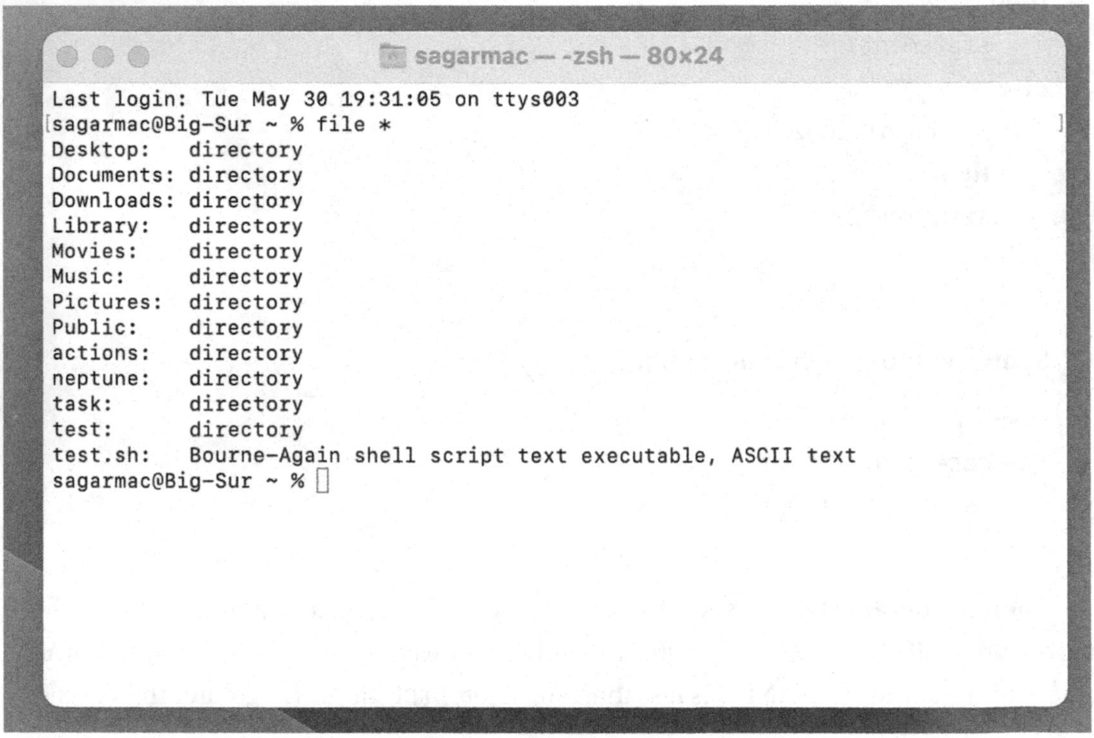

```
● ● ●                    🖥 sagarmac — -zsh — 80×24

Last login: Tue May 30 19:31:05 on ttys003
[sagarmac@Big-Sur ~ % file *                                              ]
Desktop:    directory
Documents:  directory
Downloads:  directory
Library:    directory
Movies:     directory
Music:      directory
Pictures:   directory
Public:     directory
actions:    directory
neptune:    directory
task:       directory
test:       directory
test.sh:    Bourne-Again shell script text executable, ASCII text
sagarmac@Big-Sur ~ % ▯
```

Figure 6-42. *Demonstration of a single wildcard* *

Square bracket wildcard ([]): It is utilized to specify any of the characters surrounded in the square brackets.

For example, file *[do]* shows all items in the present directory that of d, o in the file. See Figure 6-43.

Command used in Terminal: file *[do]*

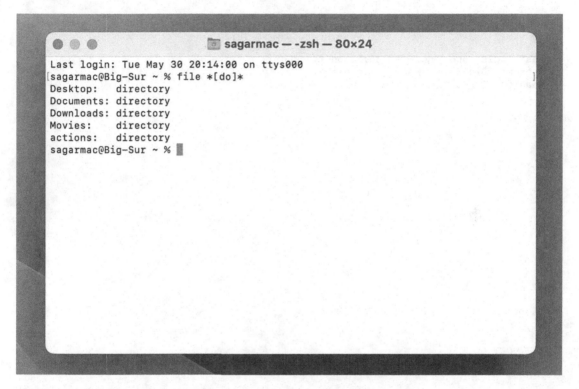

Figure 6-43. *Demonstration of a square bracket wildcard*

What is piping and its use? It allows you to use the outcome of a script/command by way of the input of the other. Piping is an enormously influential and adaptable quality of bash and is frequently used with the native commands offered by bash.

Syntax for the pipe command: command1 | command2 .... | commandZ

Consider this example:

```
ls | open -fe
```

Explanation: In order to pipe the output of a command, you can simply use the vertical line character (|), as demonstrated in the above command, which will take the output of the ls command and pipe it to the open command, which the -fe tag will tell to read the piped input and open it in TextEdit (the default text editor). See Figure 6-44.

Command used in Terminal: ls | open -fe

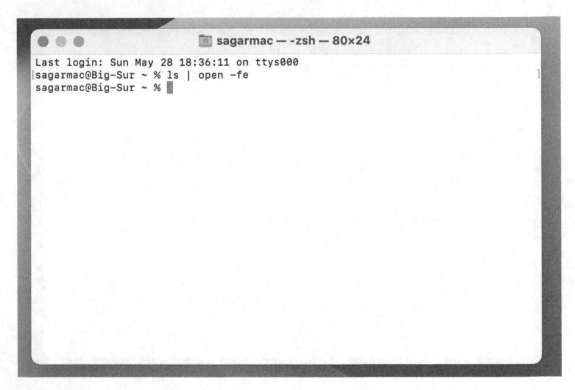

Figure 6-44. *Demonstration of the ls | open -fe command*

The outcome for echo ls | open -fe (shown in Figure 6-45) is in Figure 6-46.

Command used in Terminal: echo ls | open -fe

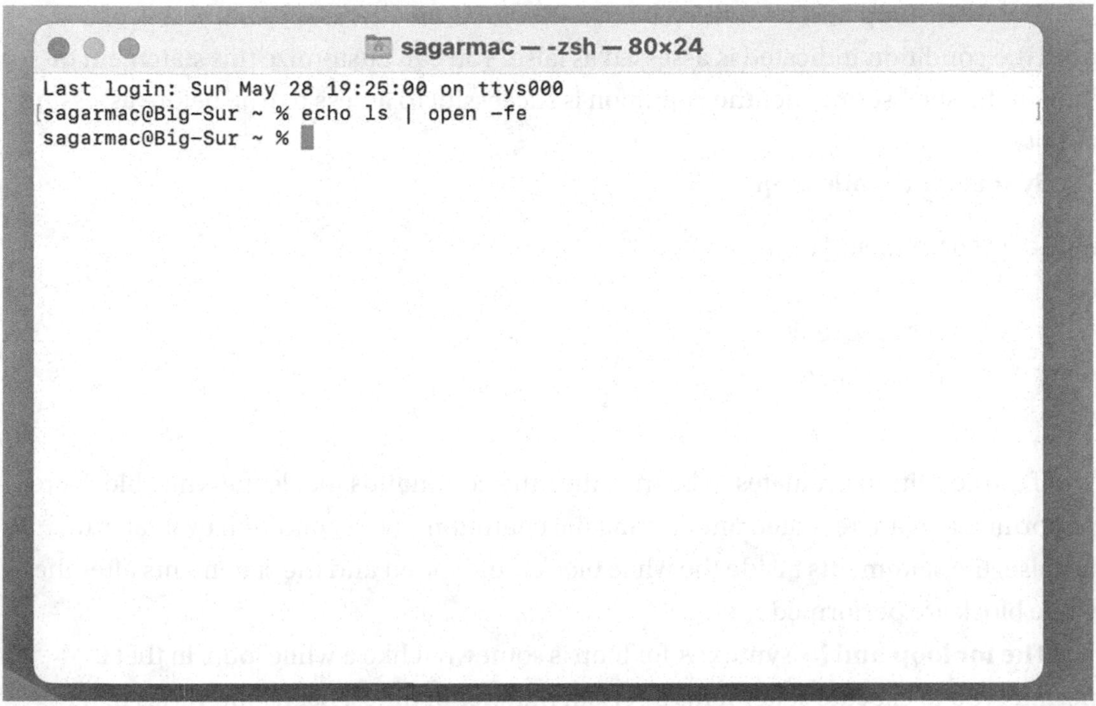

Figure 6-45. *Demonstration of echo*

Figure 6-46. *Output of echo*

The while loop and its syntax: It is a declaration that iterates over a chunk of code until the condition indicated is assessed as false. You can customize this statement or loop in the shell script after the condition is successful to assess to true before assessing as false.

Syntax for a while loop:

```
while [ condition ];
do
    # Set of statements
    # Set of commands
done
```

If the condition evaluates to be true, then the commands inside the while block are performed and are repeated after testing the condition. If the condition evaluates to be false, the statements inside the while block are skipped and the statements after the while block are performed.

The for loop and its syntax: A for loop is somewhat like a while loop, in that it permits you to execute statements a certain number of times. Each loop varies in its syntax and custom.

Syntax of a for loop:

```
for <variable> in <Value1 Value2 ... valueN>
do
    <command 1>
    <command 2>
    .....................
    < so, on>
done
```

The until loop and its syntax: It is performed as many as times the condition/command assesses to be false. The loop terminates when the condition/command develops to be true.

Syntax for an until loop:

```
until <condition>
do
    <command 1>
    <command 2>
```

```
. . . . . . . . . . . . . . . . . . . . . .
< so, on>
done
```

Creating and Executing a Shell Script on macOS

Before creating and executing the script, you must first understand the very first line in bash script (`#!/bin/bash`) and its body components. Following are the components:

Explanation of (`#!/bin/bash`): This is the beginning and very first line of bash scripts. You say this line aloud as she-bang'(shabang), hashbang. Fundamentally, this originates from the concatenation of two tokens, sharp(#) and bang (!). This grouping of tokens is present at the start of a script. It will state which interpreter must be used to perform the commands.

`#!/bin/bash` is located in the /bin directory, while the default shell to execute the commands available in file. It also describes about absolute path as /usr/bin/bash to bash shell and is typically the default location of bash shell in every Unix-based operating system/macOS/Linux.

Procedure of /bin/bash: This is the best common shell used by system admins or developers. It is the default shell for user login in the Mac/Unix systems. bash can perform most scripts. Most system admins and developers use it because it has extra features and an improved syntax.

To locate where bash is placed, you can run from the command line this code: `which bash`. The yield of this command is `/bin/bash`. This describes the absolute path to the bash shell. See Figure 6-47.

Command used in Terminal: `which bash`

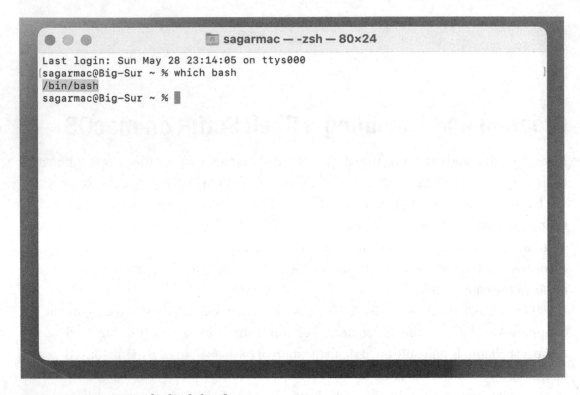

Figure 6-47. *Use of which bash*

Usage of bash: Several of the common use cases for bash are system administrators who customize systems systematically and reproducibly, software developers who automate tasks such as code compilation and debugging source code, and network engineers who must test, configure, and enhance network performance.

How to comment in bash: Comments are basically used to explain what the script is doing. To use a comment, put # and the comment. Comments are also used if you don't want to execute line in the script.

For example: # This is a comment.

Multiline comments in bash: Unlike other scripting or programming languages, bash doesn't support multiline comments. To use multiline comments in bash scripting, just add the separate comments next to it.

For example: # First line of first comment and # Second line of second comment.

Let's understand with the help of an instance. A script is basically just a set of various instructions. In the following instance, the very first line starts with a # (called a hash) followed with the ! (called an exclamation mark). It instructs the operating system to utilize bash by way of a default shell to execute the script. So echo "Learn Shell Scripting" will print the **Learn Shell Scripting** as the outcome to the console.

```
// By means of shebang to state the Operating System to
// custom bash shell
// test.sh—This is the Filename with sh extension.
echo- means to display and print the outcome
#!/bin/bash
# Bash script
echo "Learn Shell Scripting"
```

Option 1: These steps need to be followed in the same order to create and execute the shell script on Terminal using TextEdit.

Note   With the help of TextEdit, you can open and edit rich text documents built in other word processing apps, including Microsoft Word and OpenOffice. Documents can also be saved in a different format so they're compatible with other applications.

Launch the terminal and use cd to locate the directory where the script needs to be created. See Figure 4-48.

Command used in Terminal: cd ~/Desktop

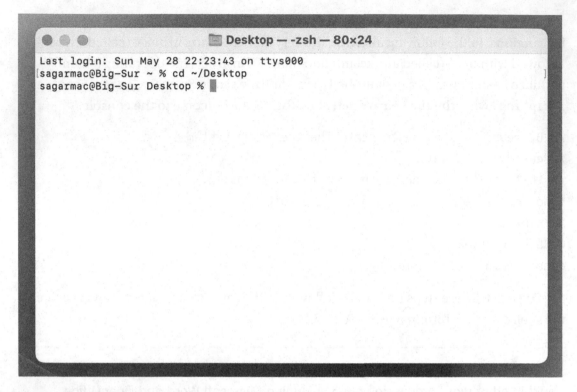

```
●  ●  ●                    📁 Desktop — -zsh — 80×24
Last login: Sun May 28 22:23:43 on ttys000
[sagarmac@Big-Sur ~ % cd ~/Desktop                                              ]
sagarmac@Big-Sur Desktop % █
```

Figure 6-48. *Navigate to the required directory using cd*

The file will be created with the .sh extension with the help of the touch command.
See Figure 6-49.

Command used in Terminal: touch test.sh

Figure 6-49. *Use of the touch command to create a file*

Build the script in the file with the help of TextEdit. In Figure 6-50, you are creating a simple script to print **Learn Shell Scripting**.

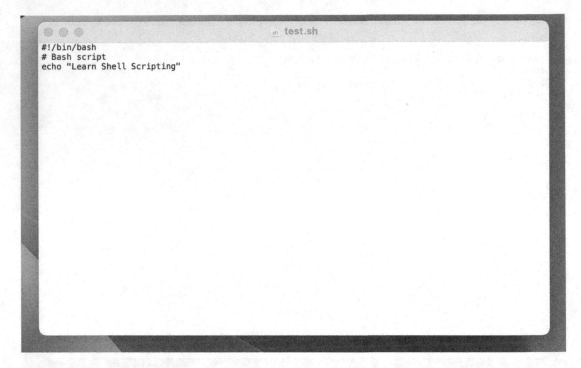

Figure 6-50. *Shell script in TextEdit*

The script will be executable with the help of command `chmod +x <fileName.sh>`. See Figure 6-51.

Commands used in Terminal:

```
cd ~/Desktop
touch test.sh
chmod +x /Users/sagarmac/Desktop/test.sh
```

Figure 6-51. *Executable shell script using chmod +x <fileName.sh>*

Execute the script with syntax **sh <filename.sh>**. See Figure 6-52 for the outcome.
Commands used in Terminal:

```
chmod +x /Users/sagarmac/Desktop/test.sh
sh /Users/sagarmac/Desktop/test.sh
```

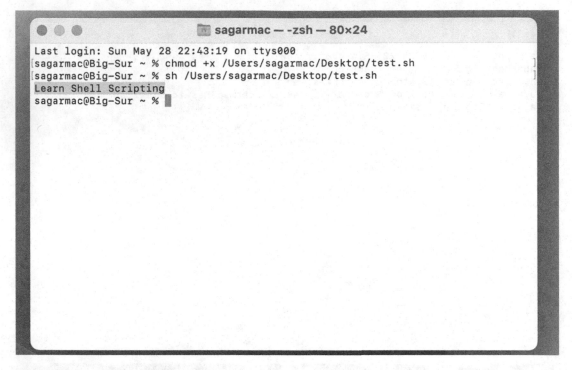

```
●  ●  ●                      sagarmac — -zsh — 80×24
Last login: Sun May 28 22:43:19 on ttys000
[sagarmac@Big-Sur ~ % chmod +x /Users/sagarmac/Desktop/test.sh          ]
[sagarmac@Big-Sur ~ % sh /Users/sagarmac/Desktop/test.sh               ]
Learn Shell Scripting
sagarmac@Big-Sur ~ % █
```

Figure 6-52. *Executing the script using sh <filename.sh>*

Option 2: Follow these steps in the same order to create and execute the shell script using a **third-party editor** tool like **CodeRunner**:

Purchase, install, and open CodeRunner from the App Store or from the source website (`https://coderunnerapp.com/`). To create a script in bash, its required to select shell script as the language from the drop-down menu located in the top left of the CodeRunner. Figure 6-53 shows CodeRunner selected as the shell script language.

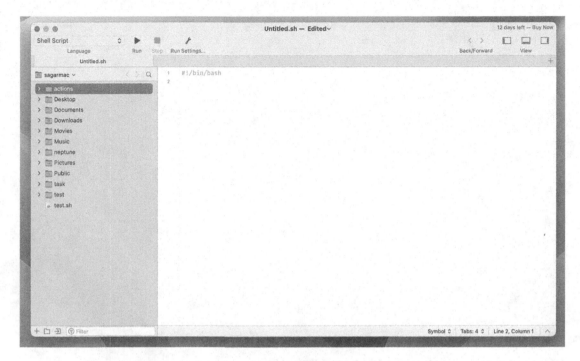

Figure 6-53. *CodeRunner as the shell script language*

It's time to create the script, save, and run it. See Figure 6-54. Please note in the lower bottom it displays the outcome as **Learn Shell Scripting**.

Note   This demo script was tested and executed on a 14-day version of CodeRunner.

Figure 6-54. *Script embedded in CodeRunner*

Figure 6-55 shows how a script can be saved in CodeRunner.

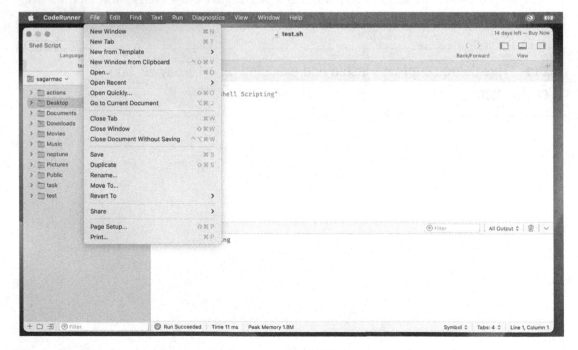

Figure 6-55. *How to save a shell script in CodeRunner*

Third-Party Text Editors for Mac

Some of the known best text editors for Macs are CodeRunner, Visual Studio Code, Atom, Sublime Text, BBEdit, Vim, Brackets, and IntelliJ IDEA.

Advance Shell Scripting and Its Components

Functions: Functions provide the easiest way to reuse code. To avoid copying and pasting the similar block of code more than twice, consider placing it inside a function. These are effectively mini scripts within a script.

Syntax of a function in zsh/bash: The following is the format of a function in bash/zsh:

```
<function name> () {
    <command1>
    <command2>
    ....................
    <command_N>
}
function name # for calling
```

Let's understand how the function works in CodeRunner with the outcome as **Time to Learn Functions**. See Figure 6-56.

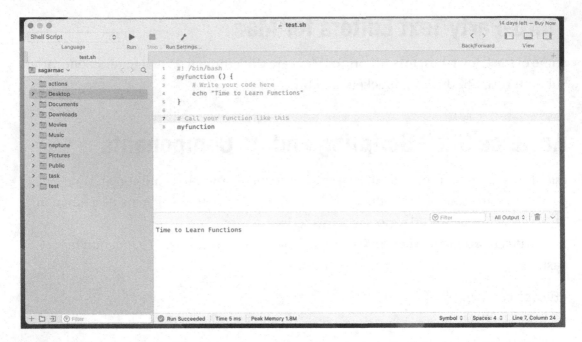

Figure 6-56. *Executing a shell script with a function in CodeRunner*

Building Elements That Create a Function

The name of the function (in this case myfunction) is shown first. It is followed by two round brackets. They are followed by two curly brackets with the commands to be executed between them. Lastly, the function is named (a.k.a. run or executed) by simply writing the function's name. Note that a function's call can only be done after its definition. So if you had called myfunction before you described what it does with the brackets, it would not have functioned.

How to pass arguments to a function: The actual control of functions is that they can be used to process data. To perform this, they primary need to be set some data and, secondly, they need to be able to perform something with it.

Giving certain data to a function is accomplished by passing arguments to it. This is completed when the function is named, by writing the data in question after the function's name. For instance, if you run myfunction Learn Functions the words **Learn** and **Functions** will be delivered to the function called myfunction.

Currently that function has been dispatched the two pieces of data, Learn and Functions, and it wants to be able to do somewhat with them. To perform this, it gives names to the data that is passed to it: $1 is the name it gives to the first argument passed to it, $2 is the name for the second argument ,and so on. See Figure 6-57.

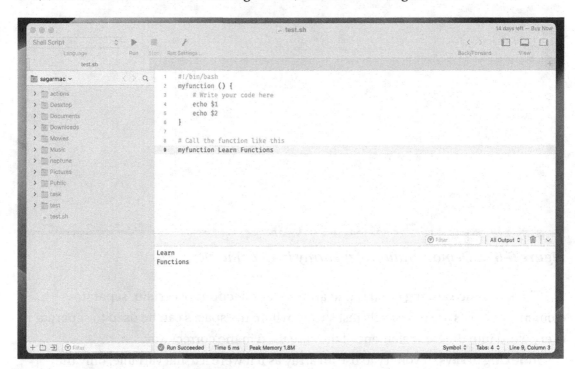

Figure 6-57. *Execution of a function in CodeRunner*

Arrays and Lists

Arrays and lists are data types in zsh/bash, like strings, numbers, and Booleans. Basically, they are both groups of elements separated by spaces. Arrays are made using round brackets and lists are made using quotation marks. See Figure 6-58.

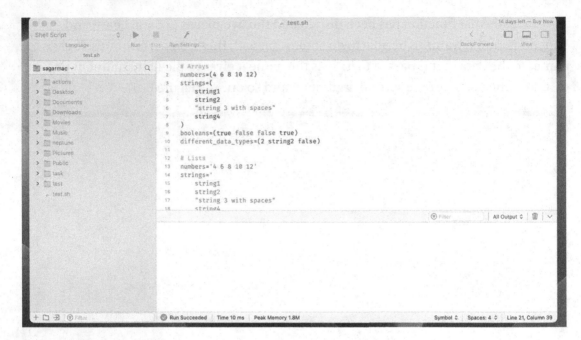

Figure 6-58. *Demonstration of an array in CodeRunner*

The difference among them is that arrays are collections of certain, separate elements and lists are essentially just strings where the spaces can be used to separate every word into different elements if they are used in the correct way.

Indexing arrays: If you try to use an array as if it were a usual variable, only the first element is available. Let's look in CodeRunner, which provides outcome as 4. See Figure 6-59.

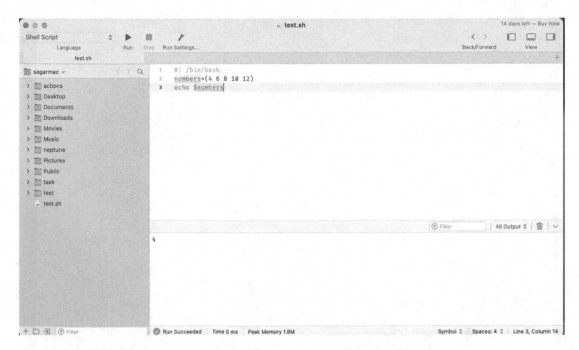

Figure 6-59. Demonstration of an array in CodeRunner

If you need to access a certain element, you can index the array. You can specify exactly which element you are involved in by writing its position in square brackets after the variable's name. For example, if you need the element in the second position in the array, you can use [2]. Let's look in CodeRunner for the outcome of 8. See Figure 6-60.

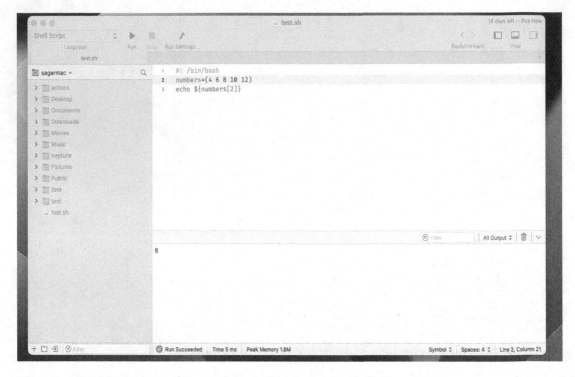

Figure 6-60. *Demonstration of an index array in CodeRunner*

Note   bash/zsh uses zero indexing, therefore the first element is in position zero and the number 8 is actually at index 2, not 3! Also it's required to include the curly brackets when making this call; if they are left out, bash/zsh will search for a variable called `numbers[4]` instead of a variable called `numbers`.

In order to use every element, index the variable with the at symbol `@`. Figure 6-60 shows CodeRunner and the outcome as 4 6 8 10 12.

Indexing lists: Since lists are only strings, they are indexed in the similar way as strings. The disadvantage to this is that the individual characters (including the spaces) count as separate elements. Figure 6-61 shows CodeRunner and the outcome as Health R.

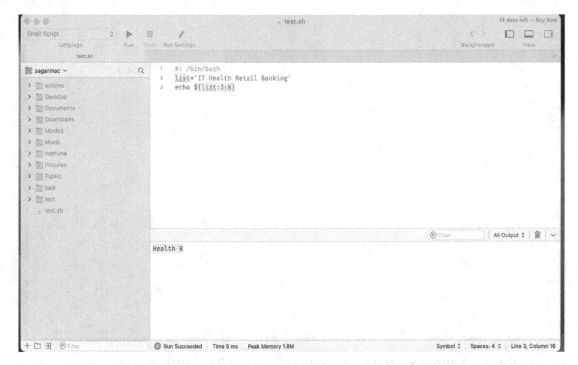

Figure 6-61. *Demonstration of an indexing list in an array in CodeRunner*

Complex loop example: Figure 6-62 shows CodeRunner where a loop runs exactly five times.

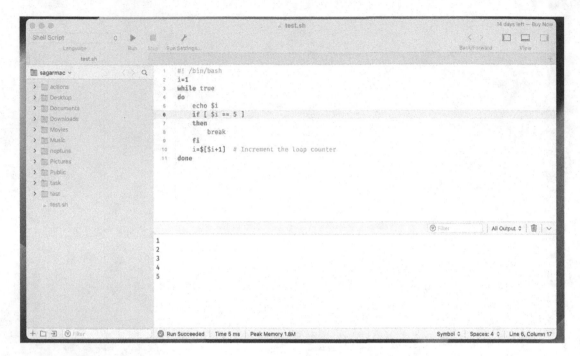

Figure 6-62. *Demonstration of a complex loop in CodeRunner*

Best Way to Debug and Troubleshoot Bash Scripts

Debugging and troubleshooting are vital abilities for any bash scripter. Although bash scripts can be extremely powerful, they can also be prone to faults and unforeseen behavior. In this section, you'll learn useful tips and techniques for debugging and troubleshooting bash scripts.

Align the set -x option: This technique is good to debug the bash script. It's basically using the set -x flag in the beginning of script. This preference enables debugging mode, which has bash print each command that it performs to the terminal, preceded by a + sign. This can be extremely helpful in recognizing where errors are occurring in the script.

Here is the syntax:

```
#!/bin/bash
set -x
# Here is the script need to come
```

Leverage echo statements: Another valuable method for debugging bash scripts is to insert echo statements throughout the code. This can aid to identify where errors are occurring and what values are being passed to variables.

Here is the syntax:

```
#!/bin/bash
# Here is the script need to come
echo "Value of variable x is: $x"
# Here additional code can come
```

Summary

You should now understand the benefit of automation with bash scripting in macOS. Additionally, you should be very well versed with the command-line utility called Terminal in macOS. You should also have good understanding about useful commands used in Terminal, which will eventually be helpful in your daily job and in automating repetitive tasks. You also know how to validate commands being executed in Terminal. Now you understand why bash/shell scripting is frequently used compared to other programming languages in macOS. You also learned how to create a simple shell script and advance shell scripting to automate tasks in your macOS environment.

This is the last chapter. You are completely equipped to manage the macOS environment in your company using the Jamf Pro mobile device management solution.

Glossary

Abbreviation	Description
CLI	Command-Line Interface
zsh	Zhong Shao
Bash	Bourne Again Shell
macOS	Macintosh Operating System
OS	Operating System
App	Applications
SSH	Secure Shell
MDM	Mobile Device Management
cat	concatenate

Index

A

Active Directory mobile account, 77
Activity Monitor, 11, 90, 108
    CPU wise processors, 112, 113
    diagnostics report, types, 118
    disk consumption, 113, 116
    energy consumption, 112, 115
    features, 108, 109
    memory consumption, 112, 114
    network activities, 113, 117
    preinstalled utility application,
        macOS, 107
    system diagnostics report, 117, 118
    update frequency, 111, 112
    users gain access, 107
    View options, 109–111
    vital tool, 107
Administrator account, 69–71, 77, 251
AirPrint, 150
    advantages, 151
    effortless printing, 151
    functionality, 151
    printing capabilities, 151
    technology, 150
.app, 77, 83, 84
Apple Business Manager, 242, 251, 252, 259
Apple Disk Image file, 80
Apple Enterprise Management (AEM), 240
Apple File System (APFS), 93, 94
Apple ID
    access, 13
    Apple ecosystem, 13

    click create, 14
    devices, 13
    preferences, 15
    sidebar options, 15, 16
    sign in, 13, 14
    successful sign in, 15
    using email account, 13
Apple Menu, 22–24, 49, 127, 130, 136, 153,
        192, 200
Apple School Manager, 242, 251, 252, 259
AppleScript
    command execution, OK button, 305
    definition, 298
    display alert on Mac computer, 302–305
    organized command language, 298
    on user Mac computer with two
        buttons, 298–302
Apple Silicon, 2–5, 176, 186, 191
Apple Silicon Mac, 53, 54, 105, 191, 192
Applications and utilities, Windows and Mac
    browsers, 10
    checking the use of resources, 11
    command-line application, 8
    deleting files, 10
    encryption, 8, 9
    File Manager/Explorer, 8
    media players, 9
    System Logs Viewer, 10
    system settings, 9
Arrays, 335–337, 339
Automated Device Enrollment (ADE)
    method, 251, 252, 259, 261